# THE BEST TRAVEL WRITING

## *Volume 10*

### TRUE STORES
### FROM AROUND THE WORLD

TRAVELERS' TALES

# THE BEST
# TRAVEL WRITING
## *Volume 10*

### TRUE STORES
### FROM AROUND THE WORLD

*Edited by*
JAMES O'REILLY, LARRY HABEGGER,
AND SEAN O'REILLY

INTRODUCTION BY DON GEORGE

Travelers' Tales
An imprint of Solas House, Inc.
Palo Alto

Travelers' Tales and Solas House are trademarks of Solas House, Inc. 2320
Bowdoin, Palo Alto, California 94306. www.travelerstales.com

Credits and copyright notices for the individual articles in this collection
are given starting on page 319.

Art Direction: Kimberly Nelson Coombs
Cover Photograph: Head of Sandstone Buddha at Wat Mahathat,
    Ayutthaya, Thailand. © Stanislav Fosenbauer.
Interior Design and Page Layout: Scribe, Inc.
Production Director: Susan Brady

ISBN: 978-1-60952-087-8
ISSN: 1548-0224
E-ISBN: 978-1-60952-088-5

First Edition
Printed in the United States
10 9 8 7 6 5 4 3 2 1

*We are all inventors, each sailing out on a voyage of discovery, guided each by a private chart, of which there is no duplicate. The world is all gates, all opportunities...*
—Ralph Waldo Emerson

# Table of Contents

# Publisher's Preface

By following the magnetic metaphor of "elsewhere" as
a guiding principle, I managed somehow to elude the
fangs and gullies of ego.
—Peter Wortsman

You might think that after twenty years of publishing
close to 150 travel books and reading thousands of
travel essays, blog posts, books, and manuscripts, I'd be good
and tired of it. But I am not—when my interest flags, it only
takes one grand story to rejuvenate me. That story can be
about any place, any topic, it can be mysterious, silly, gross,
simple, or complex. The only required ingredient is humanity
exposed in a well-turned sentence.

I need news of the stranger like an engine needs fuel, and
not the news of the news media, or social media, but news
brought first-hand by my own travels or second-hand through
the stories of others. If there is cosmic unity to be found, it is
in the staggering multiplicity of lives lived elsewhere on other
shores and the other side of town, as recorded and sung by a
good writer.

As the regular news darkens the day with panoramas of
blood, greed, and cruelty, news from the traveler lifts me into
awareness and delight, even in a cautionary tale about somewhere I would never wish to be. It summons me from stupor,
calls me to leave the mirror of home for the mirror in the eyes
of others.

It is easy to forget how much I need to be a pilgrim, a physical pilgrim, just as it is easy for any experienced traveler to wail about how places change, how San Francisco or Kathmandu or London are not what they used to be, never will be again. And it is true, true. I sometimes long with something approaching anguish for eras gone by, and that is what nostalgia means in its root—pain. But then I have to remind myself that what infuses eras gone by with magical halos, and places in the past with mystical qualities, is the landscape of humanity, ever changing, and never changing. The landscape of travel is the vast interiority of the human soul.

Serve your restless pilgrim! Serve him or her tea and a scratchy blanket before the fire. Leave town without too much baggage. Don't wait too long. Take a pen and a pad.

The stories that follow in *The Best Travel Writing, Volume 10* are but a tiny sampling of the great writing going on everywhere, every day. I hope you will find in them an offer you can't refuse, as I did.

— JAMES O'REILLY
PALO ALTO, CALIFORNIA

# Introduction

# Immersed in the Mud of Life

DON GEORGE

I've finally decided to unpack my hiking shoes.

About a month ago I returned from a week-long immersion in rural northern Cambodia. My mission had been to stay with a family in a stilt house in a village of unpaved paths, and to explore the ruins that waited in the surrounding jungle gloom. Because of time and travel constraints, I was visiting during the rainy season, but that didn't deter my explorations. Over the course of that week, I and my hiking shoes leapt over (and sometimes into) sudden streams, sloshed through ankle-deep puddles, glopped through ten-foot-long stretches of sole-sucking mud, crashed through clutching vines, stepped over furry millipedes, and stumbled on mossy picture-puzzle-pieces of massive rock carvings scattered on the jungle floor.

By the end of this adventure, my shoes looked like they'd been dipped in milk chocolate, and as I sat in my fan-cooled cottage in Siem Reap on the last night of my adventure, packing for the twenty-hour journey home, I briefly considered leaving my shoes behind. They had served me well, I reasoned, but they would not be serving me anymore.

Then I realized that doing so would be like leaving a quintessential part of my adventure—a part of me—behind. So I wrapped each shoe in three plastic bags and stuffed them into the corners of my carry-on case. When I got home and unpacked, I placed the shoes, still securely shrouded in plastic, in my bedroom closet, thinking that I would figure out what to do with them later, at a time that would make itself known.

For the past two hours I've been sitting in my study, entranced by the stories in this anthology, and now, pieces have clicked into place inside me, and I've realized that the time has come to unveil the chocolate-covered shoes.

I retrieve them from the closet and then, back in my study, heft one plastic-wrapped package and gingerly extricate the bags inside. Particles of mud—mini-mementoes of Cambodian dirt and rainwater—fall onto my hardwood floor. I reach into the innermost bag and grab a heel, grainy and grimy, and as dirt sprays around me, pull the left shoe out. Soon the right shoe is resurrected as well.

I set the shoes like trophies on their plastic bags. They are spattered, splattered, scarred, and copiously caked in mud, and as I gaze at them, the jungle comes back to me— or rather, I go back to the jungle. I feel the heavy humidity, the sweat pouring like an open spigot down my face and back, hear the mosquitoes whining in my ear, slap at them ineffectually, take my camera in sweaty hands to photograph an intricate carving of a voluptuous Khmer dancer on a two-foot by three-foot by two-foot stone block, partly hidden among lush ferns.

I'm again parting branches and vines, laboriously liberating myself from persistent stickers, wiping the sweat from my eyes, stopping for a precious swig of water—the mosquitoes whining, dancing on my neck and hands—stepping over tumbled pieces of rock, slipping and sliding, grabbing at branches to stop my fall, clambering over a half-intact wall to see a bas relief story unfold before me, warriors and musicians and fish alive in stone. I slip again, and narrowly avoid planting my palm atop a millipede. The hairy, feety nightmares are everywhere and I recall what my guide said when I asked if they could harm me: "Oh yes, if you touch one, you will die."

Through a screen of green I discern a wall, a doorway, a crumbling tower, a stony face—lips, nose, eyes—at the top of the tilting stone. I fumble with my camera as rain starts to fall, first a pitter-patter on the forest canopy and then an insistent downpour that penetrates the branches and leaves, and soaks me from the red bandana on my head to the invisible rubber soles of my shoes.

My shoes.

Suddenly I'm back in my study in a San Francisco suburb. The sun is shining, hummingbirds are flitting in the dappled branches beyond my window. The whine of a distant lawn mower dances, stingless, in the air.

And then the pieces snap together: hiking shoes—travel stories. Both take us places we never expected to go.

The book you hold in your hands offers a spectacular collection of hiking shoes. Among them, Jill Robinson transports us to an illuminating rest stop standoff with a black mamba snake in Namibia, and Lisa Alpine takes us deep into the everyday wonders of an Amazon backwater. Tania Amochaev leads us on a rigorous journey to a remote Russian village in search of roots and relatives; through Jeff Greenwald, we discover the vividly ventricled heart of a natural landmark in Arizona. Lavinia Spalding guides us on a bittersweet birthday celebration through Cuba, Erin Byrne and Marcia DeSanctis excavate the layers of poignant pasts in Paris, Michael Shapiro searches for the soul of Dylan Thomas in Wales, and Amy Gigi Alexander maps the life-saving marvels that travel can sometimes confer.

Like my shoes, all the stories herein are battered, spattered, scarred. They're immersed in the mud of life. And like my shoes, they've absorbed once inconceivable and now immeasurably enriching journeys.

So, I invite you to step into these stories, to embark on the magical, muddy adventures they hold. I can guarantee that you'll go places you've never imagined—and unwrap lessons you'll never forget.

❧  ❧  ❧

# Friends Who Don't Bite

### If we help each other, there's more time for wonder.

T he olive color of the black mamba can't be ignored. It's
the last thing I want to see in Namibia.

And it's under my car.

I perch on a picnic table at a tiny rest stop thirty miles
north of Otjiwarongo, with my eye on the snake, knowing better than to throw something to scare it off. Tall grass
punctuated with sprawling trees lines each side of the highway, and what lies beyond is protected by cyclone fencing.
After ten minutes of waiting for the snake to move, a truck
turns off the road.

"Are you having trouble with your vehicle?" asks the man.

"In a way," I respond. "I've got a mamba under my car."

The man introduces himself as Solomon, a Namibian
wildlife guide, and asks if I have binoculars so he can check
my claim. My binoculars are in the car. I hand him my camera. He looks through the lens, grunts, and gives it back.

"Indeed, that's what he is," says Solomon. "We're here for
a while. Do you have lunch?"

I reply that I have a great lunch, but it's sitting in my car next
to the binoculars. Solomon strides back to his truck, reaches

inside, and pulls out a bag and cooler. In less than a minute, he's set the picnic table and laid out his meal to share with me.

After a week, I've gotten so comfortable in Namibia that I'm not worried about driving across the country, walking through town at night, or hiking alone. Concerned emails from home ask if I'm staying safe and locking my hotel room door, tell me to watch out for strangers (which is everyone) and advise me to "be careful in Africa." I'm beginning to wonder if I'm having a one-person fairy-tale experience and missing something ominous that will teach me a lesson.

It's understandable, of course, that people are afraid of the unfamiliar. This entire continent is often prejudged or labeled based on events in a few regions. The only way to know the real truth is to pack your bags and see for yourself.

Even I had my moment of doubt before coming. When asked by the country's tourism office if I felt comfortable driving a rental SUV around by myself, I hesitated.

"I'm a blonde surfer girl from the United States," I answered. "I won't blend in. Do you feel comfortable with me driving around alone?"

The immediate, positive response was all I needed to dismiss any doubt. But when I checked in at the rental car agency and was presented with a two-wheel-drive car instead of a four-wheel-drive SUV, I realized that my tire-changing skills were more than rusty. There's no such thing as an auto service club in Namibia, and obstacles abound—from deep water holes to families of warthogs that seem to wait until the last moment to hurl themselves across lanes of traffic with their skinny tails in the air.

Noticing that the presence of the snake makes me nervous, Solomon asks me why. Surprised by his question, I sputter a little with my response about the mamba's aggression and venom. I omit telling him that only recently have I gotten a lifelong snake phobia under control. But I still get shivers when I see a photo of a black mamba. Having a live one this close to me is unnerving.

"But right now, he is your friend," Solomon advised. "Everyone is already your friend: the snake, the elephant, the leopard, the stranger. They are only not your friend if they hurt you."

I counter his optimism. "It's hard to overcome irrational fears, especially when potential danger is involved."

Solomon nods, and points out that we're two seemingly opposing animals in the world's wilderness. "But here I am, an African man, talking to you, a blonde California woman, out in the middle of nowhere in Namibia," he says. "Nobody is here to help if things go badly. And many people think that's the only way this scenario can end, as if Africa is too dangerous to bother trusting. You've trusted Namibia, so you can trust our mamba friend. But that doesn't mean you do it without caution."

We enjoy his lunch of barbecued chicken, corn and garlic bread that he'd packed for a break in his six-hour drive. The cooler is packed with frosty bottles of Hansa Urbock, a *bock-bier* that gives a subtle nod to the country's German settlers. A glance at my car tells us that the mamba is still there, so we each open a beer and toast to friends who don't bite.

"Back at home," he says, "if you have car trouble, do you wait for help?"

I remember my father's lessons in changing tires, back when I was fifteen. "Yes," I explain, "however the person who comes to help is usually a mechanic who I call. Strangers don't usually bother, thinking it's not their responsibility. And we are often too wrapped up in our own lives to think about others."

Solomon sighs, and silently points at the towering neck and head of a giraffe in the distance. He smiles when he sees my eyes widen—as if I'm five years old.

"If we help each other," he says. "There is more time for wonder. Like that giraffe. How many have you seen in Namibia so far?"

I reply that I've seen perhaps thirty. But every time I spy another animal—no matter if it's an elephant, leopard, cheetah, honey badger, oryx, jackal, or baboon—it's as if I've seen it for the first time. The excitement never wanes.

"That's how it should be with everything," he says, and looks into the distance after the giraffe.

Solomon digs in his pocket and pulls out a photo of his daughter, a four-year-old dressed in a rainbow t-shirt and red shorts, her eyes lit up by her smile. I ask if she's in school today.

"No," says Solomon. "She is with her mother this week. We don't live together anymore, so Beata takes turns with us."

I stop asking questions, thinking I've gotten too personal, but he continues.

"My wife left to be with my best friend shortly after the baby came. I want to understand, especially for Beata, but it's not always easy," he says, as he absentmindedly taps his finger on the neck of his beer bottle.

"I'm sorry," I reply. "When people you trust hurt you, it's hard to let them remain in your life without worrying about them doing it again."

I tell him that I lost a friend, someone that I trusted as well, and while we remained in occasional contact, our friendship was not the same. It was far from easy, and at first, I wanted to hurt him back in retaliation. But the experience made me pay more attention to others' suffering, as if my pain allowed me to see the pain of other people more clearly. And that made my anguish slowly fade.

Solomon smiles, and I recognize Beata's smile as his. "I feel the same way," he says. "It has made me sad, but how can I say no to the joy of my daughter, my friends, and this wide world?"

I haven't looked at my watch this entire time, fascinated with Solomon's stories. I have no idea if twenty minutes or two hours have passed. Aside from my need to get to my destination before sundown, I'm in no rush. I ask Solomon if I'm keeping him.

"If we don't make time for friends," he says as he hands me an orange, "how sad would our lives be?"

We look over to the car for our regular snake check. The mamba is gone. I silently hope it hasn't crawled into my car's undercarriage, but don't want Solomon to know that I still don't trust the snake completely.

As we pack up his gear, Solomon pulls some ostrich shell beads from a package in his truck, opens my hand, and places them gently in my palm.

"Your friends are more than these," he says, as he closes my fingers over the beads. "See them everywhere they are, and you will be happy."

He walks me to my car, and as I drive away, I see him waving. He is an unexpected teacher on my travels—one who has allowed me to see more clearly the things I can leave behind. I choose to believe his happy outlook is more innocence than naïveté.

Far ahead of me on the road, a family of warthogs runs across my path. I begin to think like Solomon.

They are all my friends, so I slow down and drive with caution.

≈≈ ≈≈ ≈≈

*Jill K. Robinson is a freelance writer and photographer. Her work has appeared in the* San Francisco Chronicle, AFAR, National Geographic Traveler, American Way, Every Day With Rachael Ray, Robb Report, Coastal Living, *and more. At home, she scoots baby garter snakes out of the road to keep them from getting squashed under car tires. Follow her on Twitter @dangerjr.*

SARAH COLLEEN COURY

❧ ❧ ❧

# The Vanishing Art
# of Losing Your Way

*Sometimes you really don't need a map.*

Here is what I remember: Heat.

Not the recreational variety, that makes you pull out a lawn chair and pour an iced tea. This was the heat that drives a thousand pinpricks through the skin; that transforms even a light cotton sundress into a cargo of oppression. The kind of heat that sunburns fingernails. This was driving across Oklahoma, the Texas panhandle, and into New Mexico in August, during a heat wave, with no AC.

The gallon of drinking water from Love's truck stop had warped into a squat, sweating gremlin on the passenger seat, which I glanced at sideways from time to time, uneasy. It was the dead of night and stars were out in force—no longer individual specks, but long seams of light. Even the stars seemed to be recklessly shoveling heat onto the world.

Buddy Holly, my forever traveling companion, belted from the speakers—we were in his homeland now. Armadillo eyes shone from dark roadside weeds, and mayflies sailed through the high beams, seeking one another with the crazed purposeful passion of a minuscule lifespan. I shunned the homogeneous interstates and kept to back roads, passing small towns situated as though they'd dropped from the sky at random, and deserted dustbowl farms with gabled roofs and black windows like wounds.

My summer internship with U.S. Fish and Wildlife in Oklahoma had just ended. I was twenty-one and bumping alone across the endless southern plains without a plan. Though Michigan was home, I headed west because, on a vagabond's whim, I had let go of the steering wheel at the four-way stop in Tishomingo. The car had veered slightly west, so I went with it, deciding to put destiny in the hands of a rusty Corsica's untended alignment.

In the pink light of dawn, I pulled off at Fort Sumner for a break at the grave of Billy the Kid. The cemetery was a sparse and dusty affair and Kid's grave was inside what looked like an old circus cage. A nearby sign explained: the headstone had gone missing twice—the first time for twenty-six years before it was found again, somewhere in Texas. The grave was scattered with tossed coins. It struck me as a scene that could only be found in the American West—the burial site of an outlaw accused of gunning down numerous people serving double duty as some kind of oddball wishing well.

I pulled the car under a ragged roadside tree and slept a while, but with no forward motion pulling breeze through the windows, the heat was unbearable. I woke with a fresh idea: keep moving slightly west, but also turn mostly north, and out of the desert. The atlas confirmed it could be done: 84 to 64 to 285, and I'd get to see Colorado. My commitment to back roads waned for a moment, and I let Highway 80 catch my eye, streaming across the map like a blue icy river above my chosen route, from southern Wyoming all the way toward northern California— where it was definitely misty and cool; where redwoods cast shadows vast enough to create their own microclimates, elven places full of lichen and toadstools and deep black earth; where my beloved sister lived. I decided to surprise her.

The rest of that day was a blur of Colorado growing greener as I traversed it bottom to top. Everything I passed looked phenomenal: Old West-type clapboard towns, distant paragon mountains, *Denver* (I hadn't seen a real city in months). But every time I longed to stop and explore, still the heat kept pushing me on.

At first I didn't pay much mind to the changing afternoon sky, partly because it was changing slowly, and partly because I was too busy staring into the endless golden grass north of Fort Collins. I've always been a fool for a good proper prairie, and this was by far the most vast and achingly beautiful prairie I'd seen. The land unfurled in spare, shaggy elegance, outlining the curves and bones of the underlying geology until it rolled off the ends of the Earth. A meadowlark on a fencepost sang a song like a flute being played underwater, pointing its beak up to heaven and wearing its bright yellow breast with a flourish like the robes of a king. If the wide open freedom of the frontier were to be embodied in one joyful sound, this would be it.

I pulled off and sat on the hood for my bread-and-cheese dinner. Looking across the waves of empty land, the old wire fences which guarded only grass and the occasional stone, the distant specks of white and brown, which must have been wandering cattle, it dawned on me that I was good and lost. It seemed I had been driving far too long on this tiny road to not have passed any signs for Highway 80, any signs for Cheyenne. Was I even in Colorado still, or Wyoming? Perhaps the signs had passed while I was staring at the grass. And hadn't the road been curving in one long and lazy swoop toward the east? The road I had chosen on the atlas showed no such tendency. Was that even east? To get

my bearings, I turned around to look for the sun. And that's
when I saw what the sky had become.

Where recently the sun had winked in and out of a benign-
looking collection of plump silver clouds, now loomed a churning chaos of brown, black and purple thunderheads sweeping
at breakneck speed in what appeared to be every possible
direction—even down. Right toward *me*, in fact, with my half-
eaten sandwich hanging forgotten in my hand. The entire sky
seemed to be expanding around me, and yet imploding over
itself at the same time, creating a vortex where lightning flashed
and radiated outward from the center. The first legitimate wind
I'd felt in days—a sudden blast, really, so cold it felt capable of
snow—enveloped me, filling my ears with empty white sound.
It didn't smell of sun warmed grass or cow-trampled scrub like
the surrounding landscape, but of frigid water and stone—a
clean ancient smell that reminded me of camping trips to Lake
Superior. Where had such a wind been born? How far had it
traveled to get here, to become this great monstrous thing?

Looking into this sky, I realized I'd never really experienced sky before. It had always been something that stayed
there, far above—often quite picturesquely, of course—but
always with a definite remoteness to it. An *otherness.*

This sky didn't stay up above at all. It was everywhere,
coming, swooping down in brooding colors to touch the
earth. I was *inside* it and not beneath it. I felt minuscule: a field
mouse, a crouching locust, grain of soil, seed of grass. And yet,
I felt like the center of the whole voluptuous, terrifying, gorgeous universe. The random no-hands turns, the driving heat,
the irrational route modifications, the obsolete and crumpled
atlas, the unmarked hodgepodge of country roads—this is
what they wanted me to see. The *Sky.* For the very first time.

Occasional fat raindrops pelting my face, I walked out onto
the prairie and stood in a new kind of happiness, touching at
once both the grass and the sky.

Eventually, I kept on driving. I found train tracks and followed alongside them for a while, stopping to photograph every train that went barreling by with the storm clouds behind it. As the light fell, I met an elderly clear-eyed woman walking a white German shepherd. Beads of rainwater gleamed in her short gray hair and dark wool sweater.

"Would you like a lift somewhere?" I half-shouted over a wind that still howled.

"I only call off my walks when it starts turning green," she said, cheerfully motioning toward the clouds.

She gave me directions. Apparently, I had missed the highway somehow, by a long shot, and was now a good bit northeast of Cheyenne and heading east—almost into Nebraska. Well hell, I thought, might as well roll with it.

I am in my mid-thirties now, and for years I had completely forgotten this late afternoon in Wyoming. But recently, as I was kneading bread dough in the kitchen, my nine-year-old son came in and gave me his best pitch for buying him a smart phone. I wasn't surprised—quite a few of his classmates already carry them. I, in turn, listed the reasons his dad and I think it needs to wait a few years.

"But Mom," he said soberly, "this is for my *safety*."

Yes, he's a smart cookie, steering the argument straight to the heart of every mother's weak spot.

"I need a phone so I can always call you if I'm in danger. And it'll have GPS, so I'll never get lost."

My busy hands froze mid-task, buried deep in the dough. This was a revelation. It had never occurred to me that my son's generation, and likely all those that follow, will very seldom, if ever, get lost. The implications of this raced through my mind. On the positive side, they *will* be able to avoid potentially dangerous situations, such as detouring unwittingly through a violent neighborhood in an unfamiliar city.

They will avoid the maddening frustration of driving around in circles; of becoming indefinitely waylaid in a tangle of one-way streets that all seem to go the wrong way; of being the jerk who made everybody in the car late by saying "No, I *really* think it's *that* way."

So why was my first emotional response to this realization a pang of regret, like any parent might feel when informed that his/her child will miss out on some really great chance? Was there really something so fantastic about getting lost?

And then the memories came.

I remembered getting lost as a kid with my mom in the town we had just moved to. How I helped find our way home using landmarks and memory, and how proud and capable it made me feel to work together with her and solve the problem.

I remembered driving as a teenager across Michigan's Upper Peninsula with my best friend on a moonless night. We got so lost among conifer-choked dirt roads that we started imagining all the horrific ends we might meet. We told gruesome tales as we passed slumped and forgotten motels, dismal prison complexes, darkened log cabins peeking out from the woods. At last we came to a crossroads with a small wooden sign bearing the name of our destination . . . and an arrow pointing both ways. It was too perfect, and we laughed at the absurdity of it all until our bellies ached. When we finally found civilization, it had never looked so sweet.

I remembered backpacking across Europe with my two sisters, and the countless instances when losing our way meant seeking out and asking a local for directions with the help of a pocket phrase book. I thought about how this had provided the ideal door from which to step out of our comfort zone, to meet new people, to speak their languages; how all across Spain, it had *forced* me to conquer some of my extreme shyness, since I was the one who had most recently taken high school Spanish. And the times this simple interaction turned into an introduction, an impromptu guided tour, an invitation, a home cooked meal and a place to stay. The very stuff of traveling.

And then I remembered something else: Heat. Buddy Holly. Absolute heat. A treeless plain. A rustling, open grass. An icy wind that smelled of water, stone. The dark and boundless sky that came, and let me hold it.

With GPS in hand we always know just where we are, where we ought to turn next, how to find the fastest, most direct route to practically *any place on Earth*. Yes, it's incredible, and in many situations it's the most important tool we could ask for.

But as a constant traveling companion, I feel it may dull our inner navigational pull, our will to diligently observe, and all the unique problem solving, independence, communication, and cooperation that go into finding our own way. And perhaps most regrettably, it leaves so little room for serendipity, a key ingredient of any good old romantic adventure.

I'm confident that my son and his peers will find alternate versions of adventure, and I'm sure they will develop skill sets that my generation never had, prompted by changes in the world we can't yet comprehend. But now I also know this: someday soon I'm taking my son on a road trip, with vague destinations and an outdated map, with an ear for advice from the locals and an eye for the subtle cues of fate, pulling us down and down some dusty road.

*Sarah Colleen Coury has worked as a small business owner, field biologist, park ranger, and gardener. Her poetry, prose, and nature and travel writing have appeared in a number of publications. She spent many years as a vagabond of sorts, traveling and living all over Europe and North America, while taking photos and writing things down. She now lives with her husband and son in their native Michigan.*

ELIZABETH GEOGHEGAN

❧ ❧ ❧

# The Marco Chronicles: To Rome, Without Love

It's love that's eternal and confounding, not the city.

I f Rome were a woman, she'd be a whore. The kind of whore who looks good from a distance or in just the right light. And while you are busy ogling her cupolas, she will deftly slip the wallet from your back pocket. She will deceive you, and she will seduce you, and she will be so intoxicating you will have a hard time letting her go.

My anti-relationship with the Eternal City began by accident. I never burned for Italy the way so many others do. I never imagined idyllic afternoons, lolling supine beneath a vine-strung pergola, chatting in a foreign tongue to new friends. And I never bought into all those stories about the irresistible charm and sexual dynamism of that mythical creature, the Italian male.

Instead, more than twenty years ago, a friend invited me on what was literally her dream holiday, not mine. She planned every detail, researched every facet. I never so much as glanced at a guidebook. But we both knew I needed that trip even more than she did. Staggered by the recent death of my brother, I landed in Italy and proceeded to ignore the place along with everything I was feeling. Then, one afternoon, alone in a café near the San Lorenzo market in Florence, I met a beautiful—and, it must be mentioned—non-Italian man who invited me to a dinner party in Fiesole, a village along a winding road, high above the city, the house just a stone's throw from the birthplace of Galileo.

That gathering became the eventual memory upon which I would later impulsively quit my job, sell my possessions, and pack my bags to construct a life abroad. It wasn't the bougainvillea dangling above the door frame that did it. Or the homemade fettuccine, fresh fennel, raisins, and cream. Nor was it the view of Florence glittering below, those overly romanticized Tuscan hills unfurling in the distance. It wasn't even the glorious golden light that gave way to the rising mist as evening suddenly surrounded us. It was the half-Puerto Rican, half-Trinidadian graffiti artist from the South Bronx.

It was the guy. Not Italy.

And it was the two of us wandering off, following a path of tangled rosemary and lavender to lie together on the still-warm stones beside the swimming pool, the distant conversations and laughter from the party punctuating our first kiss. And it was the next morning, waking in a Renaissance palazzo, spray cans scattered on the floor near the mattress where we'd slept, the walls of the room bombed with so much graffiti that I might have been in a New York subway.

Looking back, I recalled the evening with that particular man as one of the first times I forgot—if only for a few moments—to be devastated about my brother. As a result, the memory of Italy was forever intertwined with that reprieve. It became for me a landscape offering sex and solace and roads as yet untraveled. Illusive, beckoning. But memories, like men, can be alternately sharp, then shadowy; they slip so easily from grasp. As it turned out, so did the artist. And after a stint there during graduate school, Florence faded, too. Italy, however, remained.

And everybody knows where all roads lead.

Sometimes I dream of Rome. Deep in the darkest moments of a fitful, "Should I stay or should I go?" kind of night, as I toss and turn on my Italian linen sheets, Rome comes to me and sits at the foot of my bed. She is overly tanned and decked out in something by, say, Roberto Cavalli—with a plunging neckline, maybe a leopard print. Whatever it is, it's expensive *and* tacky. Nonetheless, she is smokin'.

She tosses her dyed blonde mane and in a deep, throaty voice says, "All right, Elizabeth, here's the deal. I will let you stay, but there are a few conditions."

I sit up and rub my eyes.

"You can have the clutch apartment in Trastevere that everybody will *ooh* and *ahh* over whenever the door swings open."

She gazes down at her manicured red nails, bored.

"And I'll let you have the killer university gig, teaching just two days a week, and although it will never pay very well, at least it will pay in euros. I'll even throw in four months of vacation a year."

At this point, I'm nodding and feeling sort of giddy.

"Yes," she says, "I will grant you all these things—the much coveted expatriate life in a European capital, the international group of friends, the good food, and the even better cappuccino."

And I'm still nodding and agreeing and not really listening to the rest as carefully and, of course, my Italian isn't all that strong yet, but most of the vocabulary comes from Latin, right? So, no problem, and I'm thinking, perfect, sounds good. Go on.

"But the price you will pay is this: You can only love me: Roma. You will devote all your time and energy to me and to me alone. You will never marry. You will never procreate. But your life will be the envy of everyone who knows you, *capisce?*"

And I say, "Wait, wait, I'm not sure I caught that bit just before the envy—"

But Rome doesn't answer, she just gives me that oh-so-Italian shrug of the shoulders and a hand gesture that could either mean, "It's late and I'd really better be going" or "You're fucked."

And I rewind the Italian in my head, and now I'm not so sure what just happened, and I ask, "But what if I get tired of it? What if I want to leave? Then where do I go?"

Rome just smiles and disappears in a puff of smoke.

Is it possible to love a city and abhor half its inhabitants? It's not that I don't like Italian men. I like them fine. What I don't like is dating Italian men. Truthfully, it has gotten to the point where I bristle simply hearing most Italian men speak, though that only came later. Luckily for me, I never envisioned myself marrying Giacomo della Something-or-Other and becoming mistress of a medieval monastery along the Appia Antica.

To be clear, I didn't consciously rule out the possibility of dating or even falling in love while in Rome. But unlike many of the women I meet here, especially the usual Americans, Brits, and Aussies freshly issued from the international terminal at Da Vinci Airport, I had never put Italian men at the top of my agenda. Not that I planned to remain chaste during my tenure in the Eternal City. Why would I?

Nowadays, though, after wasting so much time on the men I now refer to as The Marcos, celibacy looks pretty good. For if Rome is a terrible place to get work done, it is an even worse place to find a man. Although *find* is the wrong word. It is incredibly easy to *find* an Italian man. You don't even have to look. Italian men will find you. That part is as simple as sitting in a café. And although I don't actively discourage men who are looking for a fling, I no longer count myself among the ranks of women who are remotely interested in such fleeting endeavors. Of the dozen or so years I have lived in Italy, I have spent the bulk of them avoiding encounters with Italian men. A brief year or so after my arrival, I swore off them *per sempre*—forever. I didn't have a broken heart. The cause wasn't anything that emotional. My decision wasn't based on romantic anguish or misfortune or upon even a shred of heartfelt disappointment. I discovered that the cultural barrier was simply too vast to overcome, though it presented itself in ways I would never have expected.

I think of Italian men the way I think about most things with the label "Made in Italy"—form over function. Fabio may gleam like a sleek and stylish Ferrari—all smooth lines and the perfect finish as he sidles up beside you, motor purring, leather seats beckoning—but climb in, and you will soon discover the ride is more Fiat 500 than Ferrari. Not nearly as smooth as you might have hoped. At the risk of pushing the metaphor a bit too far, by all means, take Fabio for a spin, but do it in the same spirit with which you might rent a convertible and speed along the Amalfi Coast: Always keep in mind that there aren't any guardrails, and the fall is a long, long way down. After all, even Avis won't insure you if you plan to head "south" of Rome. Why? Because it's dangerous, that's why.

First, there's the ever-present mother figure and the Italian male's penchant for living at home until he is forty or so. Not that this was really a problem in my "relationships," because I couldn't keep anything going with an Italian long enough to spend much time with the family. And though plenty has been written about *Mammone*—the Mama's Boy Syndrome—for me that wasn't the issue. I have to say that of the Italian mothers I have met, I usually like them better than I do their sons.

Still, romance-wise, I had done pretty well the two times I'd passed through Florence, and it never occurred to me that Rome would be any different. On my first trip, I met The Graffiti Artist. Gorgeous. Not Italian, but about as hot as they come. And where did I meet him? A café, of course. A few years later, in Florence for the second time, I met Pasquale. Again, in a café. He was a Mediterranean dream—a musician with glossy black hair and sea green eyes, his face a kind of map of southern Italy, the intersection of Greek and Moorish, French and Italian. Too exotic for his own good. Pasquale quickly proved himself incapable of fidelity, though to his credit, he also proved that he was capable of admitting it, an uncommon trait among his compatriots. I still admire him for it.

Who knew Rome was going to be such a romantic wasteland? In some ways, *La Dolce Vita* seems to blame for the misconceptions about life in the Eternal City. The Italy-obsessed bandy about those three words, willfully ignoring the utter lack of romance and the undertow of desperation in Federico Fellini's masterpiece, which coined the phrase. Stripped of its irony, *la dolce vita* implies that, in Rome, a sweet life exists—and, of course, in some ways, it does. Or it can—especially if you are just passing through. But the afterglow of a wholly Roman moment—a blissful afternoon whiled away on a shaded *terrazzo* or a gorgeous meal shared with an equally gorgeous man—is fleeting. Rome has always been, and remains, a labyrinth of complex social mores, indiscriminate etiquette, streetside histrionics, and daily indignities set against the backdrop of the city's enduring ancient relics, all a timeless testament to her magnificence.

That *bitch*.

So, I may not have arrived fantasizing about some princely heir to an olive oil fortune or a marchese with homes scattered along the coast, but neither was I searching for bartenders who pretended to be painters, junkies masquerading as furniture designers, electricians who were actually coke dealers, or flight attendants claiming to be pilots. I also wasn't interested in has-been filmmakers who lied about their age and spent the better part of a day sitting in a crummy plastic chair at Bar San Calisto, rolling joints and talking smack about American politicians.

Perhaps I am just a magnet for fuck ups?

I am willing to admit that this is a distinct possibility.

Did I mention that after Pasquale, nearly all of them were named Marco?

*Marco Uno.* I met Marco Uno during my first winter in Rome. We got to know each other thanks to my daily ritual of giving myself a caffeine injection while reading the *Herald Tribune* at the café just around the corner from my house. He had sparkling brown eyes and a great smile, a rugged type who looked superb with a three-day stubble. Watching him make cappuccino was a pleasure. Simply put, he was *un bellissimo* barman.

Marco Uno courted me for more than three months, which in the modern world is a long, long time. And I mean courtship in the traditional sense. For an entire season, he flirted and tried desperately to make conversation with me. He persisted through halting discussions laced with *cappuccini* and *panini*, the dictionary on the table between us passed back and forth, back and forth, his long lashes grazing high cheekbones, as we tried to discuss subjects far beyond the scope of his English or my Italian. Topics such as the contemporary art scene in London, or politics—the low-flying planes that were then departing daily en route to Kosovo—or why the Americans were so upset that Bill Clinton had bonked Monica Lewinsky. For the record, Italians couldn't understand the whole Clinton scandal. They weren't taken aback by the infidelity; that is every Italian man's birthright. What offended their sensibilities was that Monica, according to them, was *brutta, pure cicciona*—ugly, and chubby, too.

So there I was with Marco Uno, exchanging confused conversation. I feel like an idiot for saying this, but I really did believe he liked me. Who would bother to keep up such a labor-intensive friendship? Our get-togethers weren't part of a language swap or some special yen on his part to learn English, so it seemed clear that he was motivated by the usual combination of sexual tension and an old-fashioned desire to get to know me. I thought it was sweet that it took him so long to make a move.

Finally, after a particularly raucous dinner party orchestrated by a dear friend of mine determined to get Marco and me in a room together after hours, this beautiful man and I ended up going back to my place arm in arm. He was more than a little bit drunk. I was sober. I unlocked my door, and he sauntered into my apartment, all swagger and self-assurance, immediately unbuttoning his white shirt, pulling it off, and tossing it over the chair.

Promising, I thought.

While not so sneakily checking out his rather well-formed body, I noticed the tattoo—a less-than-precise rendering of the Madonna placed strategically over his heart, the ink gone green, her face wet with tears—an image that, for me, pretty much sums up the essential problem with dating Italian men: The Madonna/Whore Complex.

Most Italian men draw a very bold line when they think of women. There are the women you marry, and there are the women you have sex with, and these two types of women are rarely one in the same. And if you are an American woman living in Italy, everybody knows how easy you are, so forget about it. The die is cast. You may as well just roll over.

Of course, I wasn't thinking about any of this as Marco Uno pulled me toward him and we tumbled onto my bed, not difficult to do since my remarkably tiny studio was dominated by what the Italians call *un letto matrimoniale,* or "marriage bed," aka a double. And there we were, after months of coy conversations and flirty lunches. *Finally.* As he fumbled with my shirt and edged up my skirt, pushing my thighs apart and beginning to grope around, it became more and more apparent that this was not going to be the tender culmination of three months of bilingual foreplay. Next thing I knew, he'd straddled my shoulders with his knees and practically cracked me in the teeth with his belt buckle, before yanking down his jeans and getting busy trying to shove his manhood into my mouth.

We hadn't even kissed.

My Italian wasn't quite up to snuff for this intimate situation, or maybe it was perfect for the rather compromising position I found myself in. After all, it wasn't conversation he was angling for. But things weren't quite moving at the speed I'd imagined. I wanted him to slow down and kiss me. It wasn't as if I thought he was truly going to be my *boyfriend,* but there had been so much build up—how about at least a hint of romance? Even if the life expectancy of our relationship was destined to be just a few more hours, who doesn't like kissing? Who dispenses with it altogether? I managed to wriggle out from underneath him and muster up the wherewithal to ask.

"*Perché non mi baci?*" Why won't you kiss me? He looked at me, a bit stunned.

"*Dai, Elisabetta, sei troppo sentimentale.*" Come on, Elizabeth, you are way too sentimental.

Sentimental? I almost laughed out loud. Now there's an adjective no one had ever used to describe me. Cynical, yes. Caustic, often. Even blasé. But sentimental? This could only mean my language skills were sub-par. Surely *sentimentale* was different from sentimental, or else this was a clear misapprehension on his part, like when Pasquale's buddies had referred to me as *dolce*.

Sweet I am not. (Even Pasquale got a giggle out of that one.) Besides, it isn't all that hard to be mistaken for sweet when you're incapable of uttering more than two syllables of Italian. But sentimental? I don't happen to believe a kiss is a sentimental act, especially when I am already in bed with a man who has been chatting me up for months. Sensual, yes. Sentimental, no. Suddenly, Marco Uno had turned into the Julia Roberts character in *Pretty Woman*. Evidently, there would be no kissing on the lips.

It was, at the least, discouraging. Even when prompted, he didn't relent. He had no intention of kissing me. Ever. I reflected for a second, briefly weighing the pros and cons of continuing on in the direction we were going. The situation was disappointing, yes, but there I was with an attractive, young guy in my bed, a guy who was clearly good to go. Why quibble over the details? I'll admit, though, that something still bothered me, something didn't add up. If all he had wanted to do in the first place was to fuck me, he could have managed it months earlier, dispensing entirely with the Italian-English dictionary, the coffees, and all those halting conversations. I liked him from the start, and I would have slept with him because, like I said, I am not sentimental.

The next thing Marco Uno did became a recurring theme in my Roman life. He refused to wear a condom. Again, it seemed, Pasquale had been an aberration. Not only had my first Italian lover admitted that he was unfaithful (actually, he admitted that he never had the least intention of being faithful to anyone), but Pasquale had also been willing to wear condoms. This one, the first of The Marcos, was insulted that I'd asked him to sheath himself, much less kiss me.

Which meant that my limited Italian was now stretched to the "no glove, no love" topic.

Marco Uno was indignant. So was I. The negotiations reached an unintelligible crescendo.

It was almost as if we were haggling over merchandise at Porta Portese, and the longer the bargaining continued, the less we agreed upon the price, however desperate each of us might have been to close the deal. Sadly, like much of what's on offer at Rome's famous flea market, Marco Uno didn't look nearly as good now that I had gotten him home. I suppose it was absolute duress and the threat of all momentum grinding to a halt that finally made him relent and tear open the package (which I provided, of course) and put on the condom. To his credit, it had taken so long for us to arrive at the begrudging condom-donning juncture, I found it rather impressive that he could still get an erection at all.

For my part, it was sheer curiosity that kept me moving forward. I needed the story to have a conclusion. And a short, short story it ended up being. Hands down, it was the most unemotional, mechanical, and speedy act of my life. Afterward, he wrapped his arms around me, as if I was his *girlfriend* or something, and fell fast asleep.

The next morning, Marco Uno rolled over, yawned, and invited me to stroll over to the café for breakfast. Basically, he wanted to make a morning-after show of me to his coworkers. I later learned the Italian verb most often applied to winning a woman's "heart" is none other than *conquistare*. To conquer.

Oh, just piss off.

\*    \*    \*

*Marco Due.* Marco Due was adorable from the moment we met. He spoke zero English, which was a bonus because trying to comprehend what soon followed our acquaintance finally catapulted me into the realm of fluency. Instead of stuttering and simply pretending that I spoke Italian, suddenly I was able to have actual conversations. Marco Due corrected my mistakes in Italian. (Note: if you are in a bilingual relationship, don't do this, especially if you are having a fight.) But there was so much else to love about Marco II. Simply put, he was polite, generous, and helpful. He introduced me to his friends and invited me to concerts. Plus, he was romantic—he even brought me to the nearby volcanic hot springs on a moonlit night.

Indeed, no favor was too great, even the kind of favor most people dread. He took time out of his day to drive me to a doctor's appointment and sat patiently waiting in a windowless room with no reading material. In Italy, a visit to the doctor's office is tantamount to sitting Shiva, so this act of kindness was no small thing. He even sifted through all the documents and red tape to transfer my scooter into his name so that he could insure it for me. Italian bureaucracy such as it is, I had found it impossible to do this myself. What I am saying is Marco Numero Due seemed quite keen, because really, truly, what straight guy would do all those things just to be nice?

As with Marco Uno, my courtship with Marco Due was somewhat protracted. But about twenty minutes after we slept together, the only time we did sleep together, Marco Due announced two things: The first was that he was completely and utterly still in love with his Brazilian ex-girlfriend. The second was that he'd had a heroin problem for well over a decade—but not to worry, because he'd been clean for all of two months.

\*    \*    \*

*Marco Tre.* One evening, I was sitting with a couple of friends at a café—another café!—near Piazza Farnese, when along came a dark-eyed, dangerously handsome, Jil Sander-clad electrician named Marco. Perhaps the designer Pumas and the expensive, minimalist jacket should have clued me in. Or maybe, as I discovered later, the erratic hours he kept. Because in spite of the tools littered across the back seat of his car, and the dashing off to see clients to quickly solve a "wiring" problem, Marco III wasn't really an electrician. He was a coke dealer. Worse, he was a dealer who owed quite a lot of money to the wrong people. I want to say that the term most often used to describe this particular group is the mafia. As a result of his debts, Marco was constantly looking over his shoulder. Literally.

A few weeks into our meeting, he pounded on my door at about four in the morning, waking me. I unlocked the door, opened it, and he rushed inside. Drenched in sweat, eyes dilated, he frantically asked if he could stay with me. *For a few days.* So, he wasn't just dealing, he was also on the lam. It seemed that in Marco Tre's world I was what amounted to a very cheap date. I wasn't interested in his cocaine. I didn't even realize people still did cocaine, aside from the Romans, who, it turns out, are seriously behind the times when it comes to *everything.*

One day, Marco Tre simply vanished and never called again. Nobody knew much of anything. Nobody had heard from him. His apartment had been cleared out, *alta moda* wardrobe and all, and he went missing. That was that. I still have no idea if he is in jail or dead or worse, but I have to admit, I wasn't too broken up about his disappearing act.

*Marco Quattro.* Marco Quattro wore an Alitalia uniform. He looked good in it, too. He often traveled, and I assumed he was a pilot, and although I brought it up several times he never contradicted me. Marco Quattro had a chiseled jaw and blue eyes and was excessively well groomed. Perhaps too well groomed. He waxed his eyebrows into an arch that was distinctly feminine, but the waxed eyebrow fetish was common among Roman men; indeed, I was hard-pressed to find one who had resisted the trend. Brows aside, the problem with Marco Quattro was that he was overtly preoccupied with a certain portion of my anatomy—one that I wasn't much interested in sharing with him. Which meant that we were ill-fated from the start.

One evening, during a small gathering that included Marco IV, my friend Sergio stopped by. Sergio also happened to work for Alitalia, and after we all went through the usual greeting routine, lots of *ciaos* and kissing on both cheeks, he quickly pulled me aside on a pretext. "Elizabeth," he whispered. "Marco's not a pilot, he's a Trolley Dolly, same as me." This followed by, "Are you sure he's even straight?"

Whenever I meet a female foreigner, newish to Rome, and she tells me she has just begun dating an Italian man, I have to ask, "Does he only want to fuck you in the ass?"

And she will look at me astonished, then shyly respond, "Wait—what? Why? Is that common? I mean, I thought that was only *my* boyfriend."

"No," I will tell her, "it isn't only *your* boyfriend."

I am continually compelled to ask this question—in the name of research, of course—even though I know it isn't any of my business. I could not care less if the woman across from me eschews the act, or if she puts up with it out of some combination of language barrier meets unfathomable sense of obligation, or if she just happens to adore the practice. In fact, if it's the latter, she has happily landed in the right country. What interests me is that I have yet to meet a foreign female who has *not* had this experience. Of course, this proclivity exists the world over, but back in Chicago where

I'm from, the act is one that any boyfriend (and note the use of the term *boyfriend*) would broach slowly, cautiously, at the very minimum after a certain level of intimacy has been established. Back in the real world, meaning anywhere but Italy, you would be hard-pressed to find a guy who would simply assume that your bum is on the menu right out of the gate, much less during a casual encounter. Gay men notwithstanding. But with Italian men it *is* an assumption. And they don't even politely ask—they just go for it.

Call this behavior whatever you want, but for me, it falls into the category of Madonna/Whore Complex—those three little words again—about which I have come up with a few theories: What with the specter of the Catholic Church looming large over Rome and virginity at such premium in the Church, I wondered if perhaps the Italian propensity to breach a different port of entry might not, in fact, be considered an actual breach? I wondered if, over time, approaching from the rear might have become a way around that pesky issue of the breaking of the hymen. But the question remains: Is Maria still a virgin if Marco only gives it to her in the ass? Perhaps I need to ask a priest to clarify.

My second theory: Maybe this anal obsession could be traced to some sort of crude attempt at birth control. For a country that, theoretically at least, doesn't approve of The Pill, Italy *does* have a radically low birth rate. And we've already established that Italians don't waste their time with condoms. Or it could be that the assumption is simply this: that all foreign women are easy, therefore all foreign women will let you do *anything* to them. Or, maybe, just maybe, if an Italian happens to be cheating on his partner, he eases his conscience by convincing himself that sodomy isn't really sex, therefore he isn't really cheating. (Kind of like being on the DL isn't really dabbling in homosexuality.) Of course, that last theory begs the question if cheating is seemingly acceptable behavior in

Italy, why bother with the back door to begin with? Aren't women pretty much designed with the perfect equipment to accommodate a penis? Ah, the conundrum of it all.

Which brings me to my gay friends in Rome. Of all my expatriate pals, only my gay friends seem capable of sustaining relationships with Italian men. You might guess this has something to do with a clemency in gay culture when it comes to stepping out—the whole "don't ask, don't tell" policy about whatever you've got going on the side. But that's not really it. From what I've witnessed, infidelity is not only accepted in Italy, it's compulsory, a phenomenon hard-wired into the national DNA. The reason gay men have a better shot at a relationship in Italy comes down to two things. Drama. And the ass. A love of both, I mean.

*Marco Cinque.* I never slept with Marco Cinque, but he spent so much time trying to sleep with me that I feel he must be included. Marco Cinque was a filmmaker who tilted back a massive daily dose of espresso and smoked an inordinate amount of hash and cigarettes. He allotted a bit of time each day to making his rounds to different bars, where he'd discuss film and politics and flex his English prowess by hitting on women.

When we met he told me he was in his thirties, though even in the most forgiving light Marco looked closer to fifty. He had stooped shoulders and a silver tangle of a beard, the worn look of a tooled, leather belt that had been left for decades under the glare of the Mediterranean sun. He owned two apartments in the neighborhood, one of which he rented out, the other of which he lived in and shared with a series of foreign female roommates. His criteria were simply that: foreign and female. Not that Marco was ever my landlord. He was merely my neighbor. We often crossed paths while frequenting one of the many cafés in the neighborhood. No matter which place I chose, there he seemed to be. Like his roommates, his locations rotated, seemingly with the sun.

Marco believed his English was quite good. He loved to discuss Italian cinema, telling me about this great film or that. But in keeping with the components typical of the dramatic arts, his association with the film business was, in a sense, fictional. Perhaps he *had* once directed a film, but for all the years I have been acquainted with Marco V, I never knew him to be absent from the cafés in Trastevere long enough to have put in a full day's work, much less direct a movie. If he'd told me he was an actor then I could vouch, here and now, that he was a man who took the term *method acting* to new heights. And I could only assume he had been researching the role of a filmmaker, one who, down on his luck, drifted from café to café preying on unsuspecting English-speaking women.

Although he meant no real harm, Marco V got under my skin. He had an uncanny way of popping up whenever I left the house. He was simply one of the many mysterious characters who exist in Rome, especially in an atmospheric neighborhood like mine. After a while, he was such a common sight that I equated him with the fountain in Piazza Santa Maria in Trastevere; it's always there when you stroll through, but looking a bit worse for wear, a bit worn down at the heel.

Marco was forever inviting me for coffees and dinners and conversations, but there was an inertia about him that frightened me. Something told me that if I did choose to sit beside him in a café, than then I, too, might never work again. And I was already having enough trouble getting things done. But it was Marco Cinque who introduced me to a few of the many Italian superstitions. The first was you should never leave the house with wet hair (not even in the summer) or you will catch a chill. Catching a chill in Italy is serious business, and the "wet hair equals chill" belief is just one of many ways a person might come down with something. From the reaction

I got when I dared to wander about with wet hair, it might even be *deadly.*

One day, coming out of my building, I ran into Marco V on the street in front of my house.

He looked at me and wagged his finger.

"Elisabetta," he said, "you must to use the *fon,* and if you do not want to use the *fon*, then in the afternoons I have a very nice sunlight in my windows."

I squinted at him, unsure of the meaning hidden in this sentence.

"You must not go out *così* with all your hairs wet. But you will come to my house and you can seat in the window where there is a very nice sun to dry your hairs."

O.K., so the first bit of vocabulary I needed here was that a *fon* (sounds like *phone*) is actually a hair dryer. Got it. Secondly, what? I am supposed to waltz down the street, freshly showered, and plant myself in a puddle of sunlight on Marco's windowsill? How does that work exactly? Does he know how often I wash my hairs? Or how long it takes all of them to dry? Was this a new scheme to get me back to his apartment after several other failed attempts? If so, it seemed much easier to buy a *fon* and avoid the conversation all together.

Once he realized that I wasn't going to come over and hang out in a towel, waiting for my hair to dry, much less get into bed with him, Marco Cinque stopped being so nice to me. I'd go so far as to say that he began ducking into shops or studiously avoiding me whenever possible. He moved on to other foreigners, other cafés, but years later, he is still here in Trastevere, holding court—espresso and cigarette in hand and, if I happen to catch his eye, he will nod at me as I pass by.

Beyond the filmmakers who never made films, there were the actors who never acted, journalists who never filed stories, architects who had never designed buildings, and students still in their thirties or forties who had never had jobs, nearly all living with their parents. Rome was all smoke and mirrors. Everybody had a title, but nobody seemed to *do* anything. And the more noble the lineage, the more likely they were to be out of work.

In spite of Rome's glorious history of producing manly men who had waged wars and captured continents, it appeared that over time another aspect of the empire's collective psyche had won out. The Bread and Circuses mentality—that love of debauchery—had been sustained through the centuries, while the intellectual forefathers who had engineered the first roads, invented concrete, and constructed the Colosseum had seemingly given birth to sons forever in a state of arrested development. The warriors had been replaced with wimps.

Taking the concept of *dolce far niente*—sweet idleness— to new heights, the men I met in Rome spent their nights smoking hordes of hand-rolled cigarettes, swilling beer, and arguing politics—in English—a language their wives and girlfriends couldn't understand. All the while, those same wives and girlfriends managed to hold down jobs and bring up children.

Patterns began to emerge. All of my friends' Italian boyfriends and all of my Italian dates—I can't really call them boyfriends, though truthfully the concept of dating is as nonexistent in Italy as a steady boyfriend has ever been in my life—tended toward holidays in Cuba and Brazil. First it seemed coincidental, then purely an affinity for the sea, a passion for the beach, maybe even a fondness for countries where the language is similar to Italian. But these vacation destinations were always frequented "with the boys," never with girlfriends, fiancées, or wives. The motivation behind these trips soon revealed itself to be a side effect of the Madonna/Whore Complex, a phenomenon I refer to as, "I like Cuba. I like Brazil . . . No, wait, I really just like black prostitutes."

This tendency exists on home soil, as well. On any given day, a drive toward the beach at Ostia will yield a bevy of prostitutes, statuesque beneath the shade of an umbrella pine, wearing a micro mini or short-shorts, ass out to the road. They never face the passing cars. I am always disturbed by this sight, so much so that I pretty much avoid going to the beach altogether. Whenever I see a customer, usually in an expensive, imported car, slowing in front of one of these prostitutes, it saddens me greatly. It is just too upsetting, gliding past all those stunning women, catching a glimpse of the shape their days seem to take.

Then there is the Brazilian transvestite situation. On any given night there are an inordinate number of trannies working the edges of the posh Villa Borghese or trawling the Terme di Caracalla, Rome's complex of ancient thermal baths. My Italian friends will sometimes look confused, claiming they don't understand the reason so many transvestites end up in Rome. I tell them it comes down to economics, simple supply and demand. They don't like that answer. Still, whenever you read those tantalizing stories about Italian politicians or the heirs to an Italian fortune falling from grace, there is always a transvestite somewhere in the mix. It's uncanny.

Sometimes I think if Rome were a female, she'd actually be a Brazilian transvestite.

So what is it about the Eternal City that beckons women of all ages to flock through its ancient gates? Partly, it's the romantic notion of the Latin lover that has prevailed through the ages. But is that really it? Whenever new acquaintances discover how long I have lived in Rome, the first assumption is always that I must have fallen in love—and that is why I stayed. People seem disappointed when I tell them this is hardly the case.

It's easy to assume that women come to Rome in search of the dark-eyed stranger, a whisper of danger about him, who sings out, "*Ciao, bella!*" and offers a midnight ride on his Vespa, but that cliché feels reductive to me. That same woman, the one who is independent enough to pack her bags and swap countries or even continents, is hardly the kind of woman who would be content to be relegated to the back of a *motorino*, bouncing along cobblestone streets. She will, at the very least, want to drive. Contrary to what I see in the movies or read in books, I have met very few foreign women who have happily coupled with an Italian male, at least not with one born and raised in the Mother Country.

I have a very good friend, an American in her seventies, who has lived in Rome for more than half her life. She loves the city and wouldn't give it up to live anywhere else. Long since divorced, she always tells me, "Get out while you still can. It's fine for me not to date, I've already had a husband and kids—but you truly must leave if you want to meet somebody."

She says it so sweetly and yet so often that I have begun to believe she is right, though I usually just shrug. Then she will put her arm around me and whisper, "After you meet him, you can always bring him back."

This import export technique actually seems to work. The foreigners who do manage to find an Italian who makes them happy usually hustle him out of the country and back to their respective homelands about as fast as I can slam down an espresso. As for the other women I know, aside from the many who have already jumped ship in spite of their best intentions to build a life here, most have had to import boyfriends and husbands from anywhere that isn't Italy. They scour Europe first, arranging dates through Internet sites in London, Amsterdam, or Brussels.

Even France will do. Sometimes, as my friend suggested, they'll leave in search of a man they can couple with, and then they set about the task of convincing him to move to Rome.

This is not so hard to manage. It is just incredibly difficult to convince him to stay once he realizes that his pay will most likely be cut by two-thirds and that it will take him more than a year to have an Internet connection installed.

I suppose that's why nearly all of my female friends in Rome are single. They are sculptors and scholars, chefs and architects; they are journalists, jewelry designers, filmmakers, and actresses. They are accomplished. They are fun. They are attractive. They are women who have never suffered so many harrowing stretches of singlehood anywhere else in the world. I am one of them.

And yet, I remain.

~≈ ~≈ ~≈

*Elizabeth Geoghegan writes in English, dreams in Italian, and wishes she could remember how to speak French. She earned an M.F.A. in Fiction Writing from the School of the Art Institute of Chicago and an M.A. in Creative Writing from The University of Colorado at Boulder. "The Marco Chronicles: To Rome, Without Love" was previously published by Shebooks and is a best-selling Kindle Single on Amazon. Geoghegan is also the author of* Natural Disasters: Stories. *She is currently at work on a novel set in Southeast Asia. She lives in Rome on a dead-end street between a convent and a jail.*

❧ ❧ ❧

# What Is that Thing?

Wild baboons got the best of him.

The first car I owned in Africa was a Volkswagen Thing that looked rugged enough to climb Aunt Fanny's Pantry in Yosemite with one tire tied behind its back. Instead of being rugged, however, it simply focused on the illusion of looking rugged. It had few amenities, a lousy suspension, and no front grille. But I loved it even though its nickname was the "Rolling Death." I loved it even though it was so ugly that years later, it was voted #6 of the 50 ugliest cars in the past half century. I loved it because of Abbott and Costello.

The old A&C routine "Who's on First?" is comic genius, and my Thing permitted me to trope my inner Bud Abbott. For example, I'd park near Addy's Tobacco Road Joint Bar, my favorite watering hole in Banjul, and a tourist would come out, look at the car, and typically start with the questions.

"What is that thing?" he'd ask. Oh, thank you British tourist, I'd say to myself.

"Yes, yes," I'd say.

"Yes?" he'd reply. "No, I mean, that thing. Parked right there. What is it?"

"This Thing?" I'd continue.

"Yes, that thing."

"A Thing." I'd say, lifting my eyebrows.

"No, no, no," he'd say, a little flustered, touching the car. "This thing right here that I'm touching with my right hand? What is it?"

"This Thing?" I'd reply.

"Yes, that thing," he'd say.

"Good," I'd say, shaking his hand. "You've got it."

"Got what?" he'd reply.

"The name," I'd respond.

"The name of what?"

"The Thing," I'd continue.

"What thing?" he'd ask.

"That Thing you're touching right there with your right hand," I'd say, smiling.

"No, no, no. What is the name of this automobile-like thing right here that we're standing next to in front of this bar?"

"The Thing," I'd say, knowing he couldn't last much longer.

"You know, chap," he'd say, walking away, "too much exposure to the sun causes brain damage."

About this time, Addy would come out and hand me a cold Heineken.

"Someday," he said in his lilting Liberian accent, "some-bahdy's gonna clahbah you."

Addy knew about "clahbahing" because he used to be the heavyweight boxing champion of West Africa. His bar was about the size of a bathroom at a Starbuck's. But he had a nephew who would guard my car while I drank cold imported beers and listened to some of my favorite songs on his juke box. I always played Janis Joplin's incredible rendition of "Me and Bobby McGee." I once played it twenty-six times in a row. When I came back the next day, Addy had removed the record from the jukebox. He'd replaced it with Sinatra singing "My Way." I knew better than to complain, so

I switched to Joplin's version of "Mercedes Benz" until that, too, was eventually removed.

Officially my car was called the Volkswagen Type 181 and was known in Germany as the Kurierwagen. Volkswagen had developed it as a rugged off-road military vehicle for the German military in the 1960s and 1970s. Although the company used World War II versions as models for it, the Type 181 looked more like the kind of war machine the Klingons would have built; the 1990s Klingons, not the wimpy 1960s pseudo-Klingons.

In addition to the military versions, however, Volkswagen also sold commercial versions of the Type 181. In England it was known as the Trekker, and in the United States it was called The Thing.

My first encounter with a Thing began shortly after I arrived in The Gambia. Between collecting for the museum and conducting my own research, I needed a vehicle to get around the country. It was *shan'hal'lak* (Vulcan for "love at first sight" . . . I was fluent in Vulcan, by the way) when I saw that 1969 dusty orange Thing parked in front of the Peace Corps office in Banjul. It was owned by a guy from Catholic Relief Services who was leaving the country and had heard I was looking for a car. I bought it that morning for 2,000 dalasis (about $1,800).

My Thing was a convertible that came with a top that disappeared two days after I bought it. My top had probably been "borrowed" by a local entrepreneur. FYI, the word entrepreneur comes from the French word meaning "to borrow my roof like a thief in the night with no intention of returning it."

A couple of weeks after I bought the car, I learned that Alex Haley of *Roots* fame had visited The Gambia the year before. During that time, he traveled to Juffere, the village near which Kunta Kinte had apparently been abducted so

long ago. You know Kunta Kinte? *Roots* and LeVar Bur-
ton before he was Geordi La Forge on *Star Trek: The Next
Generation*?

In a newspaper interview I read, Haley recounted his
arduous journey to Juffere. His trip had involving crossing
the Gambia River to the North Bank in a fragile pirogue.
For the point of clarity, a pirogue is not pirogi. A pirogue
is small, dugout canoe. A pirogi is a meat dumpling. The
two have something in common, though. Neither floats
very well.

It was a dangerous and tough trip by Haley's account, and
only the most devoted researcher would have undertaken it.
Certainly, it must have been terrifying to cross a river filled
with crocodiles and hippos a century ago. There were still
crocodiles in The Gambia, but you'd find them at Kachikally
Crocodile Pool in the tourist-oriented town of Bakau. Tourists, the sick, and barren women made pilgrimages there to
cuddle with one of the sacred seven-foot crocodiles who live
in the sacred healing waters of the sacred pool adjacent to the
sacred cash register.

Given my interest in the cultural and musical connections between The Gambia and America, I needed to go to
Juffere to interview historians and musicians and find out
what they knew about Kunta Kinte, who apparently was
making a drum when he was captured. Fortunately for me,
I wouldn't have to take a pirogue. I could also get to Juffere
via a ferry from Banjul to Barra, followed by a ninety-minute
drive along some dirt paths. Apparently, Alex Haley hadn't
noticed the ferry.

Early one morning I loaded up my Thing with my Minolta
camera equipment, Nakamichi battery-operated portable
tape recorder, tapes, some food and water, and a variety of
presents to give to the elders, including two fifty-kilogram
sacks of rice. The ferry ride lasted about ninety minutes,

including drifting for a while after the ferry's engine cut out. Shortly after driving off the ferry, I found myself ambling along a back road off another back road. The Thing handled exquisitely at twelve miles an hour. Without a top, I could look out and enjoy the dramatic panoramic view of baobab trees with vultures in them, although I didn't like the way they were looking at me.

I had been driving about 45 minutes when I saw a smoke column in the distance. I stopped, turned off my Thing, and grabbed my binoculars to get a better view. It was soon clear that it was a large grass fire, and it was blowing in my direction.

It was also crystal clear that it was blowing hundreds of frightened animals in my direction. Leading the charge was a shitload of baboons, which have really, really, large canine teeth. I tossed the binoculars onto the passenger seat and tried to start up the car. And tried to start up the car. And tried to start up the car. But my Thing had done one of its things. It refused to start up. It didn't take me long to flood the carburetor. I sat there mesmerized as the terrified primates approached. I began to imagine the letter that would arrive back in the U.S. confirming how my body was consumed by a gang of baboons. My nephews and nieces would be so proud that Uncle Mike had died in such an unusual and dramatic way; death by baboon. However, my fate was worse. Way, way worse.

As the baboon teeth were almost upon me, I lay down on the passenger seat, hoping they wouldn't notice me in their fright. But . . . but . . . have I mentioned that my Thing was a convertible with no top? Have I?

Like most primates, baboons tend to lighten their body weight when fleeing from something frightening, and before I could say baboon pee and poop, they were pouring over and around and on top of my Thing. My sunglasses were the first to be hit by something really foul, and soon I was wishing I had worn sunglasses over my nose and mouth, neck, hair, forehead, as well as shins and knees.

They fled over me and my Thing, depositing what seemed like half their body weight on me and in my car. I lay there on the passenger seat, gagging and wondering if death by canine might have been preferable. There would be no letters to my nephews and nieces about this particular incident.

I sat up, wiped off my sunglasses, and wanted to assess the damage. But there wasn't time to do that because the grass fire was continuing my way. In a moment of what must have been automotive self-preservation (*selbstbewahrung* in its native language), my Thing started right up, and I was able to hurry back down the road. When I was out of immediate danger, I pulled over to the side of the road. Almost immediately I felt the first drop.

It was mid-August, and the rainy season had begun. To appreciate the significance of an August rain in The Gambia, I should point out that the average rainfall during August is over fifteen inches, with ten more inches in September. It rains. A lot! So much so that when you ask Gambians how old they are, you ask them how many rains they've lived through.

You know that scene in *The Shawshank Redemption* when Morgan Freeman describes how Tim Robbins had escaped by "crawling to freedom through 500 yards of shit-smelling foulness?" And then Tim Robbins celebrates by lifting his face into the downpour that washes off the shit-smelling foulness on his body? Remember? That was me as the rain fell on me and my Thing that day in The Gambia. I sat there for twenty minutes, face up while the rains washed over me. All that was missing was Thomas Newman's great soundtrack emphasizing how noble and brave I had been. When the rains subsided, I started the Thing again, and I drove slowly back to the ferry, driver-side door open, dribbling a trail of dark brown and yellow rainwater behind me.

I got rid of my Thing a few weeks after I got back to Banjul. I had cleaned it thoroughly with soap and bleach, but I couldn't bleach away the memory. And every time it rained even a little, it seemed to emit a subtle, shit-smelling foulness. I traded it to a local entrepreneur/taxi driver for a 1966 Renault Dauphine, which was much smaller but had a roof. It had no illusions of being anything special; it just worked. I later learned that the Renault Dauphine was voted #9 of the ugliest cars in the past half century. But at least I was finally through with the sorry saga of my Thing. Until . . .

About two weeks after I sold it, I saw my Thing again. I was having a beer and a meat pie at a café near the Central Taxi Car Park in Banjul. The September rains were coming down in their torrential glory, and there was my Thing, all shiny and sparkly, and it was doing very well in the rain because, well . . . because it now had a roof. And not just any roof, but MY roof, the one that had been entrepreneured off my Thing, which, by the way, was the only Thing in the whole country. That's how I knew it was my roof.

*"Sach-kat!"* I yelled at the driver. I had just called him a "thief" in Wolof. The driver took one look at me, panicked and then ran to the Thing, got in, and pulled away. I jumped up from my table and yelled at him again as he pulled away.

*"Sach-kat,"* I repeated, even louder, but I don't think he heard me yell it the second time. The rain beating down on my convertible top probably blocked the sound of my voice. I could only hope that my roof helped intensify the shit-smelling foulness the rain would evoke.

❧ ❧ ❧

*Michael Coolen is a composer, pianist, writer, and actor who lives in Corvallis, Oregon. He was a Professor of Music, Ethnomusicology, and Music Technology at Oregon State University for many years until he retired on April Fools' Day, 2010. His area of specialization was the music of Africa, in particular Senegal, The Gambia, and Zimbabwe. Over the years he created and performed with a variety of marimba and steel drum ensembles, even forming a group in Copenhagen, Denmark. He has taught in the U.S., France, Denmark, Africa, and New Zealand. This tale is taken from his memoir titled* Eat, Pray, Practice: the Adventures of an Adequate Pianist.

KEITH SKINNER

❧ ❧ ❧

# Inside the Tower

### A pilgrimage to Robinson Jeffers' Tor House.

As we walked into the room, I first noticed the bed—broad, slightly concave, uncomfortable-looking—covered with a thin, antique quilt. But it was the west-facing windows, unusually close to the floor, that caught my attention and brought back the words.

> I chose the bed downstairs by the sea-window for a
> good death-bed
> When we built the house; it is ready waiting,
> Unused unless by some guest in a twelvemonth, who
> hardly suspects
> Its latter purpose. . . .

A chill rippled across my skin as I realized that we were standing in that very room and the bed before me was the subject of the poem—the deathbed in "The Bed by the Window." Robinson Jeffers had written the poem as a young man shortly after building the house. Many years later, he had indeed died in the room, thereby fulfilling its destiny.

I had first read the poem while browsing a Jeffers anthology in a bookstore, a volume entitled *The Wild God of the World*. I knew little about the man but kept bumping into him in other writers' work. Noted authors and bohemian celebrities were always dropping in on Jeffers when passing through Carmel. There was often some degree of awe or reverence ascribed to these occasions, but very little mentioned about the man himself.

I picked up the book and, by chance, opened it to "The Bed by the Window." It was an eerie poem. More than eerie—it was downright creepy. It wasn't as though Jeffers had used death in a gratuitous manner; it wasn't a cheap, dramatic device. The bed seemed to be a fetish of sorts for him as he worked through his feelings about his own mortality.

> I often regard it,
> with neither dislike or desire; rather with both, . . .

Still, meditating on death in a poem was one thing; anticipating a lingering death in the distant future while still a young man, and building a room in which to die, was quite another.

As I read through several more poems, the voice, at times, seemed almost feral. The ruggedness of the language, the starkness of the imagery—Jeffers prowled like a lone wolf or, more accurately, a rangy coyote skirting the edge of civilization: hungry, suspicious, and angry. He seemed dark and self-absorbed. If Whitman was a Telemann concerto, full of trumpets and bright brass celebrating the world, it seemed to me that Jeffers was a melancholy cello solo played mournfully in a dim, candlelit room. For some unexplained reason, I felt compelled to buy the book, though it wasn't long before it was abandoned on a bookshelf and I had put Jeffers out of my mind.

Several days before I found myself standing in Jeffers' bedroom, and nearly a year after I had bought the anthology, I was staying in Big Sur and came across an article in a local magazine about the building of Tor House, Jeffers' home. I knew the house was in Carmel but knew little of its history. The article recounted how Jeffers had purchased an uninhabited plot of land on Carmel Point and had hired a stone mason to build a house for him. He apprenticed himself to the builder so he could learn how to set stone himself. Once the house was finished, Jeffers spent nearly four years building a forty-foot-high tower on the property, hauling boulders from a nearby beach and hoisting them into place by himself using only a block and tackle.

The story about the tower was as provocative and unsettling as the deathbed poem. Who was this guy? He had rolled boulders, some weighing as much as 400 pounds, several hundred yards uphill, through coastal scrub, and then had set each one by hand—alone. This only confirmed my suspicions that the man was obsessive and unpredictable if not outright stubborn. But he had somehow gotten under my skin. I decided to stop in Carmel to visit Tor House on my way home, to see this mad man's tower, and to try to unravel the Jeffers riddle that kept resurfacing.

Our small tour group was still huddled around Jeffers' bed as if gathered to say our final goodbyes while the docent recited the deathbed poem. It was a sober moment for everyone. I looked out through the sea-window with its simple curtains and wooden window seat, across the gray-green mat of garden sprinkled with drifts of May flowers, to the gun metal surf churning in the distance. It was a stormy day and dark clouds were furrowed along the horizon. I wondered what had gone through Jeffers' mind as he lay dying, his head turned toward the window, gazing at a similar scene. Was there a sense of resignation? Regret? Fear? Or was the sight of hawks circling and pelicans diving for fish in the white foam a comfort to him, an affirmation that the natural rhythms of life overlap each other like the waves of the incoming tide? Rather than a morbid fixation, perhaps the deathbed was Jeffers' attempt to take some control over his own, inevitable fate.

What I had expected to be an ordinary tour had become
something more profound. As we filed into the living room, a
latent energy seemed to linger in the house, as if the family had
gone out for a walk together and, at any minute, the two boys
would come bursting in through the door with a dog at their
heels. This sensation was due, in part, to the way our docent
had made the home come alive for us. He told stories about
each room that portrayed the fierce love affair between Jeffers
and his wife Una and of a family life that was often insular
but very closely knit. The docent had recited Jeffers' poems in
such a heartfelt manner at different places around the property that it was almost as if the poet himself was speaking and
pointing out his favorite places—the cornerstone of the house,
keepsakes from travels embedded in the walls of the house
and the garden, and stones that had been carved with words
or quotes, then placed along the garden path.

If the house seemed infused with the warmth of family life,
the world outside, at least on this day, was more typical of Jeffers' flinty demeanor. I zipped up my jacket and cinched the
hood tightly around my face as we crossed the small yard. It
was perfect weather, I thought, to visit the tower that loomed
in front of us.

Hawk Tower was an odd structure, simultaneously squat
and gangly. Una had long admired the medieval towers found
throughout Ireland, and Jeffers had tried to replicate the style.
But the structure in front of me looked nothing like those I
had seen in Ireland, other than ruins where the ramparts had
either been breached or severely ravaged by time.

There were two ways to move about within the structure—
the wider, external staircase, or the interior, "secret" passageway that Jeffers had built for his sons. We were warned that
the passageway was dark and extremely narrow in places and
the steps, unusually steep. I chose the passageway because
Jeffers often used it himself, and I had a hunch the other

members of my group would take the stairs. I would be alone
with Jeffers and the dark, cold stone.

> Old but still strong I climb the stone, . . .
> Climb the steep rough steps alone.

I climbed past the first landing that served as a play area for
the two boys and up to Una's stronghold. Over a small fireplace in the corner, Jeffers had carved a wooden mantle with
a line of Latin from Virgil that roughly translated to "lovers
fashion their own dreams." It seemed to describe Tor House
so precisely. The stone buildings, the keepsakes everywhere,
the wildness of their surroundings—the Jeffers had carefully
created a world, a dream, solely for themselves. If the outside world chose to drop in for dinner or otherwise share that
dream momentarily, so be it. Robin and Una required only
each other's company and the promontory overlooking the
ocean; the rest of the world could be damned.

I continued up to the outside parapet at the top of the
tower, carefully navigating the steep, wet steps and pulling
myself up by the hefty anchor chain that served as a handrail.
The wind had picked up and gusts of rain stung my face the
higher I climbed. I turned southward and scanned the jagged
coast, the tree-lined shore that stretched into the distance and
wrapped around the bay to join Point Lobos.

> White-maned, wide-throated, the heavy-shouldered
> children of the wind leap at the sea-cliff.

I imagined Jeffers standing in this very spot in a squall,
pensive and content as he took in the surrounding natural
world that, at the time, laid claim to Carmel Point. Up on
this perch, he would become hawklike—calm, watchful, and
uncomplicated, comforted by the elements and the power of
wind and ocean.

Jeffers may have built the tower for Una, but it was
more than a simple material gift he had given her. It was

himself—his blustery spirit, his wild-god heart embodied in granite, each stone placed as carefully as the words he arranged upon a page. As I gazed into the horizon and considered this thought, my hands atop the coarse, damp stone Jeffers had placed there with his own two hands, he no longer seemed a mystery to me. He was neither dark nor self-absorbed as I had first judged him to be. He was this tower, strong and resolute, incorporating all that surrounded him into its surface and protecting all that was dear to him within. I needed to hear his words within these walls, feel the wind and rain against my skin as he had, and view the world from his tower before I could grasp the essence of the man.

❧ ❧ ❧

*Keith Skinner is a writer and photographer living in Berkeley, California. His travel articles have appeared in the* San Francisco Chronicle. *Most recently, "Inside the Tower" received an honorable mention in New Millennium Writings' nonfiction contest. Keith is currently working on a historical novel about the nineteenth-century Mendocino Coast.*

HANNAH SHELDON-DEAN

✎  ✎  ✎

# Notes into Lines

After all, music is the universal language.

In the middle of the St. Charles Bridge on a warm day in
Prague, we wait with our binders of music, wondering
if anyone will bother to show up. There are five or six of us
here now, out of perhaps twenty-five. We've been singing all
week, and this is our day off; we wouldn't blame the rest of
our friends for not coming. The tourists take pictures of the
statue above us, and the jazz combo carries on down the way.
You wouldn't blame the tourists, either, if they didn't want to
pay attention to us, but we're hoping they will.

In New York, I practice my choir music at home alone
between rehearsals, coaxing my brain through a process that
still feels alien, even after two years. Because I didn't learn to
sight-read music when I was younger, I'm still learning now.
It's the difference between knowing a language well enough
to translate it in your head and knowing that same language
well enough to understand the words' meaning with immedi
acy, without translation. There are so many words, each with
significance, and multiple meanings.

In front of my keyboard on the floor of my apartment,
I stitch the notes together slowly, learning every line as if
it were a melody, even though it usually isn't. Sometimes,

49

it's like trying to tie a knot using only one hand. By the time rehearsal comes around on Sunday evening, I've woven the lines into my brain, so that they're waiting for me when I open my folder full of sheet music. It's a joy every time, to stand among the other altos and hear myself singing the same thing that they are, proof that I've done my work well. It's a way of immediate understanding that doesn't come along often, in my experience. Even better is later, when I can turn my attention away from what I am doing and toward what we are doing together as a choir, a much more elaborate form of breathed pattern-making. It's an exhilarating thing, hours and hours of practice spread between twenty-something singers, condensed into a few minutes of rare cohesion.

Our first audience in the Czech Republic was an auditorium full of school children. Little kids, maybe ages six to twelve. Our repertoire for the weeklong tour is heavy stuff— lots of dissonance, lots of minor keys, lots of songs that stretch beyond the five-minute mark. Anxious about holding the kids' attention, our conductor cut the program short, down to about an hour. The school was quiet as we made our way to the stage, fighting off last night's jet lag.

In New York, we beg all around town to get attendees at our concerts. We've sung with some great musicians at some great venues, but when it comes time to fill the pews at our home field, the Shrine of St. Anthony of Padua, it's never as many as we hope. Our own friends and family make excuses more often than not, but I don't hold it against them. It's hard to know what to make of us, a gang of young, pretty, secular people singing old, strange, sacred music in a giant stone church. Sometimes it's new music, actually, but it all tends to sound foreign to pop-tuned ears. It sounded that way to me before I joined, and the mystery was part of what drew me to it. If there's a place in the United States where audiences might bother to seek us out, you'd think it would be

New York, but as it happens, they generally don't. The ones that do come applaud politely and tell us afterward that the concert was beautiful—that's what friends are for.

In the auditorium at the school in the Czech Republic, the children looked just like American children, like there could be whispering and giggling hiding right beneath their polite surface. Then we began to sing, and the children stayed quiet. They did not squirm in their seats. They knew when to applaud, and they kept their eyes on us for the entire hour. We glanced at each other in awe between songs: *Where did we find an audience like this?*

When our translator asked them, at the end of the concert, if they had any questions for us, hands went up all around the auditorium. How often do you practice? Is it hard to learn so many songs? What's that thing you hold up next to your ear at the beginning of each song? When our conductor passed his tuning fork out into the crowd, the children rippled toward it in a murmuring wave, as if he'd brought them candy. And when their teacher asked who'd like to perform for the visitors, a gang of kids appeared on the stage almost instantly, singing folk music by heart.

When we left, they followed us out to our bus, asking for autographs. One little girl drew a picture of a bear and gave it to our conductor, with the words *For your teem* written underneath.

New York, everybody knows, is a mecca of culture, a land of opportunity for the artistically minded. But New York had nothing on the Czech towns we visited. At the end of our second concert, a tearful teenage music student presented us with flowers and an angel figurine and thanked us for one of the best nights of her life. The next night, the entire population of a town in the countryside came to see us sing, and afterward, the mayor invited us over to his office for drinks. "These cakes," said the mayor's gangly young translator, gesturing to the silver trays of pastries on the table in front of us, "were made for you by my mother!" Not to be outdone, the mayor informed us that he loved to sing and usually did so publically only once a year, at the town's annual cheese festival. "But tonight," the translator told us, "he makes an exception for you!" The staff pressed more slivovitz on us, as the portly mayor launched into an aria.

*Don't they realize?* I thought of myself alone in my apartment, building my notes into lines.

The next city we visited, Karvina, was like a life-sized toy; everywhere we went, stores and restaurants seemed nearly abandoned, and around each corner we'd find ourselves running into each other and no one else. Even on a prominent billboard in the city's central square, there we were, looking back at ourselves out of an oversized black and white print of our group photo. But that night at the church, there was everyone who hadn't been wandering around the city earlier, listening, applauding, caring that we were there.

I had a nagging feeling that we were cheating them: *Listen,* I wanted to say, *in New York, we're nobody.* But there was something else: we sounded beautiful. We were singing as perfectly as we'd ever sung. Later, back in New York, we found a point in one concert recording where every woman in the group sang a single *glissando*, a sliding note, in exact unison. We replayed it three or four times to make sure, because how could that be? How could so many of us have become a single voice?

Our final concert was the biggest, the reason we had come on the tour in the first place. We were one act of an opera festival honoring Czech composer Bedrich Smetana in his home city of Litomysl. As a choral group, we weren't sure we'd interest many opera fans—and they didn't know who we were, we hadn't begged them to come, we hadn't been marketing ourselves; this wasn't New York.

There were hundreds of people there, filling the interstices of our largest Czech venue.

These are my favorite moments: when my voice fits so snugly with the others that I'm no longer sure I'm singing. I can feel the sound, but barely hear it. At the end of the back row of altos, I was so close to the front row of the audience that I felt sure, at first, that they must be scrutinizing me, noticing each breath and snag in my voice. By the end of the concert, I was certain that they could not; I was barely there, anyway.

We finished the encore for this last concert and left the church, back out onto the cobblestones outside, heading for the vestry where our New York skins were waiting for us.

"Come back—you have to come back! We're going back inside."

We stumbled back on the slippery stones, to the sanctuary where the audience was still on its feet. We were happy and unprepared; when had anyone ever demanded a second encore of us? We sang a pretty Spanish song, straightforward and cheerful, one we'd learned for Christmas shows and for anytime we needed to sound like we knew what we were doing.

To my mind there were two options: We had fooled them, or else New York had fooled us.

That evening, we sat outside at a Cuban-themed bar where they stopped serving drinks at eleven. Along the wall behind our table, there was a wooden support beam just a few feet higher than the backs of the metal chairs. I climbed up onto it and sat there with my knee leaning against my boyfriend's shoulder, swinging my other foot and drinking a minty cocktail that cost me the equivalent of about two U.S. dollars. I'm happiest, always, sitting just a ways apart from others, looking at things from an angle that no one else can see.

"Guys," I said. "In New York, someone would have told me to get down from here by now."

Just then, a Czech woman hurried over to us, looking like maybe she worked at the bar. I braced myself, ready to apologize, to get down and sit in a chair like a civilized person.

"I don't speak English," she said, in English. "But— sexy girl!"

"Thank you!" I said, and meant it, while my boyfriend smiled. In New York, we might have been offended.

That was last night, before we left for a final day in Prague before the trip's end. Here on the St. Charles Bridge, we know we've had our moment; this, now, is just for fun, and to see if we can get the tourists to toss us enough koruna to buy a single round of insanely cheap beer. It's 5:30, the appointed time. If it's just six of us, that's O.K.; none of these people know our name, and there's no pressure to do well.

It's Sunday, and the bridge is packed with crowds in both directions. Unlike the other cities we've been in this week, it's easy to lose each other here. But then Garrett appears, and Carah, and there's Justin. Steph, Lindsay, Alyssa. Audrey and her husband Gordon, and even Adam, who said earlier that he was tired of singing and wouldn't come. One by one and a few at a time, we all materialize, as if required to do so. We fan into an arch, and place a straw hat in the middle with a handful of change inside.

By the third measure—just seconds into the song—a crowd has gathered, curious and eager. We have only a few binders of music to go around; we're peering over each other's shoulders and laughing when we miss entrances and sing the wrong notes. We're a mess compared to the rest of our performances this week, but the crowd just gets bigger. An hour passes and we run out of material, and no one hesitates to start the entire set over again. As we sing through our opening song a third and final time, a man in the front row of the crowd stands with eyes closed and spine straight, choosing our voices over a stunning view of an entire city.

When we pick through the hat later, there is Czech money, Euros, Turkish money, American money, and even a single British pound. At one point, a family from Minnesota comes over to talk to us between songs, and when we tell them we're from New York, they say, "You're doing our country proud!"

Nothing will be different when we return to New York. It's not as if the mayor's translator's mother is going to tell all her friends to pack the pews at St. Anthony's next time we have a concert. We'll never see those schoolchildren again, or that family from Minnesota, and we won't put their words on our website. To New York, we'll appear just the same as ever. But New York to us, or to me anyway, will look different; I'll understand, I hope, that it has edges, and that it ends. That despite what it says to us with its winking skyscrapers and infinite currency, New York is not the world.

As I sit alone in my apartment in Brooklyn, stitching and unstitching, I am someone, and if I forget myself as I hope I can, there is every chance that some other one may close his eyes and choose to listen, and women I've never met may bake cakes with me in mind.

᳇ ᳇ ᳇

*Hannah Sheldon-Dean is a generalist to the core, and splits her time between freelance writing and her studies in the master's program at New York University's Silver School of Social Work.*

MATTHEW CROMPTON

≈ ≈ ≈

# Into the Hills

A journey into remote monsoon hills of Sikkim yields
difficulty, insight, and transformation for a lone traveler.

*The ball that we hurled into infinite space,*
*doesn't it fill our hand differently with its return:*
*heavier by the weight of where it has been?*
—Rilke

## THE CITY

The impression of Calcutta, arriving on a sweltering
afternoon in early summer, is not of an ancient city
existing, like Benares, outside of time. Instead, it feels like
a city built a hundred years ago and then abandoned, left
to moisture and mold and dust while its builders crept off to
sunnier pastures. What makes the city strange, then, is that
it feels populated, not by its original inhabitants, but by scav-
engers, squatting in the abandoned city in droves, peopling
every decrepit inch, like beings who have crawled up from the
wild to inhabit its lanes and shopfronts and markets, indiffer-
ent to the notion of civilization that they are inhabiting.

The abstract shape of the city emerges as I travel into the center—traffic, noise, squalor, chaos, heat. My hotel room in a lane off Marquis Street is roasting, chemical with the camphor-smell of mothballs resting in the bathroom sink. The pillows are lumpy sacks and the fan churns the baking air relentlessly. With the heat peaking into full force (an outdoor thermometer reads 36°C), I step out beneath my parasol and walk up RN Mukherjee Road, past the *poori* and *chai* vendors, the *nimbu pani* carts with their filthy glasses and handfuls of tainted ice.

When Hunter S. Thompson remarked on freaks at home in the freak kingdom, he could have meant this place. Calcutta—now Kolkata—is special in this respect. So far on the edges of the Indian universe that it's not on the way to anything, it attracts the real crusties and the genuinely strange. In the Eastern Railways tourist bureau near the Houghly River I meet a barefoot Korean man carrying a huge red wooden cross. I exchange a few pleasantries with him in Korean before he hobbles off, manic and sweating, his toes wrapped in a filthy bandage—"God Bless You!" he calls back after himself, "Jesus Christ! Jesus Christ! Jesus Christ!" And why not, I think? Here, everyone is welcome.

It is enough, I think, to be here in the streets, because the streets are always alive—in the morning people bathing and shaving and defecating and taking *chai*, in the afternoons hawking and pulling rickshaws and selling fruit and bearing burdens. In the evening, the heat and madness of Calcutta are barely diminished by the fall of night. As I walk the streets in the twilight I keep thinking, "There is no place on earth that smells like this, no place that feels like this . . ." The night perfume is in the air, wafting in the scent of flower garlands and the bitumen stink of burning coal from cooking fires, the resinous ghost of sandalwood. In the vivisected bazaar of the twilight city, Muslim men are lit by bare bulbs hanging behind the ribs of butchered goats, and veiled women are chased across the street by screaming-yellow Ambassador taxis circa 1961 James Bond, and again, there are no borders anywhere.

My final morning in the city, before the nighttime sleeper train to Darjeeling, I take the metro south to Kalighat and the Kali temple there. "Kali is power," an old Brahmin in a dirt-stained shirt tells me amidst the goat shit and vivid hibiscus blossoms and stippled blood decorating the ground around the courtyard altar, where a goat has just been sacrificed to the devouring mother.

"What do people need power for?"

"For everything in life, friend, for everything you need power."

And I think: do I not travel because I too am full of wishing? Have I not come here, to be apart, because I find that India is ruled by magic, still? Thinking better of goat sacrifice, I buy a lotus flower and a bundle of dried blossoms, and push with the small crowd into the dim interior of the temple, 400 years old and smelling of incense and human sweat. People are shouting prayers and mantras, incongruous for a quiet Thursday morning, but this intensity is what I love. A man presses a blood-red hibiscus into my palm, and as I move before the idol, I cast my blossoms with intent violence into the pile of offerings at its feet.

"What is your name?" the priest asks me as I stand amidst the crowd, shouting and screaming their prayers to be heard.

"My name is Matthew," I say, making sure my voice is strong and clear.

If there is a power to this moment, I want for it to hear me. All blessings are just echoes of our sincerest wishes, carried through the ether and emerging, real, on the farther side of time.

## DARJEELING

Morning in Darjeeling is a monsoon hill town dawn, the clouds like a curtain around the city, thick as fog. In the diffuse gray light I walk downhill from my hotel high on the ridge, through the narrow, twisting lanes investing the hillside like an ant farm. In the main plaza at Chowrasta, dogs lie on the damp pavement, chewing at their flanks, porters with Sinic Nepali eyes carrying burdens up the fog-slick hills braced on forehead tump lines. I take a breakfast of milk tea and greasy fry bread wrapped in newsprint from a streetside stall, watching the gaggles of domestic Indian tourists transit through the square, enjoying joyrides on broken ponies, bundled in heavy woolens and skullcaps.

Darjeeling is the easy part of travel. For three days I live the life of some low-level colonial flunky of the kind who would once have escaped to this town from the violent heat of the summer plains, taking long breakfasts with tea in the cloudy bazaar and wandering the lanes with an umbrella beneath the sporadic rains. Founded by the British East India Company in 1835, Darjeeling drew thousands of laborers from nearby Nepal, ensuring an identity at odds with the lowland state of West Bengal that eventually came to govern it, and in time, violent agitation for statehood as "Gorkhaland," resulting in limited (if to most unsatisfactory) autonomy in the form of the Darjeeling Gorkha Hill Council.

With the Chinese invasion of Tibet in 1959, thousands of Tibetan families fled over the eastern Himalaya, through Nepal, many to settle in Darjeeling, making it (along with Dharamsala) one of the primary centers for the Tibetan community in exile, undiluted by Han resettlement and Chinese government interference. Talking to a Tibetan shopkeeper named Dorje on Hill Cart Road south of town one day, I ask him what he thought of the recent resignation of the Dalai

Lama as the political leader of Tibet—curious about the views of a subject of one of the world's last great theocracies.

"He is still our religious leader, our spiritual leader, of course. But it is now 2011. We have so many young Tibetans who have studied at Oxford and Cambridge and Harvard—do they not also deserve a chance to lead Tibet?"

"And do you think that will happen with the Chinese still occupying?"

He shrugs. "We have autonomy, yes, but of course, autonomy is not independence. Independence is better."

He wraps up my Oreos in brown paper. "Anyway," he smiles, "anything is possible."

In the evenings I walk downhill through the bazaar to Joey's Pub—proper, British, wood paneled, Union Jack on the wall—and drink tall Kingfishers in the cozy, hazy space around low tables with other Anglophones, businessmen, and backpackers like some colonial social club, then stumble half-drunk up the hill in the darkness to my bed and sleep, thinking how easy it would be to remain in this congenial place living my small-town colonial fantasy, but feeling in my bones the emptiness of ease, knowing how reliably common actions lead to common results.

I began traveling, I think, as a way of seeking identity, or at least of embracing the estrangement I felt from my native conditions—an unchallenging university career that yielded few friends and no sense of belonging, short-time jobs temping or waiting tables, transplanted across the country to a home where in nearly five years I gained friends but never roots. Pico Iyer wrote in *The Global Soul* about the existential condition of elective statelessness, the vagrancy that carried long enough becomes an enduring facet of oneself, an unbelonging that, paradoxically, is itself homelike; and I find myself thinking of the sadhu back at the train station in Calcutta, just a week ago.

At nearly eleven P.M. at Sealdah Station that night, the platforms were still mobbed. The stationmaster would announce a train arriving at platform five and suddenly the mobs would bolt for it, shoving and contending in the Indian way, eager for a seat in the overcrowded unreserved second-class car in which they would be travelling overnight, to Varanasi or Lucknow or even Delhi, god forbid. I was bone-tired and sticky with sweat, 34°C outside even deep into the night, as I watched the scrum, the wolfish and pathetic packs of dark single men, the families with children, the immature soldiers with their mustaches and automatic carbines and sternly affected scowls, the women looking queenly and fiercely dignified in saris. It was through this maelstrom, the endless breaking cascade of people passing by, burdened with their baggage and identities, that I saw the lone sadhu. He was like a ghost, dreadlocked and shirtless, thin and ash-smeared, moving slowly, a wanderer without place or profession; in transit, perhaps, but unintent upon arriving. I felt a kinship there.

It's an unremarked-on fact that the regimen most associated with Eastern religions the monk's way of structured meditation and work and prayer, the so-called monastic life—is in a very real sense a later addition to the project of enlightenment, an innovation of the civilized and bureaucratic consciousness. The Indian method, if it can even be called that, is simpler, wilder, improvisational—renounce your home, your possessions and attachments, and simply wander, intent on the knowledge that God, whatever that is, knows exactly where it wants to take you. I suppose this is how, two days later, I found myself in the hills of western Sikkim, squatting at nightfall beside a low earthen stove in the kitchen hut of a thirteen-year-old boy named Ronald Bhujel.

## RONALD

Being enthusiastically received and, in time, feted by the very poor is one of the most beautiful and heartbreaking experiences in travel. Ronald, in his blue blazer and slacks, just let out from classes, had invited me to his home up a village footpath in the hills, late into a day of walking some fifteen kilometers west of Jorethang, where I had taken a jeep that morning from Darjeeling. I had climbed more than a thousand meters into the green hinterland of West Sikkim along the winding hill road, dehydrated and filthy and miserable, blinking into the sun and passed by blatting trucks. My feet were blistered and sore, and I was eager to rest.

High on the ridge amidst the terrace patches of maize and ginger where I could look down and see the thin gray-blue ribbon of the Raman Khola dividing the one-time Buddhist kingdom of Sikkim from the state of West Bengal to the south, I bathed in a low outhouse with cold water and borrowed soap, then changed into fresh clothes. Ronald was Christian, like most of his small community on the hill, and shared a single bare room with his grandmother, a poured-concrete box furnished with three narrow plank beds and a single cabinet and decorated with lurid pictures of Jesus and the Sacred Heart. On the cabinet were sun-bleached photographs of an absent woman who I took to be his mother. I drank the sweet tea his grandmother had prepared for me and asked him where his parents were.

"This is my family, yes?" he said, smiling nervously at his grandmother and adult brother, his brother's six-year-old son Aryun, whom he also called his brother. "It is a small family," he babbled a little, "a good family . . ." and I knew then that his parents had died.

In time all the households of the village, some twenty people, stopped by to say hello and chat. I entertained the children by memorizing and then writing their names in Korean

script and answered countless questions about my bald-
ness and marital status. When darkness fell, I was ushered
into the smoke-stained, biscuit-colored kitchen beneath the
three-quarter moon and given warm beer and a bowl of fried
organs, chicken heart and liver, the choicest pieces of a dish
that was itself an extravagance.

I slept that night in a bed with both head- and footboard
that was some nine inches shorter than my legs, necessitating
a great deal of creative geometry and was woken stiff-necked
at a quarter to seven by Ronald peering in the window at me,
barking like an excited puppy: "It is time to wash your face!"
At the parting, Ronald and his family refused my money, eyes
downcast, though my visit had doubtless cost them the equivalent of a week's worth of meals. As I walked down the hill
with Ronald on his way to school, he mentioned again, as he
had all night, that in three weeks he would have vacation, and
that I should return, and we would travel Sikkim together,
though I knew that this village was on the way to nowhere,
and I would not be coming back.

On the main road, when I went to say goodbye, Ronald
burst into tears. "If you can, you will come, O.K.?" he said, his
lip trembling as he fought to maintain control. "Only if you
can . . ." He was sobbing. I gave him a handshake and an awkward hug and then turned away down the road, knowing that
my merely being here was the highlight of his whole year, that
my having happened for a day into his life was a better thing
for him than Christmas and feeling the sinking adult burden
of having all a child's hope projected onto you, knowing that
you will break his heart.

I teared up as I walked away, thinking how happy I had
been for that one night, a part of Ronald's little patchwork
family high up on the ridge, squatted in the smoky kitchen
with Aryun yawning and the lights of the villages faraway all
glitter across the valley through the window. And the sense

was with me as I cried, "I'm too far away from everything, too far from everyone I know, too far . . ."

Damn.

## BARSEY TO PELLING

The paradoxical thing about trekking is that we spend much of our time whilst doing it simply wishing it would end. Few leisure activities offer, not just difficulty, but the passionate desire that the activity would cease, five minutes ago if possible. It is also unique in the level to which, having reached this point, you are committed to continue. Done reading a book? Just put it down. Through with snowboarding? It's only a few minutes to the lodge, and all downhill at that. But trekking usually finds us miles from anywhere, climbing an endless staircase of mud-slick stones through some bug-haunted jungle, and in this circumstance, the only thing less attractive than going on is turning back.

The trail from Ronald's village to the outpost at Barsey is hardly worth mentioning except in this regard, a deserted footpath through mossy rhododendrons and stands of bamboo, 15 kilometers and 1,500 vertical meters that only a hill person would describe (as they did to me) as "easy." When I reach the clearing at Barsey, three small buildings set on a hill at 10,000 feet and ringed by a low stone wall, it is both relief and anticlimax—the Kachenjunga massif hidden by the monsoon clouds and the buildings deserted except for a skeleton crew, much more living than working here, continuously scheming for money and openly contemptuous of my presence.

When night falls there is no power. I eat a dinner of *dal bhat* by the weak light of a single candle, feeling depressed, then retire to the huge empty attic dormitory where I slip into the twisting, feverish sleep of the ambiguously ill, my body achy and my belly full of gas.

When I awaken the next morning, I am far too sick to travel. In the attic on my mattress on the floor I sleep the entire day away, waking into the twilight of half-past five P.M., impossibly craving orange juice. Looking out the window, the clouds have cleared halfway to the horizon, and this little outpost feels like the end of the world, staring out at the waves of high green ridges without a single building to be seen. The most distant mountains are blue in the late-day light, and on those furthest peaks, beyond the green hills and the golden light on the rhododendrons, there are sharp fingers of snow. As I stand, shaky and feverish at the window, Kachenjunga swims for a moment out of the clouds above them, unbelievably high and white, lofty and imposing and impossible. Then just as quickly it is gone.

That moment of brightness here in my sickness at the end of the world only serves to underscore how empty and alone I am. It should feel liberating, I think, this being out in nature, miles from the nearest town, but instead it feels claustrophobic: the moment when you realize you've climbed up this far, and now you have to climb back down.

The next morning when I rise, the day itself bears all the native marks of a fever-dream—the same walled-in feeling, the same endlessness, the same inherent lack of meaning. My emotions are all mixed up, feeling ugly and loveless, keenly aware of my physical imperfections, so desperate for comfort that I curse the awful wilderness keeping me from the safety of the world.

In this abject mood I trek exhausted down the mountain, four hours of mud and leeches and stinging nettle, overgrown and jungly and airless. I find myself grown so tired of travelling that I want to quit and go home, trapped in this endless green maze in which everything seems out for blood. There are no vistas to be seen, and I would not care if there were, overtired and muddy and fed for two days on nothing but instant noodles and smoke-tainted water, gut-sick and diarrheal and so lonely it feels like I've never had any friends at all. And the horrible feeling is upon me that none of this, this traveling, this suffering, has any meaning to it at all.

I finally reach a road and walk six kilometers west along it to the tiny market town at Dentam, then take a jeep northeast along the high road toward Pelling, and as I stare down at the sharp, unprotected drop to the valley floor hundreds of meters below, I find myself thinking about my relationships, realizing that I don't even know what love to feel sad for anymore, what love to regret, it all seems so distant.

At night in Pelling it rains, adding a voluptuousness to the darkness, the insects clicking all around like castanets, and I find myself reflecting, as I often do these days, upon Paul Theroux. "Travel," he wrote, "is a state of mind. It has nothing to do with existence or the exotic. It is almost entirely an inner experience."

Back in Calcutta, it was true, I had submitted my prayers to Kali. The devouring mother demanded sacrifice, and though it was often offered in blood, it was not in blood alone that it could be paid.

I thought: "Kali Ma, have I not sacrificed love? Have I not sacrificed comfort and sex and security and friends, to live this way, to bear these pressures, to be changed? Have I not offered up my fear, everything that is weak in me, to your teeth?"

I knew that I had come to the road alone only to travel it, to cast my fixed identity aside like a crab that has outgrown its shell. Oh, but how vulnerable, I thought, the rain drumming on the roof, my body as porous as a sieve; how fearful it is to go naked, into the vagrant wilderness, before a greater shell is found.

## SEA OF FACES

Things come to fullness in time. A week later, I am in the lowlands again, on the platform of New Jalpaiguri Station, waiting, in the polluted haze and in the confusion of my memories, for a train. And in the *Times of India*, blown through the dust of the platform and past the trash and empty cups of *chai*, which I seize and read to pass the time, there is a story. It is a completely ordinary Indian story: eighteen infants, all terribly poor, dead in only thirty-six hours at a single Calcutta hospital; but it is the photograph that accompanies it that paralyzes me completely.

Poorly composed and snapped by some cub staff photog for this minor news piece, it shows a man, mid-thirties and mustached, his face a mixture of outrage and grief as he holds in both hands toward the camera the swaddled body of his dead child. Beside him, his wife, her head covered with a shawl, turns into her husband's shoulder, her features a mask of pure anguish, sobbing. Behind and all around is a sea of faces—dozens, a crowd, as there is always a crowd everywhere in India—but so wild with the symphony of powerful and conflicting human emotions that it arrests my attention completely, tears at the center of me, that I wonder at the meaning of myself at all.

God, I think, the smell of burning garbage filling my head on the sour breeze, how this place wounds me. This journey into the hills—Ronald and Aryun, the long walk, the leeches and the difficulty and the loneliness; the fear of death, loveless and alone—I know that these have taken a piece of my heart, as is the certain way of questions without answers. But there is a magic to living these questions here, lost in this most ancient of places, immersed in this most ancient of rites.

I stand on the platform in the center of myself, utterly broken and inadequate, but knowing that when I give my heart to India, India gives its heart right back, brighter than my own could ever be. And once again, as I have now for years—as the train draws up in the heavy air—as I meet the faces though the dusty windows peering into my own eyes—I thank the Universe that it has brought me through, and step, without expectations and without fear, into the waiting train alone.

✲ ✲ ✲

*Winner of the seventh annual Solas Awards for Best Travel Writing, Matthew Crompton is a writer, photographer, and occasional metaphysician now residing in Sydney after previous lives in Seoul, San Francisco, and Cleveland. His travels have taken him through the worst hotels on five continents, and he counts himself lucky to have caught giardia and chikungunya only once apiece. His writing and photographs have been published in the U.S., U.K., Australia, and throughout Asia, and his story "Camel College" appeared in* The Best Travel Writing 2011. *For his next trip, he plans to cycle across the Asia. Follow his photography, travel exploits and fevered musings at www.goingaroundplaces.com.*

≽ ≽ ≽

# Show Me, Shouyu

Two women get a strange but inspired tour of a soy
sauce factory on a rural Japanese island.

A sculpted pumpkin the size of a minivan, a restaurant constructed solely of beer cans—the islands of Japan's Inland Sea all seem to be known for something. That summer, Lindsey, a fellow English teacher, and I had made it our quest to visit them all.

We traveled to Shodoshima—"little bean island"—for its two main attractions: cycling and soy factories. That morning we'd set out along a grueling bike trail that snaked among pale green hills and along the sandy fringes of the coastline before reaching our destination, the Marukin Soybean Factory. We weren't particularly interested in soybeans, but the humongous vats of fermenting beans at this place were the stuff of legend. The pamphlet promised free group tours daily at three o'clock. But it was a long, hard trail, and riding through that thick August air was like pedaling through butter. By the time we'd walked our bikes up the steep drive to the Marukin building, I could have wrung out my t-shirt. Worst of all, it was five past three. In a land where trains are scheduled to the second, we worried we'd missed out.

A young man in a suit glanced up sleepily from behind a reception desk. His eyes widened at the two scummy foreign girls standing before him. We said hello, and when I asked for the tour in passable Japanese, he seemed to relax.

He stood. "Ah, yes. Come with me."

I gave Lindsey a look that said, *See? There's nothing to worry about. We'll catch up to the group and everything will be just fine.*

We followed him into an elevator. I sunk into a corner, hoping he couldn't smell us. Finally, he said, in English, "My name is Hiroki." The door opened and he led us down another hall into a small, empty theater.

"Moo-bee," he said, bowing. Then he rushed out of the room.

"What happened to the group tour?" I asked Lindsey.

"I think this *is* the group tour."

The lights went out and the small projection screen at the front of the room came to life. The video, backed by good-natured folk music, tracked the factory's soybean-processing history from the pre-war days. Apparently, a man with an unfortunate mustache moved to the island, saw lots of soybeans, and was inspired to build a processing plant. He passed the business on to his son, a savvy businessman whose mustache was equally appalling. The video made the place look respectable, clean, and efficient. I strained to keep my eyelids up.

Hiroki returned as soon as the credits rolled. He bowed again and made a grand gesture that we should follow him. We got back in the elevator.

In my most polite Japanese, I asked, "Will we see the real factory?" Hiroki pursed his lips and sucked air through his teeth. I pressed on. "We love soy sauce. We want to see the big . . ." I didn't know the word for "vats" so I pantomimed with my arms a shape unmistakable as either "large container" or "pregnant ladies."

He clapped. "Ahhh," he said, nodding. Then he sucked in some more air and said, "Today is a little . . . impossible."

The door opened, and we were back in the lobby. Hiroki held up his hand and told us to wait just a moment. Then he ran out of sight, the tails of his jacket flapping behind him.

"So much for the vats," I said.

"There's still hope," Lindsey said, positive as always. "I can feel it."

We heard a patter of footsteps and then Hiroki appeared out of a hallway. He was grinning. With him was another man, older and taller, whose gut extended outward like a barrel. A barrel in a very expensive suit.

Hiroki spoke formally. This is, he said proudly, the President of Marukin.

The President flashed us a polite smile, and we introduced ourselves. He did not bow; we shook hands all around. His was just a last name: Shikara. No mustache.

Shikara-san wore his belly like an executive's desk. He spoke from behind it in firm tones to Hiroki, who nodded quickly, then bowed and scuttled out the front door.

We smiled and acted embarrassed, not because we were but because the situation seemed to call for it.

"You like . . ." he began in English. "You like *shouyu*?"

We nodded. Yes, we liked soy sauce.

He stuck out his lips and stroked his cheek. "You come, my car," he said. "I show you . . ." I could feel the pun coming. "I show you . . . *shouyu*!" He laughed loudly, and we laughed too.

It was a public holiday, he told us—Respect for the Aged Day—so there were no tours being conducted. But apparently, we were special guests. A shiny black Mercedes stopped in front of us.

Lindsey and I looked pointedly at our clothes. A thick crust of dirt wrapped around my shoes and, though the sweat on my neck had dried, my shirt clung to my back.

Shikara-san waved his hand as if to say it didn't matter. He took Hiroki's place in the driver's seat, and we got in the back. Shikara-san stepped on it, and we took off on a side road into the forest, kicking up dust at Hiroki, who stood waving behind us.

Shikara-san wanted to know all about our hometowns, our travels, and our opinions of the Japanese people. He told us about himself. He was not born on the island; he was a native Edoko—child of Tokyo—and had come to Shodoshima when his father, the previous company president, had died. Lindsey remarked that he must be very busy and he replied, "Yes, but soybeans are good friends."

After a few minutes, a low gray building came into view among the trees. Shikara-san pulled up to the front of the building and parked.

He gazed at the doors. "This," he said slowly, as if we were children learning a secret, "is home of number one *shouyu*." He paused. "My grandfather build."

He got out of the car and unlocked the front doors and, finally, we were inside the factory.

It was all one giant room cast in yellow light. Except for the walls, which were stacked from floor to ceiling with large cans, the place appeared to be empty. I looked down. Bingo!

The floor was a giant cupcake tin. The vats were built into the floor, their round mouths full of dark brown goop. There were about thirty in the place, lined up in rows of five, placed side by side with just barely enough space for a person to walk in between.

Shikara-san nodded, taking our stares for appreciation. "Deep is about two meters," he told us.

We crept in for a closer look. The vats were about three meters across. Wooden lids covered some but quite a few were open. A wide plank, sitting just a finger's length above the burgundy soup, spanned the vat nearest to us.

Shikara-san walked to the nearby vat and on the plank he placed one leather shoe, followed by the other, as if he were strolling down a promenade. The right edge of the board lifted slightly and our eyes widened. He threw his left arm out for balance. In horror, we watched as one perfectly pleated right leg rose in the air, almost parallel to the beans. I could have sworn he was pointing his toes. Each moment seemed to be dipped in molasses, stretching slowly and helplessly before us.

Then he was in the vat.

Time burst free again. Shikara-san's head popped out of the goop; his arms batted at the surface. Images of quicksand drownings flashed through my mind. Will fermenting soybeans swallow a person up? Is there real danger here, and if I reach to grab him will he pull me in too, and will we drown and suffocate in soybeans?

Lindsey appeared to be thinking the same thing, and Shikara-san was oozing deeper into the mixture. As I was desperately trying to think of something to say, he wiped his eyes and looked up at us.

"O.K., O.K.," he said, blowing a drop of goo from his upper lip. Then he extended his arm and gave us a dripping thumbs-up. "Please bring Hiroki!"

Lindsey and I glanced at Shikara-san, then at each other. He wasn't going to die. We bolted for the door.

Ten minutes later, we burst through the glass doors, sweating and gasping for breath. We called Hiroki's name into the empty lobby.

When Hiroki appeared, looking concerned, I could only say, "Excuse me for disturbing you. The boss is in the beans."

His jaw dropped. He made a swimming motion, and we nodded. He ran outside and appeared a minute later with another car, this one probably his, a small blue Toyota. We piled in and sped toward the factory.

Shikara-san had managed to reach the edge of the vat. He had thrown his elbows onto the floor and propped himself up partway out of the beans. Hiroki squawked and rushed to his boss's aid. He grabbed Shikara-san's hands and leaned back with all this weight. Shikara-san rose slowly out of the muck. At one point it seemed that Hiroki, too, would fall victim to the vats—he was leaning back far over the next container—but remarkably, he kept his balance. Finally, Shikara-san was out, curled on his side, panting and covered in goop.

Hiroki helped him up and led us all outside. Shikara-san asked us to wait, then he and Hiroki disappeared behind the corner of the building.

"We're never going to see him again," I said. "I don't know who's more embarrassed. I almost think I'd feel less awkward had it been me in the vat."

Lindsey said, "No way. Those beans have been fermenting for years. Do you want to be responsible for ruining three years' worth of soy sauce?"

She had a point. I tried not to laugh, but at this point it was hard to keep it in.

Curiosity got the best of me. I poked my head around the corner and was surprised to see Shikara-san and Hiroki standing near a shed. Hiroki was holding a long green garden hose and—

"He's hosing him down," I whispered.

"No."

"Yes. Oh—get back. They're done."

Shikara-san rounded the corner first. He was still wearing his suit, which was soaked and dripping. He wiped a drop of water from his brow.

"Funny!" he said, grinning. Then, unbelievably: "Shall we continue?"

He hopped the steps and held open the factory door. A few stray beans stuck to his jacket and one hung from his ear.

Lindsey took one look at me, and we both burst out laughing. It was the kind of laugh that chokes you, that silent laugh that tires out your abs. I was helpless to stop; all I could do was look up at Shikara-san and motion to my ear. He reached up and felt the bean. Then he too was laughing.

I was relieved, which only made me laugh harder. Even red-faced Hiroki let out a giggle.

We did finish the tour after all; Shikara-san insisted on it despite his dripping suit and shoes that squished loudly in the deserted factory.

When it was over, Shikara-san dropped us off at the main building (Hiroki brought a towel for the Mercedes), and we said our goodbyes, bowing this time, and set off down the hill on our bikes. I looked over my shoulder and saw Shikara-san outlined by blue sky at the top of the hill, waving vigorously at us. Lindsey and I threw our hands up in a backwards wave and sped down the hill with the wind whipping our faces, the wide blue sea in our view.

❧ ❧ ❧

*Kelly Luce is the author of* Three Scenarios in Which Hana Sasaki Grows a Tail. *Her work has been recognized by fellowships from the MacDowell Colony, Ragdale Foundation, the Kerouac Project, and Jentel Arts, and has appeared in the* Chicago Tribune, Salon, American Short Fiction, The Southern Review, *and other magazines. She lives in Austin, Texas, where she is a fellow at the Michener Center for Writers and fiction editor of* Bat City Review.

～ぇ ～ぇ ～ぇ

# Fish Trader Ray

My Amazon man, as large as life.

"Sitten ze down!" The German's livid face was as red as an equatorial sun setting through the pollution haze of a third-world metropolis.

Flora and I looked at each other. She winked, and we wobbled the canoe back and forth with our newly acquired hip-shaking samba dance moves. Again. It was too delicious to be exacting revenge on the pissy photographer, who was tightly gripping both sides of the pencil-thin canoe. Murky, chocolate-brown river water splashed into the hull. This sent him into full-throttle hysteria.

Should we tip him overboard? I could tell Flora was thinking the same thing. No one would know. We were in the heart of the Upper Amazon Basin on a remote, flooded tributary.

He had shown up the day before. Ray had sent him. A photographer on assignment for a travel magazine. He had a lot of expensive camera gear with him.

Ray had also sent me to stay with Flora. I had arrived one week ago with a hammock that I hung from the rafters of her tiny hut. We'd hit it off, having more in common than one would suspect between a tribal Amazonian woman and a middle-class California chick. We were the same age and had the same men issues. Daily I went out on the river with her three young children to catch fish in handheld nets. We would carefully flip the iridescent wriggling fish from the netting into tightly woven, waterproof baskets. Flora sent these to Ray via the weekly mail *panga*—a long, narrow, motorized canoe. Ray was a tropical fish trader.

It was a two-day boat ride from the jungle port town of Leticia, where I had come from, to Flora's hut. I had wanted to spend time deep in the Amazon Basin. That meant getting off the well-trafficked thoroughfare of the Amazon River and into its backwaters.

Fish Trader Ray was the man for my Amazon plan.

I had met Ray in a hotel lobby in Bogotá, Colombia at the beginning of my South American odyssey four months earlier. Fantasies of rubbing shoulders with a bunch of colorful characters straight out of Graham Greene and Gabriel García Márquez novels were the extent of my travel plans. And of course, to experience the Amazon and go to Carnival.

I landed in Bogotá on a $125 round trip ticket on Avianca Airlines from Miami. I spoke zero Spanish but managed to find a dingy yet elegant hotel with high ceilings, fans, and gleaming hardwood floors in the colonial part of town. I was immediately enthralled by the mustachioed men with battered leather briefcases drinking *café tinto* and holding their morning meetings in the overstuffed lobby chairs, and the plain-faced Catholic nuns from missions deep in the selva sipping from green glass Coca-Cola bottles. Then there was Ray—a big, loud twangy-talking Texan, who looked like he desperately needed something cool to drink, wearing a pastel striped shirt with sweat stains under his armpits.

Desi Arnaz and Carmen Miranda were my only window into Latin culture. Oh, and the crazy nonstop partying Brazilians I had met the year before in Paris. Expecting salsa and rumba dancing in the streets with sexy ladies crowned in tropical fruit hats, I was dismayed to find Bogotá a slummy and polluted place populated by sullen citizens shuffling down the sidewalks. At 8,600 feet in elevation, this dreary city was chilly and overcast with nada a Busby Berkeley fruit hat in sight.

It had been a frustrating arrival, and I was piqued.

After checking in, I wandered into the streets to find my first local meal. There were no restaurants, just a few hole-in-the-wall stores in this rundown part of town. A gang of young Colombian toughs in flared jeans was milling about on the corner, eying me. The soundtrack from *West Side Story* played in my head: "When you're a Jet you're a Jet all the way, from your first cigarette to your last dying day."

Gulp. Chin up. I crossed the street toward them. "*Hola,*" I said with false bravado, making hand gestures to indicate I was looking for food. They were as surprised as I was by my forthrightness. Surrounding me like a military escort, they marched me to a stairwell leading down to a dive with six tables. In unison they poked their heads into the place and yelled, "*¡Abuela!*" A darling gray-haired woman about half my height appeared from behind a beaded curtain, gave me a welcoming smile, and gestured for me to sit at one of the plastic flower-print-covered tables. The gang departed, but not before they all kissed their grandma on both cheeks and formally shook my hand. The woman handed me a menu, and I recognized one of the items offered: tostadas.

"I'll have an order of that," I said.

Savory smells emanated from the tiny kitchen. The short *señora* shuffled out from behind the clacking curtains and set a small plate of plain toast in front of me. Where were the tortillas, meat, cheese, guacamole, topped with sour cream?

I had just learned my first gustatory word in Spanish. *Tostada* = toast.

With two pieces of toast in my grumbling belly, I headed back to the hotel tired, grumpy, and ready for a hot shower and a long nap. I turned the water on full blast and within minutes the small bathroom steamed like a sauna. As I stepped into the shower stall, a strange gurgling sound grabbed my attention. Peering through the mist I was horrified to see a waterfall gushing out of the toilet onto the bathroom tile and out the door in a steady rush across the mahogany bedroom floor. No matter how many towels I threw down to block the flow, it was unstoppable. Without thinking, I wrapped the last towel around me, scampered out of the room and down the grand staircase to the reception desk.

The clerk was shocked that I was standing at the counter sporting only a bath towel. "Americans can be so inappropriate and such attention-getters," I'm sure he was thinking as he tried not to look me up and down. My bosom was barely covered as I fluttered my hands and flapped my arms to communicate that there was an imminent disaster happening upstairs. "A flood! The toilet! Hurry! In my room!" I squawked like a parrot.

I now had the full attention of the clerk and everyone in the lobby. But nobody understood. The urgency was completely lost on them, yet they certainly found me amusing. They laughed as I continued to gesticulate that there was a serious problem and it was not me dressed only in a towel.

The sound of splashing water got them to focus. A river of water cascaded down each stair like a liquid Slinky. Now they were looking at something besides me.

I slumped in one of those overstuffed chairs in the lobby, completely ignored, and waited for them to fix the toilet and mop up the mess.

"Looks like a rough day, young lady." The large bulk of the man with the stained shirt I had seen earlier stood above me with a concerned look on his face, his thinning sandy-gray hair slicked back in an impressive helmet. "I'm Ray Johnson and you obviously don't speak Spanish. Can I help you?"

He didn't seem lecherous and reminded me of a mix of Sean Connery and Santa Claus, so I hiked my towel up a little higher and confided, "This is my first day here. Where can I get a good meal?"

"The hotel restaurant has quite decent fare. May I take a fellow American to dinner? Not now, of course. . . ."

I giggled, relieved to be speaking English and tugged at the towel again in a futile attempt to cover an inch more of my legs, self-conscious about how I must seem wrapped only in a towel.

The hotel staff moved me to a drier room, where I lingered in a luxuriously hot and uneventful shower. I gussied up in a new pair of jeans and a crisp, cream-colored linen blouse, and met Ray in the dining room. A waiter with a white napkin draped over his arm took our order. Ray counseled, "Colombian food can be very starchy and bland. They cook with a lot of yucca, which has the texture of a stringy potato without flavor. They also add fistfuls of cilantro to every dish. Try the *carne asada* with a hearts of palm salad. Have a beer, Argentinean Malbec, or a Chilean cabernet, if you like, but I don't drink."

"What are you doing in Bogotá?" I asked after we had ordered and I sipped on a lush, garnet-hued cabernet.

"I'm a tropical fish trader, along with other commodities, and I'm here to drum up buyers."

I nodded as a waiter bustled by with a fragrant, steaming dish. I could smell the cilantro. My stomach rumbled.

"Why are you in Bogotá?" he asked.

"This was the cheapest airfare destination I could find to South America. I'll be traveling for a year or two."

"So where are you going on your South American grand tour?" Ray asked with a grandfatherly twinkle in his milky sea-blue eyes.

"The novel *Green Mansions* inspired me to travel the water-ways of the Amazon Basin and explore its green veil. I also really want to go to Carnival in Bahia, Brazil and samba dance in the streets. I think the cheapest way to get there might be down the Amazon River."

He thought this was hysterical and laughed till he wiped tears from his eyes but finally responded, "You might be right, but do you know how long the river is or where you are going to launch?"

I answered seriously, "It's 2,000 miles to Belém in Brazil and I'm going in via the headwaters of the Rio Napo in Ecuador, just like the Spanish explorer and conquistador Francisco de Orellana did in 1542. Orellana's voyages served as partial influence for the Werner Herzog's film *Aguirre, the Wrath of God*. I've done my research."

He tried to stop grinning and said, "Well, you must come visit me on your way to Brazil. Leticia is a trading outpost in Colombia on the Amazon River bordered by Peru and Brazil. I live there with my common-law Yagua wife, who's from the Red Macaw clan, and our passel of kids."

He seemed sort of old to have a young family, but I kept that thought to myself. The waiter brought our dishes. The savory aroma of grilled rare meat was irresistible. Silence reigned for a few moments as we both ceremoniously picked up our silver-inlaid steak knives and dug in eagerly.

"How did you end up in the Amazon?" I stopped chewing long enough to ask.

Ray waggled his fork at me and said, "In the 1950s I was a photographer for National Geographic. We were down here making a film when our plane crashed in the jungle. Everyone survived, but I got malaria and was too ill to continue on with the film crew. Besides, I fell in love, several times, and stayed in Leticia. Been there twenty-one years."

"That's about when I was born," I said.

He chuckled and carved into his blood-red steak while still talking. "Thought I could discover an unknown tribe and make a name for myself by filming them. I'd canoe far up the rivers and ask around, hear rumors about tribes that were still virgin to the white man's eyes. I even encountered an isolated clan up near the Orinoco River delta on the Venezuelan border. They didn't cook me and even initiated me into one of their hunting trip rituals where they blew snuff up my nose with a blowgun. It knocked me out for hours, and terrifying giant anacondas and toothy, yowling jaguars populated my hallucinations. Oh, and I threw up. A lot."

Mouth gaping open, I stared and asked in disbelief, "You took psychedelic drugs with a cannibalistic tribe?"

He shrugged and said, "I didn't know. Thought it was cocaine or something, though the blowgun was a lot longer than a straw or a rolled-up dollar bill. I was in like Flynn after that experience and slept in the chief's hut, completely convinced I had found the lost tribe until one night, swinging in my hammock, I noticed light glinting off a Coca-Cola bottle hanging high up in the rafters. Boy, was I disappointed!"

"After that, I started taking tourists and scientists into the jungle since I knew it so well. Funny things happened. One lady botanist was terrified of piranha and continually obsessed about them. I reassured her they were not in the middle of the river we were traveling on but schooled in the eddies along the bank. Right then, we hit a wake and a piranha flew from the water, arced into the boat, and landed on her head, latching itself onto her forehead. Getting that fish off was one of the biggest challenges of my life. I didn't know whether to laugh or cry as I pried the piranha's pointy teeth apart. She made me deaf with her screaming. Fortunately, it was a flesh wound. The fish didn't take a big bite since there's not a lot of skin to bite into on the forehead."

"Ray, that's impossible!" I laughed.

He shook his head and said, "You wouldn't believe how weird it can get in the Amazon."

He continued, "At that point I decided it was too difficult being a tour guide, so I put the word out among the various indigenous tribes that came to Leticia for supplies, that I was buying exotic birds like macaws, toucans, and Amazon parrots. There was a big market in the States, but that ended when so many died in quarantine because of avian diseases. And you couldn't sneak 'em in anymore after customs officials upped their security checks because of the escalating drug traffic out of South America. So now, I do fish."

Several months later, still tenaciously heading to Carnival in Brazil, and having canoed down the Rio Napo in Ecuador that connected in Iquitos, Peru, with the mighty Amazon River—even mastering Spanish out of sheer necessity since my flummoxed first night in Bogotá—I scrambled up a muddy embankment to the dock leading into Leticia, looking for Ray, who I thought could introduce me to the "real" Amazon.

The early morning sun was already blazing on the Amazonian frontier town as I walked the wooden sidewalk that went back toward Leticia. Electric Blue Morpho butterflies burst from the rain puddles while mangy mongrels skulked about, picking at piles of fish bones haloed in clouds of botflies. Indians in feathered headdresses and ear plugs, their skin painted in red achiote, hustled past on their way to the open-air market, carrying spider monkeys, black caiman, emerald-green macaws, and even a terrified hissing jaguar kitten, trussed on poles or trapped in basket cages swinging from the Indians' blowguns. One shirtless *mestizo* in ragged soccer shorts had a twelve-foot anaconda draped around his shoulders. He caught sight of me, and before I could wave him off, he wrapped the snake around my neck, holding onto the back of its head so it couldn't bite, and asked for money for a photo. The reptile was uncomfortably weighty and smelled of snake urine, which has its own distinctly unpleasant pungent odor. As I looked at its skin, I noticed ticks bloating out from underneath its scales. Repulsed, I wiggled out of the snake's tightening grip. Bursts of gunfire, coming from a ramshackle bar perched on stilts overhanging the river, punctuated the cacophony at the dock. This roughshod town assaulted all of my senses at once, invoking Hieronymus Bosch's paintings of hell.

Salty sweat poured down my face, stinging my eyes. I managed to make my way to the deserted main plaza and sat, panting, on a bench under the pathetic shade of a scrawny palm tree. Scratching under my shirt, concerned one of the ticks had hopped off the snake for a warmer host, I wondered how to find Ray. He didn't have a phone or an address, and had simply told me, "When you get to Leticia, just ask for Fish Trader Ray."

I motioned to a young boy kicking a ball across the otherwise-empty plaza. "¿Dónde está Fish Trader Ray?"

The boy looked puzzled and then asked, "Pescadero Raymundo?"

He motioned for me to stay where I was and ran off down a side street. Minutes later, Ray appeared on an exhaust-spewing motorcycle with his wife and several kids hanging off his wide girth like a bunch of ripe bananas.

Ray hesitantly greeted me, but then a huge smile broke across his face and he embraced me in a sweaty bear hug, introducing me to his family. He said, "You found me. I almost didn't recognize you. You've lost a lot of weight since we met in Bogotá and your clothes are pretty beat up. Still going to Carnival?"

We all sipped Coca-Colas at an outdoor café, the kids playing with a shiny black rhinoceros beetle that scuttled in the dirt under our table. The frosty, curvaceous bottle in my hand yielded the most delicious, sugary-sweet, icy-cold soft drink I had ever quaffed. Surprised that he had paid for our drinks in dollars, I asked him why, and he explained, "The dollar is more common than pesos because of the drug cartels coming through here to the States. Leticia is a hub for outlaws, contraband, and cocaine."

Ray entertained me by pointing out CIA agents trying to blend in as American businessmen in dark suits, their bulging necks and biceps giving them away.

"Why are they in this godforsaken place?" I asked.

He raised his eyebrows and talked out of the side of his mouth in a whisper. "You don't want to know. They protect the drug trade and make sure the government officials are cooperating."

"My tax money is paying for that?"

This further heightened my desire to get out of town pronto and return to the green tangle of the jungle. Give me poisonous bugs, blood-sucking bats, carnivorous fish, and strangling snakes anytime over men with guns.

"Ray, I really don't want to stay here. I'd love to spend time with you and your family but this place scares me. Do you have any suggestions for how I might get farther into the backwaters of the Amazon? I want to see the rarer flora and fauna, and then head toward Brazil and Carnival. I've been practicing my samba steps. . . ."

He nodded sympathetically and said, "Leticia is a very dangerous place. There's a mail boat traveling downriver leaving late this afternoon. My buddy Marco, the captain, will drop you off at Flora's, about a two-day boat ride from here on one of the more obscure branches of the Japurá. She collects exotic aquarium fish for me and loves visitors."

Ray walked back down to the wharf and got me settled into Marco's twenty-foot-long *panga*. He waved goodbye

with his weather-worn Panama hat, surrounded by his reti-
nue of barefoot children and his short, stoic, native wife.
Another gunshot emanated from the stilt bar, as if a starting
pistol was announcing our departure. Leticia quickly—and
thankfully—faded into the distance. That town was no place
for a young woman—unless she was plying her trade.

The sunset across the twenty-one-mile width of the Amazon River was a fantastical light show of tangerine spectral
colors. The languid water's surface shimmered in a coppery-
peach glow. I curled up on a lumpy sack of mail, appreciating
the tranquility and dreamily watched as the constellation of the
Southern Cross faintly appeared in the gloaming of twilight.

We chugged along the sluggish waters of the Amazon
River with dozens of other craft, from slipper-size dugouts
paddled by plumage-bedecked natives to rusty cargo container ships struggling upstream to Iquitos or Pucallpa. My
only company in the stern of the boat was a wild peccary in a
slat cage who, thankfully, gave up squealing after a few hours,
and Marco's pet capuchin monkey, who made a game out of
looking for nits on my scalp. His gentle preening soothed me
during the hazy, heat-baked days. I had to lie on my pack, as
the mischievous monkey also enjoyed digging through it with
his dexterous digits—squeezing out the toothpaste or chewing on the soap bar. His most naughty and annoying trick was
absconding with my silky underwear, placing it on his head
like a beret and keeping just out of my grasp. We shared a
passion for cashews and boiled palm nuts that I cut up and fed
to him. He was too cute to be mad at for very long, especially
when he innocently batted his coal-black eyelashes at me.

Toward the end of the second day we detoured up a coffee-
colored river confluence and into narrower tributaries, finally
arriving at a small hut on stilts above the riparian jungle terrain.

There was no terra firma to disembark on, so we motored
right up to the porch railing. Marco introduced me to a

compact, smiling woman with bright white teeth, mocha-toned skin, and peculiar pale green-blue eyes that flashed an invitation of friendship. Flora reached down, gave me her calloused hand, and hauled me up from the boat's rim into her twelve-square-foot thatched roof shack. Marco confirmed he would come get me in a week and hook me up with a ride to Manaus midway between Leticia and the mouth of the Amazon River in Belém, where a bus would provide transport to Bahia in about three days. "Just in time for Carnival!" he emphasized as he shoved off, in a hurry to get back to the main river branch and visit his family. The monkey screeched goodbye with a furrowed brow as he watched me, and my pack contents, fade into the dusk. He was wearing something on his head. . . .

Flora seemed pleased to have me as a guest. She was isolated here with just her three young children, all under age five, for company—her only social life the occasional visitor Ray sent or the infrequent passing trader. The tribe she came from lived much farther upriver, and she never saw them. I never asked why she lived by herself, but I got the impression she was an outcast due to her mixed blood.

She spoke passable Spanish, so we communicated easily. I agreed to contribute to the food kitty and also help her with household chores, fishing, foraging, and child care.

When we weren't out fishing we cooked, swept, wove baskets, and lounged in the hammocks, sharing stories. And braiding my hair. The kids were fascinated by my back-length blond tresses and fooled with them constantly. I teased that they should open a beauty salon. This sent them into giggle-fits, as the only women for many miles in this riverine no man's land were Flora and I.

Flora's tipsy canoe was the only way to get around. Carved out of a single tree trunk, it floated just a half-inch above the waterline. Balance was essential when we sat, stood, or paddled.

At night, after the children were asleep, we'd slip into the dugout with flashlights and glide silently into the lagoons surrounding the shack, looking for black caiman. Their eyes glowed a spooky citrine-green in the distance like iridescent marbles hovering right above the obsidian-dark waters. We'd quickly shine the flashlight into their eyes to mesmerize them before they disappeared below the surface. Then we'd paddle over and gently tap on their prehistoric boney heads. This would break the spell and, plop, they'd sink underneath the inky water.

That was about it for nightly entertainment.

My visions of the magical realm of the jungle that *Green Mansions* had stimulated were real. How glorious the gigantic, two meters in diameter, Reina Victoria lily pads were—each one a universe inhabited by jade-green frogs and giant-legged bugs—and how strange and mythical the pink river dolphins appeared, quietly rising up and sinking back into the muddy malachite waters as our canoe wove through the mesh curtain of vines and drifting roots. I was finally living the fantasy that had inspired the long and arduous journey I'd taken to get here. Traveling through Flora's watery world was worth every bug bite and petrifyingly scary moment.

Over her brazier set on the floorboards, we shared meals of smoked monkey stew, boiled palm nuts, dried pirarucu—the largest freshwater fish in the world, and my favorite: grilled capybara—the world's biggest rodent. We also did what women do all around the globe—we talked about men. Ironically, she had the same boyfriend problems I did. Hers was a bigger dilemma, as she also seemed to get pregnant and have children by the various Casanova traders who canoed past.

The week at Flora's passed quickly. I was ready to travel onward to Carnival, especially once the sour German arrived the day before I was to leave and put a crimp in our fun factor. He took up half the hut with his camera gear and shoveled all the stew onto his plate leaving a thigh bone and some sauce for the rest of us. He spoke in a bullying baronial tone of self-importance ordering us about like servants, but Flora needed the money he was paying for her guide services, so I couldn't shove him over the railing and feed him to the caiman like I wanted to. Thankfully, Marco showed up when promised and had consigned a boat ride to Manaus for me. I hugged her wild, spunky kids goodbye and promised Flora I would stay in touch with her via Ray and return to visit her special watery world someday—maybe with my own future children in tow.

I did arrive in Bahia on the first day of Carnival as Marco predicted and danced nonstop in the streets for a week. Several pair of shoes were worn out as I tried to keep up with the battery of booty-shaking, sexy samba mamas who paraded around town 24/7 in their stilettos, towering headdresses, skimpy costumes, and mile-wide electric smiles. Shimmy, shimmy, smile, rotate, wave to the crowd; then run, run, run to catch up with the frenzied drum bands on the motorized parade floats and shimmy some more. It reminded me of the moves Flora taught me to prepare me for Carnival, standing up in her tipsy canoe, scaring that silly photographer. Shimmy, shimmy, shake, shake, giggle, guffaw! Sisterhood discovered deep in the Amazon.

The Amazon and Carnival faded into a blur of further larger-than-life adventures traversing Iguaçu Falls and the glaciers of Patagonia, over the Atacama Desert to Bolivia, and months later, flying home from Ecuador—a full circle from where I began my Amazonian quest.

I went back to California and started an import business. For seven years I commuted to South America, and whenever I could find a flight from Colombia or Peru to Leticia, I'd take a detour and visit my friend Ray and his growing family. Leticia held a certain backwater charming seediness that grew on me the more I explored the region. Flora had married one of her Casanovas and moved to Iquitos, and I never saw her again.

The last time I saw Ray was thirty years ago, right before I sold my import company. He was hoisting me into the cargo hull of an unpressurized plane on a dirt runway filled to the gills with odoriferous planks of salted pirarucu fish. Throngs of Indians pushed and shoved to get on the plane that provided the only transport to Bogotá on a random schedule. Luckily, they were much more diminutive than Ray, who tossed me like a football, launching me over the indigenous feathery finery and headfirst onto stacks of smelly fish. As the plane sputtered and the propellers whirred, we lifted upward. There was Ray on the runway below, large and pasty-white, enthusiastically waving his sweat-stained Ecuadorian Panama hat, grinning and squinting upward toward the blazing orb of the sun. His kids taller, his wife shorter. Fish Trader Ray. My Amazon man. Straight out of a novel.

≈ ≈ ≈

*Lisa Alpine is the author of* Wild Life: Travel Adventures of a Worldly Woman *and* Exotic Life: Travel Tales of an Adventurous Woman *(winner of a BAIPA Book Awards Best Women's Adventure Memoir). Writing, dancing, gardening, hiking, family, and travel are the passions of her life. She divides her time between Mill Valley, California and the Big Island of Hawai'i. Find out about her writing workshops and book events at www.lisaalpine .com.*

TANIA AMOCHAEV

✺ ✺ ✺

# My First Trip to the Homeland

She goes in search of abandoned treasures behind the
Iron Curtain.

I wondered yet again: Had I really agreed to fly on a one-way ticket into a remote backwater of Communist Russia of 1977, a country repressed by fear and impoverished by incompetent bureaucracy, one my father fled as an infant and couldn't believe his daughter was braving?

My family, Don Cossacks, had lived for centuries on the Don River between Moscow and Stalingrad. The Cossacks, although mostly peasants, were staunch supporters of the tsar and represented the last stand of resistance to the Communist Revolution, losing the final battle in 1920.

When I was a child, my grandmother told me stories of that final battle. How the family, following the White Army, repeatedly left their village and returned. How by the last retreat there was no time to dig up the silver she had buried under the back doorstep to their house, abandoned to the dust of history. My grandmother was long gone, but that silver in its dirt grave halfway around the world lived on in my mind, my sole keepsake beyond the small gold stars she had always worn dangling from her ears. I wanted to see where our story began and to retrieve what she was forced to leave behind. I wanted to dig up that dirt.

The plane heading north from Stalingrad, to the town of Uryupinsk, was a ten-passenger WWII biplane converted for commercial use. In front of me sat a man staring intently into the open cockpit, leaning in as if he would steer from his seat if he could. I had seen him and the two pilots in the cafeteria drinking a quick shot of vodka before departure.

"What are you doing?" I asked.

"I am the observer," he replied, proudly.

The Communist party had observers everywhere. They had broken my camera, pawed through my luggage, read my notes. Now this guy was making sure of what—that the pilots didn't hijack us?

The plane rattled into action and weaved over the runway. The noise was deafening, it shivered and groaned. Only 300 miles, it took an interminable three hours, and the shaking didn't abate. A confident flier who rarely felt queasy, I started retching and then vomiting almost instantly, my head in a bag for the entire trip. Perhaps it was I who should have had that early morning shot of vodka.

We finally landed, but I couldn't get up, I couldn't think, I could barely breathe. Everyone deplaned. Finally, holding on to the bag, embarrassed to leave it behind, I crawled to the door. We were in an abandoned field, dead grass all around. At the bottom of the stairs a man with a paunch and an official looking chauffeur's hat waited.

"*Ah, vi Amerikanka!*" he said. You're the American.

"*Kak vi znali?*" I replied. How did you know?

"There was no one else left."

He introduced himself as Yura, the chauffeur for the president of the flaxseed oil factory, and the proud driver of the only private car in the district. He explained that his boss had loaned him to me for my stay. Did I want to go to my hotel or straight toward the village of Kulikov?

I desperately needed to wash up.

"I have a hotel?" The town had no cars. The airport was a dirty field. My expectations were low.

"Yes," he explained, proudly. "Our town has a hotel because we have a sister city in Czechoslovakia and our visitors need a place to stay."

No American had ever visited this modest but clean hotel, far beyond any approved tourist areas. The price was one ruble, less than two dollars at the official exchange rate. The forms were in Russian. I transliterated my town of Minneapolis into Cyrillic: Минияполис. There was no line for state or country.

The receptionist peered at it carefully, then said, "That's in the north, right?"

I was impressed with her knowledge of U.S. geography and said, "Why, yes. How did you know?"

"I could tell by your accent. It is vaguely Siberian."

I had never set foot in Russia before, and my father had left as an infant, but my knowledge of the language was good enough that this woman, who had never been anywhere else, clearly took me for a native. It was an amazing testament to the uniquely powerful Russian concept of *Rodina*, or homeland.

The showers in the hotel were off for the day, and there was no hot water, so I washed up in the sink. Before setting off, I asked Yura if we could buy some water, and we stopped in five stores, all empty and deserted. What did these people eat? Finally he took me back to the hotel, where they gave me a large bottle of apple juice and a chipped glass.

There was no map that included the remote village of Kulikov where my father was born, the one I was seeking. However, I was fluent in the language, stubborn and determined. So far I had found this, and little else, in common with these people, my "countrymen."

My father's brother Shura was eight when they left, the oldest son and now patriarch of the scattered family. Always confident, he had sketched a map and proudly pointed out their home, telling me it was "the only two-story house in the village." My grandfather, whom I had never met, was a *kulak*, a peasant who took advantage of land reforms passed in 1906 to develop a wheat trading business and rise above his class. Uncle Shura drew in the *ambar* or granary, the symbol of his father's success and, ultimately, of their survival. It was across from his aunt's house, near the creek and the church, and around the corner from the train station. This final detail, that the village was important enough to have a train stop, was the clue that still had me in the hunt.

Yura knew the train station. "The Jarizhenskaya station," he said, "is near your village of Kulikov. Do you know any other details?"

I did. The previous evening in Stalingrad I repeated an act I had performed in countless cities of the world: I scoured the phone book for an Amochaev. I had never before found anyone beyond my immediate family, but Stalingrad had two, and I had met one of them: Oleg. While neither of us knew enough about our families to figure out if we were related, his mother lived in our village of Kulikov, and I had agreed to look her up and tell her he was well and would write soon.

"We are looking for Maria Afanasievna Amochaeva at number 6, Gorkii Street in Kulikov," I told Yura.

We quickly reached the outskirts of the city and bounced onto a dirt road.

"This," he said confidently, "will soon be the highway to Moscow!"

Soon was a relative term as weeds abounded and no equipment was in sight.

"And what do you think of this car?" asked Yura.

It was a comfortable Volga limousine, and I told him how fortunate I felt that his boss let me have the use of it.

"Do you own a car?"

"I do."

"Is it like this?"

"Oh, no," I said. "It is much smaller."

"Of course," he nodded, undoubtedly visualizing the tin cans of Eastern Europe rather than my flashy sports car. "Did you wait a long time for it?"

"No, we don't actually have to wait for cars."

He mulled this over for a while.

"But you do have shortages, don't you?" He searched for common ground.

I wracked my brain and remembered a true story. "Last year," I said, "there was a run on toilet paper. It was started by a rumor that the company was going out of business." I didn't mention that it was a comedy hour gag gone awry.

"Yes, that happens a lot here."

"But could you buy a truck? Or a bus?"

"If I could afford it, I could."

"Surely that can't be. *Ne mozhet bits.* How would you do that?"

I had never actually considered this subject. "I'm really not sure," I said, "I guess I would go to a company that sells them."

"Would you need permission from the powers, *ot vlasti?*"

"Well,"—now it was I who stretched to find common ground—"I would have to get a special driver's license to operate a large vehicle."

"Ah. They would probably use that to prevent you from buying one," Yura said, knowingly, in collusion with me against the bureaucracy.

I found myself torn, as so often happened on this trip, between wanting to share a bit of my life, but not wanting to point out just how desperate theirs seemed to me. It was a fine line to walk. The previous evening Oleg had proudly showed me the latest miracle installed in their apartment, to the envy of neighbors: a sink where cold and hot water merged into one faucet rather than coming out separately. I tried to be appropriately impressed.

As I was leaving he opened up the top of his greatest treasure, a small piano bought with his black market earnings as a dentist at night and on weekends. He withdrew a clear plastic sleeve with four colored felt pens and offered it with both hands, saying: "This is for you, to take back and remember us by."

"That's . . . those are the ones Cousin Igor brought back from Germany!" his wife stuttered, the pain of loss clear in her voice.

He insisted on giving it to me, and I could not tell him that I had a drawer full of felt pens. I thanked him as deeply as his consideration in parting with this treasure deserved. But I already sensed I would regret my inability to express gratitude for the thought and still leave the treasure intact.

My conversation with Yura, meanwhile, was interrupted by the appearance of the train station. A man walked along the tracks, and we pulled over to ask about our destination.

"Can you tell me, *tovarisch*, how to find 6 Gorkii Street?" Yura asked the elderly man.

"Where do you think you are, Moscow?" came the gruff reply. "We are in the boonies, *mi v derevnye*, not the big city. Who are you looking for?"

"We are looking for Maria Afanasievna Amochaeva," I interjected.

"Ah. Why didn't you say so? She is in her front yard with Efim Ivanovich, as always. Take the first right, it's a hundred *arshins* up the road." I thought *arshins* had died with the Old Testament, but the driver knew it was a measure just short of a yard, and we easily found them sitting at a table in front of a small house, sipping tea.

Convincing them of my identity was much more problematic.

"What do you mean, you're from America but your father was born here? That's not possible, there's no one in America from here!" said the frowning woman, her gray hair circling her head in a neatly tucked braid.

I knew she was almost right, and that the escape was a close call. My grandfather had loaded the family, including four children and his mother, on his hidden horse cart and fled across hundreds of miles of war-torn country to the town of Yvpatoria on the Black Sea. In late 1920, carrying a large bag of wheat and a single suitcase, they boarded one of the last ships taking refugees out of the country. They survived by mixing the wheat with salt water and baking it on the ship's steam pipe exhaust vent. The ship tried to dock in Istanbul, but was refused entry. Gallipoli was taking only military refugees, no children.

Finally, they landed on the Greek island of Limnos. My great-grandmother looked at the barren shore and refused to disembark. She returned with the ship, which went for one final mercy run, and was never heard from again, disappearing into Communist Russia. Many of the refugees died of starvation and disease, but the wheat fed my family until they were given asylum by the King of Serbia, where I was born.

I started explaining: "Well, his father took them away during the revolution . . ."

"Likely story." She spat at the ground.

"Why would I lie to you?"

"Why wouldn't you? And who's he, with the fancy car, driving you around like some kind of princess. What are you doing here? We don't know anything. We have nothing to say."

There was something about her steely strength that reminded me of my grandmother, but her words were devastating in their implication. She clearly assumed I had been sent for some nefarious reason. Was this as far as I would get?

"Marusia, Marusia, wait a minute. Let the young lady tell us what she wants. Maybe she can explain." That was her friend Efim, tall and thin and around the same age, which I seriously overestimated as around eighty. He quickly became my ally, loosening up as my chauffeur wisely withdrew.

"Well, all I know is that my grandfather's name was Ivan Minaevich Amochaev," I explained, "and that he had a house and an *ambar* here. When the Red Army defeated the Whites for the last time, they escaped to the Black Sea and almost forty years later ended up in America. My uncle was eight when they left, and he drew me a map." I turned to Efim. "Why doesn't she believe me?"

Efim swept his upturned palm across the emptiness that surrounded us. "Well, you see, *dorogaia*, dear, no one survived."

"What do you mean?"

"When the Reds came in they lined up all the men, and boys over twelve years old, and shot them. No one got away. You're the first person in nearly sixty years who has ever arrived, claiming to be from here." His words suddenly explained the silence of decades, all the letters gone unanswered. I had trouble grasping the scope of the tragedy before he continued. "But you have nothing to gain that I can imagine, so I am prepared to believe you. Do you have that map?"

"Oh my God! Were you here?" I wanted him to keep talking, I needed to learn more.

"We were infants," he said, "but we grew up with the stories of the horror. Marusia lost her father, her brothers. She can't bear to think about it all." I appreciated the enormity of what I had just heard and knew I would learn nothing further about this tragedy.

I pulled out my map, we huddled over it. "Theirs was the two-story house, right here. I was told it had become a tea house, a *chaiovnia*, after the revolution."

"*Milaya*," Efim said, dear one, "there has never been a two-story house in this village, but let me see this. There was a tea shop at that corner. Let's walk over there."

We wandered around with the map. I realized that my uncle's little boy mind had enlarged his father's home beyond anything in this village, but we found the house, even the *ambar*.

The town hadn't grown since my family left, and the remaining skeleton matched the sketch. The neighboring village of Amochaev became the collective farm, and the young people had been moved there, Efim explained. Most of the homes in Kulikov were abandoned, the church was torn down, and there was no need for a school any more.

"We're just left with dust and memories," he reflected. "And we don't let the memories go back too far."

Stalin's collectivization campaign, which destroyed the final private ownership of land by peasants and wiped out all *kulaks* as enemies of the people, took on a more vivid form than it ever had in my history classes in Russian School in San Francisco.

I shot a few pictures and walked around, trying to imagine who I might have been, who my father might have been. The gap was too wide; we simply wouldn't have existed.

I approached the house, the forlorn and crumbling single story white *isba* that would eventually disappoint Uncle Shura. I circled the faded wood fence that surrounded it, checked the gate. It was all shut tight.

"Who owns this now?" I asked.

"No one owns anything, here, golden one, *zolotko*," Efim said, inadvertently using my father's childhood nickname for me. "No one has lived there in a long time. Everything belongs to the state, we aren't allowed to go inside or touch anything." I could tell this gentle man would be uncomfortable if I opened the gate and walked up to embrace the house, as I envisioned doing.

So I didn't. They had been beaten into submission by a system that spread fear and terror as a way of life. In an abandoned backwater miles from anywhere, that authority still controlled their actions, from their fear of strangers to blind obedience to power. My father, forced to flee a Communist dictatorship yet again as an adult, carried some of those scars. I, on the contrary, had grown up in a country that took my family in with little more than the clothes on our backs and allowed me to become a woman unafraid of challenges, knowing how to aim high and break barriers.

I had become someone who might prove valuable even back here, in Russia, and I was given permission to do the unimaginable, rummage around alone in places far beyond the few zones open to tourists.

Now I was at the heart of so many memories: my grandmother's, my uncle's, mine. This rough wooden fence with its missing slats, leaning precariously, was no barrier to me. It would be so easy to open that gate, or climb over it. To dig a hole at the back door stoop. To search for my treasure, my grandmother's silver. I had no idea what it really was, just that it was something I had wanted my whole life.

But taking liberties unimaginable to these scarred people would rob them of their dignity.

And so, I just stood there for a long time, quietly memorizing the scene. The dirt lanes. The few old-fashioned Russian houses—the *isbas*, unchanged since Czarist times. The abandoned train station. Finally I had to move on, and we returned to Marusia's house. I drank her tea, ate her apples. I told them about her son Oleg, who had not been back since the train stopped running several years earlier. They asked me nothing about America; it was far beyond the range of their imagination. They accepted a few trinkets and, in parting, each one kissed me three times in the familial old Russian way.

As for me, I left Russia with a small bag of dirt and dust, a memento for my father and uncle of this place that once held all we were. I brought it back to our new homeland.

❧ ❧ ❧

*Tania Amochaev is a writer, photographer, and traveler. Born in what was once Yugoslavia, she fled that country with her family and lived as a young child in a refugee camp in Trieste before emigrating to America. Her parents were also political refugees as infants, her father from Russia and the Bolshevik Revolution, her mother from Istria, now Croatia, which was given to Mussolini as a spoil of World War I.*

~❧ ~❧ ~❧

# The Tea in Me

Transformation can be a long process.

## PACKING

I t looks like a dance floor, a thirty-foot-square section of smooth wood among the rough planks that make up most of the flooring, all surrounded by giant locomotive-like drying machines. I've been waiting at the cool, dark packing station just inside the front door of the tea factory, and alternately in the warm April Sunday morning sun just outside, for my packing shift. Packing represents the final step handled here at the factory, completing my education in the processing of my favorite tea.

At 4,600 feet above sea level in the Himalayan foothills of India's Darjeeling region, I'm at the 150-year-old Makaibari tea factory perched on a slope just below the town of Kurseong. I'm just over a week into my physical travels across northern India, but a dozen weeks into the personal journey that began with giving notice on a twenty-year career, and planning my solo wander across a land that has existed in my mind as a magical and challenging destination, no more or less real than Narnia or Brigadoon.

After an hour of waiting, four large full tins of finished tea from the sorting room—carried two ladies at a time—are dumped on the shiny floor, filling the air with the rich, dark vegetal scent of black tea leaves. A man, barefoot, wearing gray dress pants, a white t-shirt and, amusingly, a Starbucks baseball cap, shovels and sweeps the tea into a single well-blended mountain of the finest grade Makaibari Estate, First Flush Darjeeling Tea. We wait, he and I, for the inspector to ensure the quality of the grade, and then begin filling twenty-kilo foil-lined brown paper bags, one scoop at a time into the chute engineered into an upper corner of each bag. Easy at first, it becomes very difficult once the bag is over half full and has to be repeatedly shaken and shifted—the entire bag lifted and dropped—in order for the tea to settle and make room for more. We've been joined by a woman, swiftly scooping tea and maneuvering the large bags with an urgency and confidence that compensates for her diminutive size and arms that are, at their widest, the size of my wrists.

"She filled two in the time it took you to fill one," the foreman teases after watching my slow struggle with the process, "and then finished yours off for you." It's not true! I started two different bags, handing one off to each of them for the challenging final touches. It is true, though, that each of them has done twice the work I have. He smiles, "She says you should only get half pay."

Packing is the only part of the process that—as far as I've witnessed—employs both genders. The gender roles are strong, each stage of the process (plucking, withering, rolling, firing, sorting) is handled either by men or by women, never both. The process begins and ends with women, and the distinction can be drawn along the lines of precision. If the work is delicate enough that human hands are involved, they must be women's hands. The gross handling of larger actions (and larger machines) is done by men.

In any case, here I am, one man interested in experiencing each step of tea processing as my own process unfolds, far from home.

## PROCESSING

Tea is both art and science. It is the careful, methodical refinement of a bulk raw material that is pure potentiality. If handled correctly, it can become a brilliant and universally captivating expression of this potential. It is a delicate and many staged process, however. When it's harvested, how—and *how quickly*—it's processed, the precision of brewing, etc., all affect the degree to which the essence is optimally revealed.

I see this clearly from my position here on the tea estate, surrounded by dramatic hills carpeted with hundreds of acres of what many consider the world's finest tea. The drama of the place comes from the geography, the grade. Simply put: it is steep. These are young mountains, the Himalayas, and that must explain their boldness. These foothills burst out of the plains below with such urgency that a flat surface is nearly impossible to find. On a clear night I can easily see Siliguri, a plains city only twenty-two miles down Pankhabari road, yet more than four thousand feet below me. The roads attempt to follow the ever-ascending ridges, and this is where the towns are. The tea villages and fields are in the startling, swooping valleys.

That's where I've spent these last several days, above nearly vertical fields of the robust little shrub, *camellia sinensis,* in a village homestay just down the road from the factory, the oldest one in the region, still processing tea today the same way they have for more than a century.

"Makaibari" is stenciled in white paint—each letter three feet tall—on the green corrugated tin roof of the rugged old building. Truly unchanged for well over one hundred years, even the machinery inside is pre-1900. The factory opened in

1859, not coincidentally the same year tea production began in the region. Mechanization came in the next few decades, and that's about it. The rest has happened day in and day out with very few changes over the next dozen decades. The place is run by the vital and eccentric Swaraj Kumar Banerjee, the "Rajah of Darjeeling Tea," a man in his early sixties, graying hair around his sharp, handsome Bengali face, and often a somewhat devious smile like a child with a secret. Known simply as "Rajah" Banerjee, he is the fourth generation Banerjee to run the estate, and the man responsible for bringing organic agriculture to India's tea lands, indeed changing the way things are done outside the factory in the fields.

Rajah and I were crouched in the dirt outside of his office one afternoon as he counted types of uncultivated flora growing between the bushes. ". . . three, four, five . . ." Then turning to me, "You have a brother? Same genetic make-up, same cultural upbringing . . . right?" I agreed on all counts. "Tell me, placed in a room together, facing, talking, how long would it take before you had a disagreement?"

"Two hours?" I considered.

"I bet it's more like fifteen minutes, but O.K." He resumed plucking fronds and flowers, all in reach from his squatting position between bush and building, all voluntary growth, ". . . six, seven, eight . . ." He stopped at fifteen. "*This*," he declared, handing me the bouqueted cluster of flora, "is what happens naturally." He was referring to the stability of a complex ecosystem vs. the fragility of genetic homogeneity, like brothers or chemical-dependent monocrops. "*This* is what creates sustainability: diversity!"

Diversity is subtext, however, as are the words *mulch* and *dung* and *compost*. To distill Banerjee's ever ready lecture to a single word it would be: soil. "Healthy soil is healthy mankind," is his mantra. The result is better tea, healthier workers, and a product that just might be reproducible for another 150 years, and then another after that.

Days later in his home, in a smoke-filled living room with two enormous taxidermied tigers and two very alive German Shepherds, I sipped sparkling wine with Banerjee and his wife, and their daughter-in-law and six-year-old grandson visiting from Bangalore. "My father was one of the greatest hunters in India," he proclaimed as I inspected the very large, catatonic, dusty creatures. "He took down eighty-six such beasts in his day."

I was glad to hear this placed him among the best of hunters, the notion that this might be an average performance made my stomach turn. "I think he might be singlehandedly responsible for putting these on the endangered species list," I said.

He smiled, accepting the jab, but was unapologetic about the contradiction. This man with his impressive legacy in organic agriculture and fair trade business practices, this champion of biodiversity, remained very proud of his family's legacy as well. Even those elements that depleted the local tiger population.

It's Makaibari's environmental record that intrigued me into coming here. That and the ad hoc homestay volunteer program. A love of tea, too, factors in. Particularly Darjeeling's lighter body, golden-brown liquor, floral astringency, and tannic bitterness. But I come without substantial expertise on the beverage, and my work here is not directly related to tea. I'm volunteering among the villagers—many employed by the tea company, but experts, each, in a single process, not a finished product—thus I'm not substantially progressing my tea knowledge save for a few shifts on the factory floor. My expertise on the topic of timing and handling comes from an uncanny sense of fellowship as we, leaves and I, are plucked from our framework and set on course to reorganize ourselves into something new. In fact, that is precisely my work here.

The story for both of us begins after the roots and branches have been well established; after the various feats, cultural and agricultural, that brought us to this point of readiness.

## SUPPLY AND DEMAND

Three months earlier at a corner table in Boulder, Colorado's Dushanbe Tea House, I sat flanked by my sons, both of them smiling and joking and masking their competition over a shared scone and a small cup of Devonshire cream: sixteen-year-old Henry's self-assured attack on the thing, and Simon at thirteen demonstrating a more reserved—yet frustrated—politeness. Across the table, mirroring my *chai* sipping, sat their mother, my ex-wife CC, her tall frame and long brown hair framed by the tall windows and long drapes—pulled back to expose the cold January morning and the half-frozen creek outside. I looked forward to these family meals; they were good opportunities to catch up, but they tended to be scattered. We often failed to drop deeper than friendliness or remain on a single topic for more than a few uninterrupted lines.

That morning a new element was added to the mix: anticipation. There in my hands was a *Lonely Planet Guide to India* and a yet-to-be-opened card. On the table sat the handprinted gift wrap and raffia that had just come off this belated birthday present.

Our food arrived, just as the scone battle was won, and my two handsome sons dove into their breakfasts while they quietly watched me. I opened the card, a plain, store-bought birthday card, to reveal a $5,000 check and words that tumbled my heart in a way it is so rarely touched. "This is a thank you and an exuberantly offered investment in the second half of an already incredible life . . . now it is time to go and do something for you. Something a little crazy that feeds the soul and rocks the foundation." Here were words of gratitude and generosity in the handwriting of the woman I'd married nineteen years earlier, the woman with whom I was still raising these two remarkable boys. A woman now married to another man yet with whom I have a somewhat stilted closeness and friendship, like an honorary siblinghood—but clouded by the historical fact of deeper intimacy. Most of all, here was gratitude for a "decade and a half of doing things to ensure our security and happiness."

These words cut beautifully into the deepest wound from our divorce where my very loyalty to my work, my commitment to career in its conventional nine-to-five, day-to-day trappings, was the source of discontent for her. She couldn't "respect"—her word—that relationship. And even today, seven years later, the wound trembles. This was the single most painful communication in our divorce. At the time all I could hear was the ingratitude and irrationality of it. Here I was "ensuring our security," while she had left the paying work world in what was a long ascent to finding her true work, her passion. This search was honorable, but fettered me that much more, it seemed, to my office and my paycheck.

The searing word "respect" had long since been recalled, and time had erased my defensive reaction to it. I could see the complexity of our situation with greater clarity, and this gift testified that she could too. No doubt my career loyalty was honorable, but it was also sad and compromising as it became a defining box so sturdy it began to sprout bars. I did want out but lacked the courage to make the break.

"We are gifting you with a trip to a place that defines WILD—human and otherwise," read the card.

India was not their idea, it was recognition of my number one travel dream. But India is not an extended weekend trip.

It's not even a trip one can do justice to within the three weeks
of paid vacation granted by my work. My mind raced with
excitement and gratitude—*Was this level of generosity really
happening?*—and doubt and even irritation. For in this gift
was a directive, and in that was a lack of understanding, perhaps even a subtle criticism, of the demands of my career. *It's
not this simple*, I thought. *You can't just say "go to India" and
expect that my busy life will allow it.* My head spun with the
responsibilities that would make accepting this gift impossible. There was work and the money and benefits it provided.
There was Melissa and the stumbling, fumbling romance we
were struggling through. And there were the kids.

"We will help you as 'ground support,' your cheerleading
squad and the ones who keep the home fires burning." So,
inherent in the gift was permission to temporarily downshift
my family responsibilities. And with it, this excuse to maintain the status quo was removed. But still, I left the restaurant
feeling both excited and uncertain how this would unfold and
if I'd be able to pull it off.

It was three weeks later that I decided not only would this
trip to India happen, it would be part of a more substantial
breaking of the branch: I would quit my job of fifteen years
(my career of twenty) and turn it all inside out. "I wanted my
life," as in Mary Oliver's *Dogfish*, "to close, and open / like a
hinge, like a wing, like the part of the song / where it falls
down over the rocks: an explosion, a discovery; / I wanted / to
hurry into the work of my life."

## PLUCK THIS

Tea must be harvested at the right time. That is right now,
April, for the finest Darjeeling, what is called "first flush" tea.

It starts in the hills where women pluck the emergent
green tips. Yesterday I accompanied a few of these ladies as
they harvested the fresh first flush leaves and buds. Baskets

on their backs, strapped around their foreheads, both hands engaged in this rapid but specific plucking, many of these women exceeded—some by a couple of decades—my forty-two years. Carrying nothing but a small camera, I tripped and floundered behind them, scraping my legs against the firm branches of the tea bushes. I felt like a harbor seal hiking with mountain goats.

This place, the hills of Darjeeling, is like none I've witnessed. Each time I step outside, I'm struck by it. "Hold on," I'll say. "Let me take a picture." I say this because I keep thinking that somehow, *this time,* I'll be able to capture the magnificence of it, because, *this time*, the light is different. The light is often different: there's sunrise and sunset and there's mist. Sometimes the mist is so strong you can see only a few feet away, and like thick San Francisco fog it rolls over the place, a black-and-white filter stripping color out of the little that remains visible. Mostly it's the rolling blankets of clouds that amaze, flowing into the nooks of these recklessly steep hills, sometimes swallowing the entire town of Kurseong in its perch at the peak of the next hill. I'll muse as I sweat in the hot sun, that the people in town—less than two miles away— are cold and wet in that midday black-and-white fade. Sometimes the clouds are above me, but below the surrounding hilltops, transforming the landscape into an animated Japanese scroll painting.

A week and a half ago—the first Wednesday of April—I arrived in New Delhi en route to where I am now. The Wednesday before that was the middle of my final week at work, the last of some 750 Wednesdays I'd made my way into my office. Now on a tea estate on the other side of the world from my former job, my family and my girlfriend, I watched these durable, weathered women busily pluck tips from the bushes only days after the fresh leaves and buds had emerged. These first leaves of spring, the first flush, represent some of the finest tea and will command high prices for their delicate flavor.

There's a later "second flush," May harvest that is considered just as good by many. In fact, its richer "muscatel" character has always been my choice for a fine cup. This is a relief, too, because I fear I missed my own first flush and began to wilt on the branch a bit. A bright green leaf of potential, I believe I remained too long, especially in my job.

## THE BRANCHES

It was confusing to find myself in a career, reasonably well paid, working for a company of good people driven to do good in the world, yet to be disenchanted. It was only my second company in two decades of nonstop forty-five-hour work weeks, commutes, cubicles, and eventually my own office. I ran the eco-friendly products division of the company, selling goods to consumers who wanted to be part of the solution, not part of the problem. This was not blood money, it was an honest, right livelihood. Almost.

There was compromise in every direction. The product *could* reduce energy consumption, for instance, but may itself be manufactured of nonsustainable materials and shipped half way around the world. The consumer culture *could* be affected, inspiring people to live more simply or closer to the land—and likely was—but increasingly the job became one of failing budgets and discussions of profitability. My primary focus had shifted from eco-green to financial green and my interest faded.

I wilted. My potentiality began to droop. Not so much directly from the work, but indirectly from the stagnation that results by not finding passion in what I was doing. And the fear that kept me where I was, afraid to risk my employment, to jump ship, to reach out and find a better expression of myself. This fear deflated my spirit, and that rippled out into other areas of my life, other relationships. Like romance and family.

If the quality of output (my sons) is any testimony, my parenting is commendable. But exhausted and stagnating, I am often less present than I'd like to be, less attentive to their needs, less patient. Less aware in general, really, but nothing is more important to me than my sons: Henry as he forges his way, in the second half of his second decade, into a sense of self-reliance, yet still craving—in subtle ways—the parental boundaries of childhood. Simon, having just entered his teen years, asserting his own style despite the strong pull of his brother's character. Both of them unfailingly impressive in their brilliance and competence—in everything they attempted—yet too often disenchanted and discouraged—with school, with friends. With me.

The days or nights with them that were defined by my impatience and short temper are tragic moments in my parenting memory, burned in my mind. Thich Nhat Hanh says it's possible, firmly grounded in the present, to transform the past. He says, "the traces of a bad drought can only be erased by a bountiful rainfall, and rain can only fall in the present moment." I love and need this. But presence, a simple word and a simple act (or non-act), is so difficult to achieve—all the more so when palpably dissatisfied and restless.

Romance, too. Such a conflicted dance this has been for the last decade. Divorce, adolescent emergence (yes, at thirty-five), a constant dizzying centrifugal spin engaging woman after woman, and the breakaway and recoil that inevitably followed. And recent history, sharing this dance with just one beautiful and patient woman. Pulling, pushing; wanting in, wanting to escape. Desiring her in one moment and desperately needing aloneness and quiet in the next.

Six weeks before I left on this trip, Melissa and I went on a painfully ironic Valentine's Day walk. It was an unseasonably warm afternoon, and we were walking along a winding path between square, ordered backyards and rolling, golden open space. "Do you think we need to break up?" she'd asked in the office, prompting the walk.

Melissa is a beautiful woman, no less so that afternoon, and we are capable of coasting blissfully together. But not always. Too often the familiar tentacles of anxiety constrict in my upper chest when I'm faced with the pressure of our relationship. On the walk I explained to her that without knowing why, I felt an ill ease too much of the time. "I beat myself up trying to understand it, to find the reason. But really, the *why* of it isn't as important as the *fact* of it."

She stopped and looked at me, her blue eyes the color of a bottomless well of generosity, and asked, "What do you want to do?"

"I think we need to end it," I said, feeling a great conviction to keep away for the next several weeks leading up to my trip, and to go to India unencumbered by a relationship that competes for limited space in my limited heart. "To spare each other."

I don't know if I thought then of the half-dozen other breakups I'd engineered in the last few years, and the greater number of fade outs from undefined relationships. If so, I may have noticed the glaring common denominator. A few days later I would admit to myself a hope to take time away and to finally find the ability, some months down the road, to be in a relationship, and to find Melissa still willing to be in one with me. But if I had this awareness that Valentine's Day, I withheld my confusion. We both needed my decisiveness. "Yes. I do think we should break up."

"O.K.," she said. I watched her lips—heart-pink against winter white skin—the symmetry of which had magnetized me for two on-and-off years. "I love you," she added. Then flatly, without venom, "Good luck, you sad and foolish man."

We kissed. I smiled, gently despite a torrent of conflicting emotion. My head smugly received the drama of the event and the clarity of the decision with a misbegotten satisfaction, while my heart raisined one more dark, retreating step down into my gut.

Wilting on the branch, indeed.

We continued to see each another almost daily at work, and the attraction prevailed as it had before. We got back together—albeit somewhat tentatively—at the end of February, perhaps stronger (us), definitely still confused (me). And now, 8,000 miles away, I feel closer to her than ever.

## STORM CLOUDS

After the first flush harvest there is a nonproductive period of four to five weeks, called *Banji*. In his book, *The Rajah of Darjeeling Organic Tea: Makaibari*, Banerjee describes the climate during this period: "Fast moving rain-bearing clouds sweep up from the Bay of Bengal, and on collision with the Himalayan foothills, inundate the Darjeeling district with short but fierce bursts of precipitation." Ah, yes. I've stumbled back from Kurseong twice in these storms. He continues, "These are the awe-inspiring Norwesters. In a flash, dark clouds appear out of clear blue skies. The lashing is intense, with copious rain accompanied by streaks of lightning and deafening thunderbolts. God help those who do not unhook their electronics, as they blow up instantly. Within an hour, it is all over and the sun appears with clear skies. This is a magical moment. Overnight, the region is a riot of green and is abuzz with the emergence of all life forms."

This is when the emergent second flush shoots signal readiness to harvest a tea darker in liquor and fuller in flavor, the rich Muscatel Second Flush.

Certainly I've ridden out my own *Banji*. A general climate of complacency hit with occasional storms of doubt, fear, and even misplaced anger when I'm stretched to my limit.

A bitterness sets in at these times, but maybe also a richness. Self-plucked late in the season, I now find myself halfway around the world, unemployed and alone, and ready to refine my character.

## WITHERING HEIGHTS

The refining process isn't immediate, of course. The first and longest step is "withering." The leaves are laid out to dry under a mild air flow for about fourteen hours where they shrivel and lose about 70 percent of their moisture. They are beginning to decompose, to rot. At just the right time the following morning, the men overseeing this drying and oxidizing process drop the still-damp leaves through a hatch in the floor to the rolling machines below.

In this room, to the vibrating groan of monstrous machines, the leaves are churned together under moderate pressure. The mechanized rolling process hastens a more aggressive breaking down—the controlled death of the leaves—and is the height of the fermenting process, imparting the flavor style and caffeine. "This process of death," says Banerjee in his book, "releases the enzymes that are so essential for developing the aroma and infusion of the tea." Timing is critical to ensure that just the right amount of fermentation takes place.

What exits here is a shadow of its former self. Yet without the decomposition, the ultimate potential of that once bursting green leaf cannot be harnessed. For Darjeeling tea, the withering and rolling process takes less than one day. For me?

My last few weeks at home were hell. I'd given two-month's notice at work that was followed, not by the great liberation I'd imagined, nor a dark apprehension about my unemployment, but by a holding pattern. My life was a movie playing in slow motion, punctuated with dramatic scenes of worry as I wrestled the practicalities of the trip into place.

I'd given *myself*, on the other hand, only three days between my last day at the office and my flight. This proved insufficient for any physical response—call it let down—to my life's upheaval. My body, more aware of the situation than my brain, addressed the oversight with a profoundly inconvenient sickness (sinus infection, deep body aches, extreme exhaustion) for my last two weeks at home. Even as I readied myself and attended going away parties in my honor, I'd withdrawn. I began to emerge only somewhere between Newark and New Delhi airports.

Worry tackled me again in Makaibari by way of ATM failure. Days of marching up to the town of Kurseong to release my card into a machine and breathlessly await the bad news: "INCORRECT PIN," written in aggravatingly plain English across the screens of all four machines in the small town. Each time followed by a deflating sense of hopelessness combined with the familiar upper chest choke of my anxiety.

And then my homesickness. Part three, perhaps, of my decomposition.

My first Wednesday in the village I awoke from a long deep slumber, and after a moment of orientation, I lay in bed and cried. Tears running into my ears as I stared at the ceiling, or alternately as I stared with closed eyes into the beautiful smiling faces of Henry and Simon; and as I reached over, imagining the warm and comforting snuggle of Melissa's body. It'd only been a week, but add to that the vast distance, both geographical and cultural, and the fact that there were nine more weeks in my journey, and the whole recipe became a bit more than I could imagine.

*Why am I doing this? Why am I so far away from those I love?* I wondered. Somehow I'd imagined I could book a trip like this, like a twenty-year-old, and become that twenty-year-old.

But that is a time all about outward growth, expression, and expansion. A time when we are immortal and eager to run from home and establish ourselves as adults, as independent in the world. A time to push away from those we love and go explore.

I'm not twenty. And while I certainly wanted to shake things up and push away from the constructs and confines of how I'd been defined, I did not want to push away from Henry and Simon and Melissa. My money situation had drained my inner reserves, and I was destined to settle into weariness.

Later that morning I headed off for my first volunteer teaching stint in the village school, a modest single-story building housing four small classrooms. Availing themselves of my assistance, the school director and two teachers retired to a small office and heated their early lunch on a tiny, shoddy stove.

As the scent of curried potatoes and fresh flatbread *roti* emerged from the stench of dirty fuel, I found myself among the sweet smiling faces of a dozen uniformed children, trying to explain the math assignments in slow English. Then I sat at the desk grading their work one at a time as they yelled "finish!" and brought their workbooks to me. Exhausted by it all, I played with the globe that sat, almost cruelly, in front of me. I wanted to see if indeed Chicago was closer to New Delhi than New York is (made curious by a shorter flight time), but all I saw, little finger and thumb stretched across the top of the small globe, was that I could not, in the northern hemisphere of this massive planet, be any farther from Boulder, Colorado. My eyes filled with tears again. Not "finish!" yet.

How much more withering will I have to endure before a good firing ends the emotional decomposition and sets me on my new course?

## FIRING AND SORTING

For tea, the breakdown is brought to a sudden end as the leaves undergo a firing process, a tumble down five layers of a conveyer system through a large coal-fired oven at approximately 100°F. This takes just over thirty minutes, after which the tea is roughly complete and ready to brew, but needs to be sorted and graded.

It is then wheeled into the sorting room, the most magical room in the factory. Tin-lined wood floors and large sorting machines are bathed in natural morning light from tall east-facing windows, while a dozen or more barefoot women in brightly colored saris move about carrying various baskets and tins and handmade grass whisk brooms through the sorting process. The room is filled with the vibrating hum of machines and tea dust in the air, and the choreography of the process is delightfully theatrical. Even the sunken floor adds to this sense; it's like a black box theater—but a brightly lit set—with a thoroughly Asian performance art taking place. One of those theatrical endeavors whose brilliance titillates my senses, yet whose meaning escapes me: something about the meeting place of artisanal handiwork and larger-than-life technology, all in constant motion, a ritual dance of woman and machine alike. What flows out of this room, after hours of scooping, sifting, shaking and picking, is the beautiful finished product of some of the world's finest tea.

## SHIPPING AND HANDLING

This is the fantasy, of course. That by simply taking the leap, things will all be sorted out and then cleaned up the way the ladies clean up the sorting room after each batch. Will I be so deftly handled? I have nine more weeks of travel ahead of me before returning home. I await the firing that will end my deterioration, and then perhaps I will adeptly sort it all out, the next chapters of my adult life. This, I suppose, is the hope of any good pilgrimage: that we will find some clarifying truth to hang our next actions on.

This first flush tea, packed into these twenty-kilo bags and ready to ship out into the global market, will be brewed—and hopefully enjoyed—by someone, somewhere; the finally released, fully realized potential of that recently plucked-from-the-branch leaf. But perhaps it's too lofty an order. To take a wholly Indian view of it, it doesn't ultimately matter—as long as we do our best in any present incarnation of the process—because even the finest teas become compost and piss shortly after that first satisfying sip, ready to start over again.

What I do know is the branch has been broken, the withering is underway and what will emerge—well sorted, expertly prepared, and fully appreciated, or not—will be a version of me at least a little richer in character. And maybe that's enough. When I set out on this journey I wanted to know, returning to Mary Oliver's poem, "whoever I was, I was / alive / for a little while."

≈ ≈ ≈

*Bill Giebler lives and writes in Boulder, Colorado. His work on food, travel, and the environment has appeared in* Organic Spa Magazine, Green Living Journal, Edible Front Range, *and more. "The Tea in Me" won the Grand Prize Gold Award in the Eighth Annual Solas Awards.*

≈ ≈ ≈

# Code 5oo

One person's desert wonderland is another's grave.

The first thing Brooks County lead investigator Danny Davila wants to know is whether I have a weak stomach. We are sitting in his cramped office at the sheriff's department in Falfurrias, Texas, on a sweltering July afternoon. Before I can respond, he slides a three-ring binder my way. "The Dead Book," he calls it. Inside are dozens of laminated photographs of the remains of the thirty-four undocumented immigrants who have died in the county's scrub brush in 2012, presumably while sidestepping the nearby U.S. Customs and Border Patrol checkpoint.

"This is the American dream," Davila says, spreading his arms wide, as if to signal beyond the cedar-paneled room, "and this is where it stops, right here." He thumps the binder with his forefinger.

I grasp the Dead Book with both hands and open to a random page. A dark-skinned man in yellow briefs is curled in the fetal position atop a blanket.

"We find them naked sometimes, but it's not because they were abused or anything," Davila explains. "It's just their last-ditch effort to try to cool off. They don't know that makes it worse."

It almost looks as though the dead man was caught in a moment of contemplation; his muscles are relaxed and his gaze is soft. But then I look closer, and I see that ants are swarming his eyeballs. I turn the page quickly, scan some typewritten reports, then stop at the next batch of photographs. An engorged hand, roasted purple and protruding from the dirt, its fingers extending skyward. A face that is half-skull, half-meat, and a full set of teeth. A belly so swollen it has split like a chorizo on a grill. Every image traumatizes me further, yet I keep flipping the pages to prove that I can handle the gore. Twenty minutes ago, a rancher called in a Code 500; the thirty-fifth body of the year has been discovered. If my stomach is up to it, I can accompany Davila on the retrieval.

By year's end, there will be three Dead Books perched atop Davila's desk, along with a "Missing Persons" binder full of photos and emails sent by anxious families in Mexico and Central America. The year 2012 will break all records for Brooks County, with 129 bodies found somewhere along 942 square miles of ranches and roads. Not only is that body count a 260 percent increase from 2011, but it comes at a time when migration across the U.S. border is at a historic low—nearly half the rate of even four years ago. In 2012, the entire state of Arizona recovered just 28 more bodies than they did in this tiny Texas county.

So why has Brooks—a full hour-and-a-half drive from the Mexico border—become a killing field for immigrants? Davila thinks Arizona's notoriously stringent regulations could have something to do with it. Then there's the weather. Texas has suffered its worst drought ever these past two years, and temperatures routinely hit triple digits. Coyotes tend to tell their clients that they'll only need to walk a couple of hours to avoid the checkpoint (as opposed to a couple of days), and that the trail cuts through a nice ranch. Unprepared for the harsh conditions of the South Texas desert, many immigrants succumb to heat exhaustion and then die when the other travelers continue on without them.

The rise of the Mexican drug cartels, which have largely taken over the smuggling business, has led to even more deaths. Ten years ago, immigrants could hire local guides in Mexico to walk them across the border for $1,000 apiece; today, they usually wind up with cartel minions who not only charge exorbitant rates, but occasionally orchestrate kidnappings halfway through the journey so they can extort even more money from families back home. Davila can tell horrifying stories about immigrant abuse. One woman he recently apprehended managed to escape after the coyotes "had their way" with all the women in her group.

The narco-factor is the hardest to quantify, because almost none of the bodies discovered in Brooks County undergo autopsies, which cost at least $1,500 each. It simply costs too much to determine whether a person died of exposure or as a result of violence. The county's entire operating budget is just $585,000 a year, barely enough to pay its employees. Davila, after eighteen years on the job, makes only $27,000. Moreover, wild pigs and vultures usually find the bodies long before the authorities do, ravaging potential evidence. In the reports filed neatly on Davila's desk, the cause of death is invariably listed as "hiking through ranch illegally," even when the more accurate culprits might be climate change, sadistic coyotes, or U.S. immigration policy. No matter the cause of death, one thing is certain. "Hiking" is deeply murderous in South Texas.

"I don't know if this body is a stinker or a bloater or what," Davila says as we climb into a black Ford F-150. He never knows what awaits him on these runs: scattered bones, a freshly vacated corpse, or something in between. Davila's supplies are in the cab of the truck. There's a camera tripod, a camouflage jacket, a flashlight, gloves, a body bag, and a gun, all coated in dust.

We zip down County Road 201, past the Brooks County Detention Center and a string of bail bond agencies housed in trailers, toward town. Historically, Falfurrias has been famed for two things: a nineteenth-century faith healer named Don Pedrito Jaramillo and a dairy that sold its sweet cream butter across the state in yellow-and-blue boxes. While Jaramillo's shrine still draws dozens of pilgrims a day, the dairy has since become a Whataburger, and the downtown strip largely consists of dollar stores, loan offices, and pawn shops. Of Brooks County's 7,200 residents, nearly 40 percent live below the poverty line. It's not hard to fathom why smuggling is so lucrative here.

"You find someone lost in the woods and you take them home, call their loved ones, and say, 'Hey, for five hundred bucks, I'll take them to Houston.' Then you wait for the money to be wired over, and you put them on a bus," Davila says. "I'd say 40 percent of the population here is involved like that."

Indeed, I'll turn on the news the next day to learn that the wife of the justice of the peace in nearby Kenedy County has been busted for transporting ten undocumented immigrants in her Hummer. She charged $500 a head.

As someone born and raised in Falfurrias, Davila finds it all disheartening. "That's the hardest part of this job, policing your own, the people you grew up with," he says, shaking his head and stroking his mustache. He's a handsome man, late thirties with thick black hair and dark olive skin. Though he routinely sees unspeakable things, he seems inherently upbeat, always joking and grinning. His name is stitched across his shirt and his rubber bracelet reads PEACE. Leaning over the steering wheel, he flicks on the radio. *This heat has got / Right out of hand.* It's Bananarama, the '80s British pop band. The song is "Cruel Summer."

A ranch hand wearing a rosary as a necklace ushers us in at the gate of a sprawling ranch, one Davila asks me not to name. We're among the last to arrive—the Border Patrol, the justice of the peace, and the sheriff are already here, and the undertaker is on the way. The body is located in the far recesses of the property, so we must travel in a caravan so no one gets lost. As we amble down the caliche road, Davila points out where gaping holes have been cut into the barbed-wire fence. Some ranchers have left out ladders in the hopes their fences might be spared, but the hikers don't seem to use them. It's the same with the water. Afraid, perhaps, of being poisoned by the big tanks painted blue especially for them, the immigrants opt to break the valves off windmills and drink that water instead. Although every rancher I've met out here expresses compassion for the immigrants, they feel a grudge against them, too.

At 3.3 miles, we switch to four-wheel drive, take a right, and begin off-roading through the brush. My heart is beating in my throat, and Davila doesn't help when he notes that this seemingly deserted ranch is actually teeming with smugglers. "There ain't *someone* looking at us," he says. "There's a whole *lotta* people looking at us."

He is constantly reminded that the smugglers monitor his actions. Not long before our meeting, a stranger approached him at the store and said, "I noticed your antenna is bent, what happened?"

Davila laughed it off—"I hit a butterfly," he told the man—but the point was clear. People know what kind of car he drives, and where and when, which is especially disconcerting given that he has a young daughter. I ask how he deals with the stress, and he quips, "I take a lot of blood pressure pills."

In time, we see a navy hoodie dangling from a fence. The truck ahead of us parks and so do we. The brush has grown too thick for driving. It's time for us to hike.

I smell the body before I see it. The scent wraps around my face like a hot towel, burning my eyes and singeing my throat. It is violent and rancid and frightening. I start breathing through my mouth instead of my nose, but that transfers the sensation to my tongue. Now I am eating death instead of smelling it.

Trailing behind Davila, I enter the woods. The brush is so dense, I must clear it with my arms before each step, half-swimming across the loamy soil. Brambles crack beneath my boots. It is ninety-five degrees.

Maybe forty feet away, I can see a black pair of jeans. An occupied pair of jeans, stretched out in the dirt. One foot remains inside a sneaker, but before I can spot the other, I see the arm. What's left of the arm. Not long ago, that arm must have hugged and danced, carried firewood and groceries and children, but now it has been eaten to the bone, with just a few pulpy morsels remaining. The hand, meanwhile, has been ravaged not by animals but by sun, baked so black it almost looks blue. My eyes drift toward the mid-section of the body. At first, I think it is wearing a child-sized t-shirt, but then I see the belly has bloated to colossal proportions, so engorged that it has exploded along the jean line. Slick black beetles crawl in and out of its crater.

It's the face that unravels me. From the nose down, its remaining skin is black and leathered, but the top half is strangely untouched, the color of a bruised peach. There are deep holes instead of eyes, and the mouth is open as if silently wailing. The hair is streaming all the way down to what used to be elbows, thick and black and damp. *It's a woman,* I think, and with that realization comes the overpowering urge to scream, to continue the sound her own mouth was making before "hiking through ranch illegally" forever quieted her voice, to continue the collective wail they all must have been making before winding up inside the three-ring binders of Brooks County, Texas. I bite my lips until they bleed.

We gather around the woman—Davila, the sheriff, the border patrol, the justice of the peace, the ranch hand, and me—yet we stand a good fifteen to twenty feet away. We lean forward, as if over an imaginary railing, but no one steps any closer. It could be that we are respecting the privacy of this tragedy, or taking care not to trample any evidence. I've been told that these bodies harbor all manner of wildlife, including snakes and spiders. Perhaps no one wants to get bit. I've also been told that people's spirits hover long beyond death—the spirits wait for someone to find them, then affix to the shoulder of the living. Perhaps no one wants to get cursed. Or maybe we're just sparing ourselves further revulsion. Like everyone else, I stand close-but-far, despite a pressing impulse to run up and hold what's left of the woman's hand.

The justice of the peace asks for the time. We all scramble for our watches and cell phones, grateful for the distraction. After much discussion we decide it is 12:35 on July 3, 2012, which the justice of the peace jots in her notebook. Although this woman has clearly been gone for days—three, by Davila's estimation—this will be her official time of death. And because there is no obvious sign of foul play, no hatchet sticking out of her skull, for example, her death will be attributed to "hiking through ranch illegally."

Just then the undertaker arrives on the scene. He is an older man, slight of frame, and he carries a white bed sheet and a large cardboard box. Breaking through our imaginary railing, he walks right up to the woman's feet, sets down his parcels, and slides on a pair of blue rubber gloves. He briskly searches her pockets, inches from the beetle pit. First he finds some dollar bills: a twenty, a five, three ones. He piles these atop the woman's thigh. Next he pulls out an LG cellphone and wipes it clean. Running his fingers along her bra line, he checks to see if anything is tucked inside, an ID maybe, or a list of phone numbers. There is nothing.

Now comes the task of slipping the woman into the bag. He unfurls the sheet and lays it out beside her, though ultimately it must go beneath her. Carefully, he rolls the woman onto her side—but that makes her scalp fall off, hair and all, with a strangely soupy sound. She has become liquid. All of her is leaking and dripping, colored fluids as well as beetles. The undertaker catches her scalp and swiftly slides it back into place, as though assisting a lady with an errant wig. While the rest of us simply stand and stare, Davila bounds over to help. They push the sheet beneath her, then roll her back on top.

"She's small," Davila announces. "Probably Guatemalan. Or Honduran."

The two men swaddle her in the sheet, half bones, half stew, and then stuff her into a black body bag with gold zippers. Davila, the sheriff, and the Border Patrol agent fan out thirty feet and scan the brush for approximately half a minute before heading back to their respective trucks. There is no evidence in sight. We leave behind only an empty water bottle, and a host of beetles. No words are spoken. No rites are given.

Over by the Ford, Davila wipes his shoes on a patch of huisache. "Gotta make sure there's no bodily fluid on me, 'cos it will stink," he explains.

We notice the undertaker struggling with a gurney, and Davila hurries over. Together they prop it open, lay the body bag on top, strap it down, lift it up, and roll it into the back of the van. Davila introduces me to the man from the funeral home, whose last name is Angel, pronounced *An-hell* in the Tejano way. I want to say "how fitting" and applaud his professional graces, but before I can speak Davila tells him I am a writer.

Angel shakes his head. "A lot of people write stories," he says softly, "and nothing ever gets done."

I hear this a lot, and though it never fails to shatter me, I usually try to brush it off with a self-deprecating remark and a smile. But there's something about being a Mexican American in this landscape—a product of "illegal hiking" myself—that emboldens me to hope that maybe, just maybe, something will change this time in Washington. To hope that by writing about this woman, I will memorialize her, this woman who went hiking through a ranch and got annihilated, this one member of the 129 who will die in the brush in Brooks County in a single year. Even if we never learn this woman's name—or whether she's Guatemalan or Honduran, or for all we know Chinese, I will think of her feet and her face when I brush my teeth and try to fall asleep. Does this count as something getting done?

I wish to say this and a great deal more, but there isn't time before Angel retreats to his driver's seat, where he removes a pair of badly soiled gloves. He already knows he'll be back tomorrow.

❧ ❧ ❧

*Stephanie Elizondo Griest has mingled with the Russian Mafia, polished Chinese propaganda, and danced with Cuban rumba queens.* These adventures inspired her award-winning memoirs Around the Bloc: My Life in Moscow, Beijing, and Havana; Mexican Enough: My Life Between the Borderlines; *and the bestselling guidebook* 100 Places Every Woman Should Go. *As National Correspondent for* The Odyssey, *she once drove 45,000 miles across America in a Honda hatchback named Bertha. She currently teaches creative nonfiction at UNC-Chapel Hill, and can be found online at www.MexicanEnough.com. "Code 500" originally appeared in the Fall 2013 issue of* Oxford American.

❧  ❧  ❧

# Diego Forever

An adventure in the Prado with
Velázquez and his damn sexy mustache.

O f course I would fall for him. There is something
about his mustache, the way it curls up at the edges,
and how it skirts the top of his dashing little smirk. His brown
eyes twinkle, or at least appear to be twinkling, which I have
come to understand is a major feat when painting a portrait.
Particularly a self-portrait. It's Sunday, after midnight, and I
have to give a presentation in twelve hours. The last thing
I need is his pixels burning like a Spanish sun into my computer screen. Yet in a fated series of keystrokes, we've found
each other. There he stands with a glove on one hand, MJ
style, and the other naked, curled regally on his hip making
it impossible to look away. Clad in black, his figure pops off
the ochre background in opposition to the majority of his canvases. A one-off. An original.

Every girl falls in love with at least one moody brooding
artist in her lifetime, and in my lifetime it's Diego Velázquez.
Never mind the fact that nothing about his life suggests
moody or brooding, just artist, but at that he excels. He's
been dead for over three hundred and fifty years, and I find
this to be more than a minor inconvenience. At nearly one

in the morning I am filled with intense longing, and before I know it, I'm checking fares to Madrid. Two hours later, I fall into bed having resolved to ignite a spark with the dapper Spaniard, to throw ourselves into the libertine bustle, and to experience the ways only a mustache can tickle. Our incompatible blips on the time/space continuum leave me with two choices: 1) Get a tattoo on my left breast of a dagger impaling a heart wrapped in thorny roses. Scrawled above in swirling tattoo typeface: "Diego Forever"; 2) Go to Spain and lick his canvases.

I take option two because everyone knows that tattooing your lover's name on your body is the kiss of relationship death. And besides, the thrill of going to Spain to walk in the footsteps of *mi amor* is intoxicating. Then again, so is the seventeenth-century paint with its pigments made from the pulverized bodies of insects and stone ground minerals. At the very least, these paint chips will guarantee a serious buzz. The demotion of the Spanish monarchy and the end of the Inquisition makes it much easier for me to get close to his paintings. Close enough to huff the iron oxide at least. I'm torn between my happiness over the demise of political and theological domination and my desire to actually step back into time, to dodge the bishops' red coats, and to sneak into the palace to fritter away an afternoon with Diego himself.

Velázquez spent his time working for King Philip IV as the court painter and left behind a trove of portraits, most of which hang in Museo Nacional del Prado in Madrid, Spain's oldest, largest, and most famous museum. Outside the main entrance, I stand before his dominating copper sculpture now oxidized into a beautiful patina. He leans forward in his chair and looks down at me from behind that mustache. One elbow rests on his knee with a paintbrush in hand, a palette lies across his left arm, and that silly little collar made famous by his boss juts from his neck. I imagine removing it altogether, followed by the buttoned vest, and eventually the knee breeches. It's June in Madrid, and Diego is doing nothing to help the rising temperature.

According to the Prado map, about half of the museum showcases Spanish painters. I beeline it for the second floor where Velázquez keeps company with his fellow greats: Rubens, Titian, and of course, Caravaggio, who was so influential in Velázquez's work that most of his pieces are described in artsy circles as "Caravaggioesque." *Mars, God of War*, completed in 1640, is just such a painting. Unlike Diego's self-portrait, the background is mostly black, and Mars appears in a wash of light that shines on his bare arm and leg as if revealing something true and mysterious in all those layers of muscle. With the dark background now forgotten, I stare at his physique. Wearing his helmet, and nothing else, he sits on an unmade bed in a swath of pink silk with his loins covered in bright blue fabric. This is not the eternally youthful and triumphant Mars, or Mars in the garden wooing Aphrodite. No, this is Diego indulging his love of paradox—Mars, the god, waking up from a disappointing one-night stand.

His shield and weapons lie in a heap at his bare feet, and his right hand holds the handle of something that finishes off canvas. It could be an axe, a mace, or a toilet plunger for all I know. After reading the placard I learn it's a general's baton of command. Obscured in shadow are his eyes, but lo! What a mustache! The same handlebar style as Velázquez himself. I cannot take my eyes off him.

Like many of Velázquez's paintings, I want to step inside the world he has created. I want to ask Mars if he would like a few aspirin and a *café bombon*, the Spanish coffee confection designed to cure all ills, and to tell him in frank terms that this will do nothing to win Aphrodite's love. She will drop him like a hot rock if she finds out about his escapades. Maybe I'd tip back his helmet to see his eyes, or sit on his lap Santa

Claus-style and ask him for a pony that I don't really want. More than likely, I'd be glancing sidelong looking for an isolated corner in which I could lure Diego during the afternoon siesta. It grieves me that I can do none of these things.

A group of kindergartners in matching red jackets enters the room with nary a glance to Mars. Instead, they sit cross-legged in front of another Velázquez prize, *The Thread Spinners*. Mars, dejected, looks at them forlornly as they point out the spinning wheels, the balls of yarn, and the ladder in the background. It's all part of their culture curriculum which includes nothing but ambivalence toward the war god. People file in and out, read his placard, glance at him, leave. Even the school children rise, get into their hand-holding-stay-together formation, and move on.

For a moment, we are alone. I lean toward the slate gray walls, the braided keep-at-least-two-feet-back cord grazes my kneecaps. I lean into Mars and his brushstrokes. "Give them twenty years," I whisper. "They're too little to understand. Would you want to explain to them this hot mess you're in?" The second wave of red jackets interrupts us, and we both know how this is going to play out. We watch as they form a semicircle in front of *The Thread Spinners*, their eyes focused on nothing but their teacher. After a lengthy goodbye I linger another moment, blow Mars a kiss, and head for the next salon where I know Diego is waiting.

Just through the door is the biggest room in the building that has an art deco skylight roof. The gray floor tiles give way to a red-and-gray marble streaked with blue. Unlike the area with *Mars* and *The Thread Spinners*, this room is a hive of activity, chatter, and the clicking of camera shutters even though photos are strictly forbidden. Voices bounce off the walls and floor, all indiscernible, even when standing within arm's length. This room, like the four previous, is dedicated to Velázquez. Here, his work as a court painter shines. I scan the walls: Philip with his dog and hunting rifle, Philip standing at a desk, Philip standing and looking important. It's a Philip IV parade with few exceptions.

It wasn't *Mars* or Diego's self-portrait, the one with the short hair, the funky collar, and the singular gloved hand, that made me fall so hard for my conquistador of the canvas. It was his most celebrated work, the last painting he is known to have completed, *Las Meninas*, finished in 1657. It's here, in front of the masterpiece, that I find my troop of five-year-olds wedged in among the tour groups and budding artists, staring up at Princess Margarita who could have been, in another time, their classmate.

Velázquez creates the same dark background as Mars, and places Margarita in the foreground in high light. She is surrounded by two attendants and flanked by two of the court dwarves. Behind them, her chaperone and a palace bodyguard shun me as they peer through the shadows whispering secrets to each other. If only they gave me a chance, I could give them so much more to whisper about. But they don't, and in the humdrum of palace life, the dog falls asleep at the dwarves' feet. All of the action takes place in the bottom third of the canvas, culminating in a scheme of blues, whites, and browns. The illusion of light streams through a nearby window, and also from an open door at the back of the room, where José Nieto Velázquez, the Chamberlain of tapestries, has paused, like me, to look in on the sitting.

The dark top presses down on the figures, punctuating their diminutive statures and the pressure that is already on Margarita, who is only five years old. Little does she know that in ten years she will marry The Holy Roman Emperor, have four children, and die before she turns twenty-two. Here, she's infected with a boredom that can only be cured by chasing a cat through the garden, or by throwing pebbles in the fountain. She'd likely give anything to don a red coat and

clasp hands with an assigned buddy for the remainder of the
Prado visit. Her loyal attendants continue their coaxing. One
curtsies while the other offers Margarita a red cup, and for
just a moment they get her to stand still. She looks at neither
of them, pinning her curious gaze on the group of her fellow
kindergartners. I watch her, waiting for the moment when
she runs across the room.

What is most striking about this painting is all the pictures within it. Most are shadowed copies of portraits lining
the back wall. A mirror shows the King and Queen of Spain.
Some argue that it is a reflection of a painting, but I think
they are there, standing shoulder to shoulder with me, keeping an eye on their little girl, and quite possibly offering up a
1650s Spanish equivalent to the ice cream sundae if she's good.
Their presence only confirms my suspicions about her desire
to dart off and play, to go outside and get dirty.

On the bottom left, behind a canvas twice his height, stands
Velázquez with brush in hand.

We stare at each other. Time and space do that romantic-
comedy movie thing where everything slows down, and the
man's laughter next to me stretches out like a line of taffy. A
woman raises her map in dramatic slow-motion speed. Jaws
hang agape. My heart thuds in my chest as the room around
me slowly comes back into focus. The Japanese couple move
on to Phillip with his dog and rifle. The school children find
the red cross painted on Velázquez's chest. They don't know
it, but it represents the Order of Santiago bestowed upon him
by the King's decree in November of 1659 just a few short
months before his death. I watch fifteen pairs of eyes focus on
the painter who stares back at us, at them, and at me.

There he stands in his black coat with the gray satin under-
shirt, his high waisted belt, and like his statue outside, a palette
rests on his left arm. I gaze upon his oval face, the curly hair
and crazy collar, and of course, that mouth-watering mustache

that started everything. Finally we are together, and in that split second I realize there is no hope of us ever being alone.

It's then that I imagine Velázquez's voice in my head, breaking the ice with this, "They want to call this painting *Las Meninas*, but I think Meta Velázquez is more appropriate. Who else but me could paint a picture of me painting a picture of the royal family?" Then he laughs, but not an evil genius laugh, the laugh of an uncle who always plays pranks and knows coin tricks. I wonder if he knew how controversial his statement would be. By painting himself with Margarita, he claimed the status of the artist, and art itself, was just as significant as royalty. He must have known, that sexy rebel.

"Can you believe this? I am surrounded by a circus of children, dwarves, sleeping dogs, and the King of Spain. It's a crazy gig," he goes on. I wonder what his wife thought of it, and of me lusting after her husband. Did she appreciate his facial hair like I do? Did she wish he would paint her? How could she not?

Diego considers the beholder. A profound statement lies curtained off behind his lips. Who wouldn't want to sit for that guy who peers out from behind the canvas? The one who stares you straight in the eye, not looking over his brood of models, but straight at you, the viewer.

"Step inside," he says. "Come into my world."

Who am I to resist?

～＊ ～＊ ～＊

*Kelly Chastain is a graduate of Pacific University with a B.A. in Creative Writing. She works in both fiction and non-fiction, and has been published in* The Burrow Press Review, Isthmus Review, Cactus Heart Press, Outside In, Silk Road Review, *and others. Currently, she blogs at kellychastain.com, and is working on a historical novel, a series of memoir vignettes about growing up on a farm, and travel writing essays from a recent trip to Portugal.*

KATHERINE JAMIESON

꙳ ꙳ ꙳

# Woman Rain

She was a weather system unto herself.

When speaking of the Georgetown car park, the central hub of transportation for their country, Guyanese use the word "chaotic," which they pronounce with a hard "ch," like "charge." "Da place chaotick! Watch for the teefman, he'll pick ya pocket quick, and gone!" my friends warned me. In the car park, rats scurried between mountains of trash, music blasted from thirty different minibuses, and every so often a madman stormed the market screaming about Queen Elizabeth. Still, I went there often; I could not stay away. It was the most vital place, the filthiest place I had ever been.

Once I stayed past nightfall and lost my bearings in the dark. Bodies thronging in the thick evening air, mosquitoes biting through my sunburn, and the rising smell of sweat, sewage and trash overwhelmed me. I was in tears when a young woman saw me. "Gyal, what 'appened to you?!" she asked as she took my elbow and pushed me onto a bus. I thanked her, but I could not explain. What had happened to me?

I had come to Guyana three months earlier to work as a teacher for teenage girls at the May Rodrigues Vocational Training Center of the YWCA. There was no headmistress at

136

the school and no one to help me define my job, ostensibly to set up some kind of "Youth Development" project. After an initial burst of energy, during which I attempted to catalogue the entire library of donated books, my idealism was waning. When school let out I spent the rest of my days wandering through the city and here, at the car park, watching.

"White gyal! White meat! Nevah eat a white meat yet!" the men would yell at me. I had learned to signal to them, to give a half-complicit wave to their calls and then forget that I had been noticed at all. This allowed me to watch without feeling that I was being watched, to imagine that I somehow blended into the scenery, though I was likely the only white here among thousands. It was a camouflage of ignorance; and though I couldn't admit it then, I was camouflaged only to myself.

The day I met Eulis, I was standing on the outskirts of the melee in front of a branch of Guyana's local fast food restaurant. Out of the corner of my eye, I glimpsed a short figure approaching me in a black-and-white checked housedress. We made eye contact, but I looked away quickly, pretending I had not seen her. She took a long time to reach me, listing side to side as she walked, while schoolchildren wove around her as they ran by. Eventually I had no choice but to acknowledge the four and a half-foot woman inches away in the dust of the street. I stood on a little concrete plateau of cracked sidewalk and braced myself for the lilting demand of the Georgetown beggars: "Sistah, ya 'ave a little piece for me, sistah?"

"Hello, good aftah noon, Miss!" she said, laughing. "Ya must watch ya don't get buhn up in this sun! Sun hot, hot!" Another giggle.

"I'm alright," I said, shading my eyes to see her better. Smiling, she revealed a mouth full of gapped and broken teeth. Though she must have been at least seventy, her high rounded cheekbones made the skin of her face look smooth.

She gripped a faded umbrella in her left hand, and a glass Coke bottle poked out of the wrinkled, black plastic bag in her right.

"I'm sorry," I said, trying to pre-empt her. "I don't have many dollars, but I can give you this." I offered her a few small bills. She frowned when she saw them, her dark skin puckering into deep wrinkles.

"Ya 'ave a husband? Y'all could use a cleaning lady for wash de wares an' so! I used to clean 'ouse for a nice white lady, and she was very pleased with my work," she said puffing up her chest.

"No, I don't have a husband. I have a roommate, and we're really not looking. . . ."

"But y'all must need someone for dust, an' sweep up, an' scrub walls, an' beat rug?" The woman cocked her head to the side skeptically. "Ya must be busy, ya 'ave job with the Embassy or so? I could come when y'all are at work, just one day a week, do every, every ting."

I hesitated. Though I had only lived here briefly, the demands of cleaning in Guyana had been impressed on me early. The jungle exists in vast tracts throughout 95 percent of the country, and life on the coastland is always imperiled, plant and animal perpetually on the verge of reclaiming that lost 5 percent. Ants and cockroaches swarm at any crumb that reaches the floor. I took my showers with salamanders and frogs. Tarantulas and centipedes skulked in my cupboards. In rainy season, waves of black and gray mold grow over any moist surface, and during the dry season dust from the unpaved roads billows in through the windows. I had seen small clouds puff up when people sat down on our sofa.

"No, we really don't need a maid, but thank you," I said. The woman screwed her face up in a look of mixed dejection and disgust.

"All right then, but if ya change ya mind, I'm shopping 'ere in da mawrning," she said, reaching down to her umbrella and pushing it up over her head. "Good aftah noon," she said, and listed back in the crowd where she was quickly lost in the rush of people and animals.

All afternoon I couldn't forget her plaintive questioning, her queer, high-pitched voice, her unnerving cackle. But my real discomfort with the woman's offer originated in the possibility of hiring a "servant" in a country where I was supposed to be serving. Having a maid seemed like something an ex-pat would do, not someone with a mandate to "live at the level of the people." I wanted to believe that I could do my own work, like a Guyanese woman. I remembered my family's maid growing up, a very sweet Salvadoran woman named Edis who still cleaned for my parents. She had become something of a family friend, inviting my parents to her wedding, her children's christenings, and her own naturalization ceremony. The fact remained though: she scrubbed our toilets.

I was relieved that I had not given in to the woman. It was much easier than grappling with difficult questions about service, privilege, and poverty. Better just to scrub our own shower, mop our own floors. I liked the illusion of solidarity with the Guyanese that I had been cultivating and this strange woman had disrupted it; I resolved to avoid the car park in the mornings.

A few hours later, though, on a tree-lined neighborhood street, I saw a familiar short figure approaching. By the time I thought to turn around, she was waving her umbrella and walking as fast as she could in my direction. "Miss! Miss! Like the good Lord brought us togeder again! Who could believe it, to see you 'ere so soon aftah we fuhst meet. . . ." she laughed and laughed. And then she was before me again, a short woman who seemed to take up my whole field of vision.

"Yes . . . what a strange coincidence," I faltered, noticing the heightened desperation in her eyes. She told me she had gone by her nephew's to see if he had a "little piece" to spare, but he couldn't give her anything this month.

I had no crowd to protect me now, no bustle and honking to distract me from her palpable need. "Ya sure ya don' need some help with the house. . . ." she asked, her wide brown eyes fixed on me, her face twisted into a hopeful grin.

My decision had nothing to do with a clean house. It was simply that she was old and poor, and I was young and rich. Guilt played a part, and pity also. Looking at her stocky, compact body and wrinkled face, made me think of my own grandmothers living in retirement communities in Florida and Maryland, not out begging to clean houses. Some vague economic principle occurred to me: job creation as the truest expression of development. What could be so wrong in offering work to this woman? Wasn't that better than leaving her to beg on the streets?

"Well, I'd have to ask my roommate Maureen. . . ." I began.

"Oh Miss!" she laughed, clapping me on the arm. "Ya won't sorry, Miss! Y'all gon' like having a nice, clean house!" She pumped my hand in a strong, vigorous grip, laughing as she introduced herself: Eulis Idina Saunders, age 65, resident of the St. Luke's Catholic Home on Vlissengen Road. With the tropical sunlight fading into the evening sky and the whistling frogs beginning their song from the trenches, I could almost believe that I had made a good decision.

"You hired us a maid?" Maureen said when I told her the news over dinner. "Why?"

"Well, she seems like she has a lot of experience," I explained, looking down at my plate. "And it'll be helpful for us. We won't have to worry about the house getting so dirty."

"Were you worried before?" Maureen asked, raising her eyebrows. Of the two of us, she was much more likely to be found scrubbing the black mold off the windowsills. The second of five children from a working class, Irish-Catholic family in Cleveland, she had been responsible, like all her siblings, for her own regimen of household chores. For her, having a clean house was a matter of pride and propriety, as important as applying make-up and styling her hair, which she did every day of our two sweltering years in Guyana. Maureen had already mastered the art of hand washing, bleaching and ironing loads of laundry, including towels and sheets, every week; the challenges of cleaning in Guyana did not intimidate her.

I had been raised in an upper-middle class suburb of Washington, D.C., collecting piles of clean, folded clothes from the dedicated Edis. House cleaning had always been an invisible process to me, something that happened while I was at school. My sense of duty to household chores was more theoretical than practical, and meeting Eulis had provided a convenient out. "Look, it could at least save us some time," I argued, and Maureen had to agree. Just doing our personal loads of laundry was a three-hour project every weekend, and sweeping and dusting the house could easily take up a whole day. In the end, we agreed that she would at least meet Eulis, and I offered to pay her full salary for the first few weeks until we decided if the arrangement would be permanent. "I think you're going to like her," I said optimistically. "Really."

Eulis arrived at precisely 6:55 A.M. the next Monday, jangling the rusty gate at the end of our walkway. "HELLO! HELLO!" she called as she walked toward our apartment, the "bottom house" of a two-story duplex. "GOOD MAWRNING GIRLS! Ya tired, Miss Katrin!" she cackled, "Like ya stay up late last night! I had to go on the road and catch minibus early fuh meet y'all here! I was worried I couldn't find the house, but look, I found y'all easy! Is nice house for

the two y'all, nuff, nuff rooms. . . ." she went on talking, as
Maureen emerged from her room, rubbing her eyes. "Hello,
hello, you must be Miss Mawreen!" Eulis said, pumping her
hand up and down. "Y'all is pretty white women, but ya must
protect your skin!" she said, looking at Maureen's freckles.
"Eh, eh, look de cyats. . . ." she said, as our three kittens scampered through the middle of the apartment. "I didn't know
y'all had cyats?" she said, laughing, looking at me.

"Oh, we just got them . . . they're just kittens," I said, reaching down to pick up one and kiss him on the head. Eulis wrinkled her nose and made a clicking noise with her tongue.

"Oh, Miss Katrin! Animal is a dirty ting! Ya must not treat
dem as children!" she scolded me, laughing again. Maureen
shot me a look.

"Maybe we should take a look around the apartment," I
offered.

It was a quick tour. We walked her through the three bedrooms, one empty for guests; the pipe jutting out from the
wall that served as a shower; the tiny closet that housed our
toilet without a lid. Then there was the dim kitchen area
with its gas stove and metal sink, the small living room with a
wicker sofa and low table. Finally we showed her our cleaning supplies, a small collection of worn out sponges and soaps
provided by our landlord.

Eulis nodded at everything she saw, commenting on the
quality of the furniture, and the lacquered wood floor. "I am
very happy to work for y'all, but dere are a few tings me just
not able with. . . ." she said as we finished the tour. Maureen
and I sat back on the couch as she began her ground rules.
Eulis did not do laundry and she did not cook and she did
not clean windows. She did not do dishes, and she did not do
stovetops. She made it clear that she had no love for cats and
planned to kick them out while she cleaned. Our traditional
pointy broom, made up of the spines of palm leaves, would

not be suitable; she would need a "push broom" with a handle. She needed Vim for the bathrooms, Bayclin for the floors, and Baygon for the cockroaches. Maureen and I listened and nodded as she went on and on. Again, Eulis' sheer force of character won out, and we agreed to pay her to come once a week.

And so it began, each Monday Eulis opening the gate at 6:55 A.M., calling, "MAWRNING MISS KATRIN! MAWRNING MISS MAWREEN! MAWRNING GYALS!" Her worn, brown rubber sandals slapping the concrete, plastic bags rustling against her housedress and then three strong raps, as her calloused knuckles met the wood door with a crack. I would pull myself from bed, opening the door to: "HELLO MISS KATRIN! HOW YA DO?" and Eulis would amble in and drop her bags on the kitchen table. "Ya hear da news last night, terrible fire on the East Coast, nuff, nuff people dead and da big cricket match this week coming. . . ." Still talking, she wandered into the back room for the cleaning supplies. "All de lawless young people gon' be parytin', like I won't go on the streets for the weekend, such madness dis country come to. . . ."

Eulis liked to talk most of the time she was cleaning, whether we were fully awake, or even in the room with her. Despite the running monologue, though, she was a hard worker, trundling through our small apartment with her bottles of brightly colored cleaning products. She soon earned a reputation among our Guyanese neighbors, who were also treated to her morning serenades. "Small woman got a big mouth!" one of them laughed to me, "How y'all take it?" Other American volunteers who stumbled out of the guest room on Monday mornings got the full Eulis treatment: an interrogation about their lives in the States, a passionate analysis of the Guyanese political situation, and a strong encouragement to marry young. In her weekly lectures, she would drop aphorisms for us to digest, about hard work and "how people stay," the challenges of grappling with the limitations of human nature. Most of her thoughts were prefaced with "Ole people say . . . ," a local version of "Confucius says," that connected her opinions to a lineage of wise and weathered Guyanese.

Unexpectedly, Eulis' hire ended up making me feel better about my life in Guyana. My job was still vague, and I was starting to doubt that it would ever change. Eulis' arrival each Monday was something that I had set into motion, a routine I could count on. I was so hungry for a sense of accomplishment that I began to think that hiring a maid somehow counted in the equation of my service to Guyana. This blind appreciation led me to be oblivious to her actual work, which, similar to Edis' efforts throughout my childhood, I simply took for granted.

As the months passed, we came to realize that as strong as Eulis' opinions were about what she would not clean, she had even stronger convictions about what was absolutely necessary to clean. She insisted on dusting under our beds every week. "Ole people say . . ." she would begin, followed by a discourse about regular under-bed cleaning, usually involving premature disease and death. Before she could slide under the wooden frame into my bed's nether regions, she had to remove duffel bags, rusted umbrellas, cracked sandals, broken flashlights, and my standard-issue medical kit. She worked herself into the corners on her stomach, only her stubby legs and the hem of her floral housedress sticking out and rocking up and down with the movement of her torso. When she finally emerged, she wiped the sweat from her forehead, dusted off her housedress and re-stored everything to its place. The whole process took about twenty minutes.

Eulis' second, non-negotiable Herculean task was to clean the shower curtain top to bottom, on both sides. Any question about the significance of this task would put a wrinkle in her brow. "Miss Katrin, ya must realize dat mold is growing! Ya cyan't see it yet, but it is dangerous mold, and soon it black up da ting!" Unable to reach the curtain, Eulis had to drag a chair into the little shower area, and remove it ring by ring from the stall. Then she would lay it flat on the kitchen floor, sprinkle it with soap powder and water, and scrub it with a hard brush. She writhed, her arm and leg muscles torturing the thin plastic into the rough cement floor. Ten or fifteen minutes later she would rise again, damp, soapy and dripping with sweat, to rinse the curtain and hang it back up.

Eulis' personality would have seemed to predict a flashy, big-picture cleaner: a waxer of floors, a scrubber of tiles, everything sparkling at the end of the day. But in truth her aesthetic of clean was concerned with nascent filth in obscure places, and little else. And there was no arguing that she didn't work hard. By her general dishevelment and the strong smells off her body after a few hours of cleaning in the tropical heat, it was clear that she had purged our apartment of all sorts of imperceptible scum.

The problem was, the house didn't look all that different after she had cleaned it. Eulis had a disdain for the dirt you could actually see, as if it were simply too obvious to be worth her time. After a combined hour of arduous toil under our beds and the guest bed (regardless of it if had been slept in), she would leave crumbs on the table or a thick layer of dust on the bookshelf. This drove Maureen crazy. "Did she clean the shower curtain again?" she would ask when she got home from work. "These tiles are disgusting!" She started to take on some of the tasks that Eulis refused, which made her even angrier. When we raised our suggestions to Eulis she would puff up her chest defensively. "I been cleaning houses for twenty years, and de ladies 'ave always been very happy with my work!" Maureen's dissatisfaction, Eulis' stubbornness, and my apathy made her salary more and more contentious as the weeks wore on.

As tensions rose, Eulis became representative of a larger societal scorn for North Americans. Though respected for our education, we were generally considered doltish when it came to household management. We stained our clothes, hung them so they took twice as long to dry, left the house with noticeable wrinkles in our slacks. We didn't even know you needed to wash your curtains and walls at Christmas to remove cockroach eggs, or beat your rugs outside every few months so they wouldn't stink with mold. We swept around furniture, rather than moving it, our *roti* did not bubble and flake, and souse and black pudding were entirely out of our league. Yes, we might be able to read or do calculations, but any Guyanese woman could outperform us when it came to the things that mattered, the things that meant clean or dirty, rich or poor, and, in some cases, life or death. We knew that our neighbors laughed behind our backs at our unconventional cleaning and laundering techniques. By refusing even our most basic suggestions, Eulis was laughing in our faces.

By this time Eulis had been working for us for seven months, and both Maureen and I had established ourselves at our jobs and become friends with young, hip, Guyanese who mocked us for putting up with such a difficult maid. The initial charm was outweighed by our annoyance with being woken up every Monday morning by a woman who refused to do the work we were paying her to do. The cross-cultural luster had worn off our times with Eulis, and we were losing patience.

As relations deteriorated we became less careful, less kind. I forgot to buy more cleaning solution when Eulis ran out, causing her to grumble for an entire morning that "ting worth doing is only worth doing right." We let the cats run freely in the house while she cleaned, so that every five minutes we

heard her shoo them away, even if they were across the room.
Over the Easter holiday, we forgot to tell her we would both
be leaving for the week. After pounding on our door for ten
minutes and getting no response, she assumed we had died,
though the neighbors assured her we were just on vacation.
"YOU 'AVE DONE ME A GREAT INJUSTICE! YOU
'AVE DONE ME A GREAT INJUSTICE!" she sang the
next Monday morning, waving her pocketbook over her head
as she stormed up our walkway. Only after a long explana-
tion, profuse apologies and a round trip bus fare refund were
we able to quiet her.

A few weeks later we moved to a smaller apartment in a
more upscale, safer area of town. We decided this was good
opportunity to try to talk to Eulis about our ideas for cleaning the new space. The next Monday she arrived on schedule.
"Good mawrning, Miss Katrin!" she said, stepping into the
apartment. "Like ya get nice sunlight in da place! Ya shouldn't
keep the back door open, too much of dust flyin' in. . . ." She
paused, noticing Maureen sitting on the couch already dressed
for work.

"Eulis, we just wanted to talk to you for a minute about
some things," I said. She hesitated at the front door, her face
tense, and then came to perch on the edge of the red velvet
couch looking at us both warily.

"We wanted to discuss how this space might have some different cleaning needs than our old apartment," I said, trying
to be gentle.

Her face tightened as she looked first at me, then Maureen.
"Y'all aren't happy with how I been cleaning?" she asked.

"No, no, you've been doing a great job," I said. "We just
thought that now that we're in a new apartment it might be
time to think about other things that might need cleaning
too." She glared at me. I looked down at the rug.

Maureen spoke up. "These are things we've talked about before, but now that we've moved we thought you might be more . . . flexible." Eulis' eyes were narrowing, her lips thinning in a look of suppressed outrage. Maureen went on. "You know about the shower tiles, well we just want you to scrub them a little, so the soap scum doesn't build up. And the stovetop could always use. . . ." she continued listing the most common battlegrounds in our cleaning standoff.

"But don't I always mek da sink shine?" Eulis burst out, sputtering with anger. "Like y'all too busy tinking of stovetop to see anyting else!" she yelled.

"Of course, of course," Maureen said backing down a little. "The bathroom sink looks great. Now maybe you could just do the same with the kitchen sink?"

It dawned on me that our disagreement with Eulis would never be resolved in a pleasant conversation on the couch. She would always believe she knew better than we did how to clean our home: this was her country and her career. Of course she didn't want to compromise the only part of her life that gave her any feeling of power to two American girls young enough to be her granddaughters. As far as we were concerned, so much of our lives in Guyana was about accepting limited options that we couldn't bear to relinquish our last bastion of control: our own home.

"Like y'all believe since ya move here ya gon' up!" Eulis said under her breath.

"No, that's not it, Eulis, we don't mean to offend you. . . ." I added. But it was too late.

She shook her head, for once silenced by the magnitude of her anger. "Y'all get me too vexed for work!" she said. I protested but she was already picking up her umbrella and pocketbook and walking out. "Goodbye Miss Katrin and Miss Mawreen," she said in a low voice, then pulled the door hard behind her.

"Me nah able," she said, shaking her head, when she visited me at school the next day. My students looked on curiously as I tried to reason with her.

"Eulis, we still want you to work for us, in fact we want your job to be easier. . . ." I said. She was already shaking her head.

"Miss Katrin," she said, her voice wavering with anger. "Twenty years I work cleaning houses and no ladies ever sit me down for 'talk' like yesterday." She spit the word "talk" out like it was a bitter root. "No, me nah able with y'all." Though she had no other work and only a meager pension from the Government, Eulis quit her job as our maid.

Maureen was unapologetic. "She left, Katherine. If she wants to work she'll come back, but we don't need to go after her." But I couldn't forget the look of betrayal on Eulis' face the day she visited me at the school. When I went home to the States that summer, our failed relationship was still on my mind. I ended up telling Grammy, my 80-year-old grandmother, about Eulis, omitting any mention of our recent falling out. "Oh, Katherine," she said, her watery blue eyes growing even more watery. "How hard it must be to live alone down there!" She shook her head, "No children or grandchildren either."

As she did every year, Grammy sent me a care package that Christmas. Buried among parcels of flashing fairy lights, plastic trees, and tinsel, was a bag with little red-nosed reindeers on it. In her spidery, arthritic handwriting, she had printed, "For Eulis, with love from Grammy (Katherine's grandmother)." Her letter read: "I remembered how you had told me about your dear maid, Eulis. Please pass on this little gift to her from me."

It had been almost half a year since our rift with Eulis, and the idea of seeing her again brought up mixed feelings. I put off giving her the gift, taking as my excuse the fact that she had no phone. For months, the bag sat behind a low table in my now dusty room. Occasionally, though, I would see the green ribbon curls poking up and feel a pang of guilt for withholding from Eulis what was rightfully hers.

Finally, one day after work I got up the nerve to seek her out at the Catholic home for the elderly. I found her in a sitting room looking out the window, fanning herself with a magazine. She was wearing one of her familiar housedresses, her hair pinned back in little white twists on her head. "Miss Katrin!" she said, raising her eyebrows and widening her eyes. "Me ehn't tink I'd see you again dis lifetime!"

"I brought you a present, from my grandmother. . . ." I began, raising the bag in the air.

"No, Miss Katrin!" her face darkened and she waved ominously toward the two elderly women smiling and peeking around the doorframe. I followed her into her bedroom where she took the bag from me. "Dese ole people here is terrible," she said, glancing furtively toward the door. "If dey see you give me tings, dey goin' come after me all de time." She looked at the wrapping paper and the note. "Long time since Christmas pass. . . ." she mumbled. But the contents pleased her; my grandmother had sent a rain poncho, a box of candy canes, and an angel figurine with wings of gold.

I told her news of the house, the cats, and the other volunteers she had met. She mentioned our last conversation in hushed tones. "When y'all wanted to 'ave long talk, I knew dere was problem ahead." She offered a few theories as to why our working relationship had failed: "Like y'all had to do tings you own way," and, "It must have been dat other girl. I believe she never did tek to me." Her anger seemed to have been mollified by the peace offering from my grandmother, though, and when I left she walked me to the gate and waved goodbye.

A few weeks later, Eulis visited me again at the school and asked for my grandmother's address. In her thank you note she listed each trinket that Grammy had sent, underlining it in red and explaining in detail how she would use it. Touched by her appreciation, Grammy decided to continue sending packages through me, necessitating more trips to the Catholic Home. As it turned out, Grammy's inclination toward sentimental, religious and mass-produced gifts was a perfect match for Eulis. She wrote back about every token as if it were the most beautiful, useful item she had ever received.

Our working relationship ended, Eulis and I were able relax with each other, and gradually she began to open up to me. Over sodas and water biscuits she would tell me stories about her life in Guyana, which had been a series of "great injustices." She had been born into a large family, one of a set of twins, but the boy had died at childbirth. "I was de blackest one," she told me. "Maybe he would have been as black as me, but I was alone with my color. My other brothers and sisters were different, more fair."

"I was smart, ya know," she said. "Smart! I used to write nice papers and do all ah my assignments. I passed my exams, but da man was wicked." The Headmaster of her school had reported that Eulis had failed Maths, which kept her from graduating from secondary school. As a young woman, she had been sent to live with her aunt and uncle in the country to keep house for them. "He trouble me," she said in a whisper, leaning forward. When she told her aunt about his advances the woman asked her to leave.

Later she had found work as a nurse in the hospital. On hearing this, I finally understood Eulis' fixation on the shower curtain and under-bed region, and her vitriol for our cats. She had been trying to rout pestilence from our house, not just dirt. Again, this career path had led to frustration. The other nurses had turned out to be "wicked badcration," and gossiped about her incessantly. She quit and went back to cleaning other people's houses.

Of all of Eulis' regrets, the greatest was not getting married. When she worked for us she assumed that every male volunteer she met was a boyfriend. "Miss Katrin, like you and de dark-hair one, Mistah Gabe, would make a fine couple!" she would tease. "Y'all must marry, don't hesitate!" she told us again and again. Growing up she had listened to other women's stories of difficult relationships. "Husband worries is the worst worries, they told me. Husband worries is the worst worries—so I never bother with men." Now she regretted her decision, because she had no one to take care of her in her old age, no children, no "grands," and no husband.

Having had my own complex dealings with Eulis, I could imagine how she may have played a part in some of the injustices heaped upon her for the past sixty years. But hers was also a familiar story of a dark-skinned girl growing up in a post-colonial society. Then Eulis had made the most counter-cultural choice she possibly could. Married or not, women her age commonly had ten or twelve babies. Though she regretted her decision, she had clearly escaped some of the ravages of extreme poverty. She was uncommonly healthy, highly intelligent, and more vibrant than many Guyanese women half her age. Although she would never see it this way, Eulis had the marks of a truly independent woman.

Toward the end of our two years in Guyana, Eulis initiated a final act of peace making, offering Maureen and me a parting gift: a serenade for future happiness. We planned it weeks in advance and Eulis insisted on having the performance taped for posterity. On a day in our last month in Guyana, she again knocked on our door at seven A.M., and tottered into the house. "HELLO! HELLO! Good mawrning! Good mawrning!" As we lounged half-awake in our pajamas, Eulis stood in the middle of our living room, her chest lifted, hands straight at her side. She explained that her song, "Where'er You Walk," would ensure us good fortune, including marriage to respectable Christian men, I assumed it was a hymn, but later learned it is an aria from Handel's Semele.

> Where'er you walk
> cool gales shall fan the glade
> trees where you sit
> shall crowd into a shade
> Where'er you walk

Though not exactly melodic, Eulis' voice was booming and clear. As she sang, her face became concentrated and serious, and she lifted her head and closed her eyes when the highest notes coursed through her rigid body:

> Where'er you tread
> the blushing flower shall rise
> and all things flourish
> and all things flourish
> Where'er you turn your eyes

It was a benediction, the best way Eulis knew to express her hope for us in the face of a world gone wrong. In her operatic voice, she offered us a song of faith and protection, the only gift she had to give.

In a strange turn of events, I continued to hear from Eulis through my grandmother for several years after I returned from Guyana. Though they had very limited understanding of each other's lives—Grammy had never traveled beyond Europe, and Eulis had barely left Georgetown—the two women had an epistolary chemistry. Unable to compete with my grandmother's material generosity, Eulis compensated by writing letters twice as long. She offered a vivid picture of the politics, weather, and challenges of life in Guyana.

> Granny Jamieson, whenever I write you these long letters, I do not write all on the same day, I usually start to write days before, and

every day, I write a piece, and when I am finished, then I write the
date of the letter.

I am person who loves to write.

At Eulis' request, I received her letters secondhand. They are
written in beautiful, even script, a remnant of her education
under the British colonial system. Her grammar and spelling
are Standard English, and show no trace of Creolese dialect,
the only language I ever knew her to speak. On the page, you
can imagine a more moderate tone, though she indicates volume and passion by underlining her main points in red ink.
Multiple pages are attached with a tiny bronze safety pin,
enclosed with thick packets of clippings from *Stabroek News*
or *The Guyana Chronicle*. Her meticulous nature is just as evi-
dent in her writing, as it was in her cleaning.

My dear Granny Jamieson,

I received a notice which is also called a parcel slip, from a post-girl
on 28th of November, and she informed me to go with it at Customs
of the General Post Office (G.P.O) to uplift a parcel. On the 29th
of November, I uplift the box. Thanks for sending me the yellow
raincoat, with hood attached to it, but I am very sorry I cannot wear
it, because it is very large for me. I think medium size would fit me,
therefore I gave it away.

Other contents of the box are 1 red face towel, 1 cream hand
towel with red flowers, 1 black and gold cloth, 1 calendar, 1 Christmas card with the two angels praying by Jesus' bed, 1 Gospel of John
book, 1 card with basket of flowers, 1 thank you card with a little
boy and girl on it and 1 blue (please turn over) card marked Gibson
Island at the back of the card. I also received a U.S. $20 note in one
of the cards in the envelope, and 4 Daily Word books. I also received
the little holy manger figures which are 2 angels, 6 different kinds
of animals, baby Jesus, the holy Virgin Mary, all of them are very
beautiful. Saint Joseph was absent from the figures. Many thanks for
all your beautiful gifts. Jesus will continue to bless you abundantly
for your kindness to me.

Her letters always included some strong wishes for my
welfare:

> I am sorry that I cannot send a Mother's Day card to Katherine, because she is not a Mother. One of these days when she marries to the very good husband that Jesus will send, and after marriage gets a baby, then I will send her a Mother's Day card.

And some powerful complaints about the continuing great injustices of her life:

> Water is not coming in the house, and I have to fetch many buckets of water for myself and the old lady. I fetch the water from the next yard. I also have to raise my hands high using 3 1/2 buckets of water to flush one large bowel movement for the old lady, because for years the flush system of the toilet is not working properly. The Committee knows about this problem for all these very long years, and is not paying a plumber to repair it. This is also a very hard job. Sometimes she gets 2 bowel movements a day or 3. The faeces are normal stool. Therefore a lot of my time is taken up, and I am also very tired. I do not want the Committee to know that I am giving out this information about the home. This is neither a paid job, nor I never volunteered to do this job, which is looking after the old lady.

She remembered out first meeting, though somewhat romanticized from what I recalled:

> I used to be Katherine's maid cleaning the house, and I have found Katherine to be kind-hearted, loving, friendly, she showed concern for me who is an old person, because when I first met her in "quick-service restaurant" standing in the queue to order things from the cashier, I approached her and asked for work, and immediately I observed that she was willing to employ me, in order to help me out financially.

In another letter, she reflected on our disagreements about her cleaning:

> Katherine also showed concern for me in another way, because when I was cleaning the plastic curtain of the bathroom she told me not to fatigue myself too much in cleaning in it, but I told her that because I like to do work very clean, I do not mind if I fatigue myself. This also showed that she had a tender feeling for me, because I am old.

And Eulis had a poetic sensibility that came through in unexpected moments:

In Guyana the intermittent showers are also called the "Woman Rain." This is because when some women quarrel, they quarrel and stop and quickly begin to quarrel again about the same thing, and then stop again, just like the <u>intermittent showers</u>.

Finally, Eulis told my grandmother about my departure:

> The day before she flew out of Guyana, she visited me at my home, she gave me a "Thank you card," a U.S. $20, and I think she also got a friend to take a photo with herself and me, she threw her hand around my neck, and I also threw my hand around her neck. She flew out of Guyana the next day. When the visit was over and she was leaving the yard, I stood up at the gate, and watched her until she was out of sight. I miss her very much.

My grandmother has since died and Eulis has stopped writing. I have her letters, though, tens of pages of her script on tiny, frayed notebook pages chronicling her life and the life of the country I lived in for two years. I can still hear her voice when I read them now: her operatic cadence, punctuating laughter, her strong opinions on a world that she believed had forsaken her, but to which she absolutely refused to surrender.

*Katherine Jamieson is a graduate of the Iowa Nonfiction Writing Program where she was an Iowa Arts Fellow. Her work has been published in* The New York Times, Newsday, Ms., Narrative, Meridian, Brevity, *and in* The Best Travel Writing 2012, The Best Women's Travel Writing 2012 *and* The Best Women's Travel Writing Volumes 9 *and* 10.

DAYNA BRAYSHAW

❧ ❧ ❧

# The Crap Between the Love and Us

There's no escape on a forty-nine-foot sailboat.

The waves were as big as houses, and the wind kept picking up the tops of them and driving them sideways into the boat, their slam like cannon fire. Day seven, no sign of land, and the autopilot had just broken with one long, lumbering groan. The captain, a fifty-nine-year-old crab fisherman who looked seventy due to a life spent at sea and a recent stroke, was cursing and gripping the bucking wheel, "Well just in the goddamn go to hell perfect time to break," he muttered as the first mate —who was also my boyfriend and also most likely a sociopath—gripped on to one side of the heaving boat and glared at me as I gripped the other side, wrestling down nausea and the white-cold growth of soul fear that comes when you think you are going to die and also, I understood later, when you realize you've fallen in love with a sociopath.

It has been said enough for it to be well-known by most: You will meet The One at the point when you've given up trying.

The lesser-known thing is what the hell we actually mean when we say "The One."

I had met my One at a bachelorette party, just days after a colossal breakup with who I'd hoped was The One but turned out to be The Zero, much to my devastated surprise and his, also. My devastation was softened only by the comfort of knowing I would soon be far away, immersed in something that had nothing to do with Love—at an intensive, two-year dance training in Israel that I'd gotten into just barely by the grip and sweat of my own prayers. I was due to fly out in two weeks time, when The One waltzed in and changed the course of my life forever.

It was the bachelorette party of my first close friend to get married, and we were at a cabin on the beach, late afternoon, in Tacoma, Washington. She was shaky and nervous and everyone was bringing her glasses of wine until she looked close to tears with drunkenness on top of her terror. I was sipping a white wine spritzer in an attempt to quell my own nerves, ensconced as I was in a steady chatter of pedicures and wedding prep conversations, flower arrangements and "At MY wedding we. . . ." discussions amongst the pregnant bridesmaids, when the entertainment showed up. Three guys in Speedos with ukelele, guitar, and bongo drum, singing in Spanish. *Contigo tenia todos y lo perdi.* Their backs were to the sun and the bongo player—a tall, broad-chested guy with eyes bright as the bay behind him—noticed my squint and handed me his sunglasses in one swift movement between beats. I thought, *Well, this party just got better.*

He kissed me hard as the sun set over the bay. I took him home with me, and then the next day to the wedding, and all the old friends from high school looked greedily at us, and the bride said "I wish my husband would kiss me like that."

I'd been housesitting for my parents for the summer, but they came back from their vacation sometime later that week, arriving in the middle of the night, disheveled and jet lagged as I popped out of my room, dragging The One—"Look what

I found Mom!"—cause he was the type that was fun to show off, real tall with shiny dark hair and eyes that made everyone look twice, even dudes. My mom's tired eyes missed most of that though. Her tired eyes said, "Oh Dayna, another one?" and she smiled weakly at him as he gave her his best charmer smile, all straight white teeth and love-me-I'm-a-good-person openness in the way he hugged her rather than shook her hand.

We didn't sleep for a week. I took him through my home-town, to the farmer's market to eat soba noodles, to the beach and the forest and the new cupcake shop, and we were stupid and happy and kissing everywhere. My world his eyes, his lips. The way we laughed. I loved the edgy quality of danger beneath his cheer and sharp intelligence. He told me of killing a mugger in Guatemala and I didn't flinch. "If you want to have my back in a fight, you gotta come up behind him, hit him sideways in the neck . . ." he instructed me. I was Bonnie to his Clyde. The darkness of him right there, but subdued somehow, like he had a grip on the neck of some wild beast and he walked like that. His stories sounded insane, extravagant—"When I was five I'd run away from home to sleep with the homeless people in the canyon," or "In the mountains of Colombia, when I was translating the spiritual texts of an indigenous tribe who is dying out I. . . ."

After traveling for the last four years myself, my stories, too, sounded extravagant and made up, for I was unable to tell something simple without a detail that others deemed brag worthy "In Paris I was waiting for a table when . . ." and everyone would roll their eyes. "Oh here we go. When you were in PARIS" stars, stars, bells, etc. So I was relieved to be with someone who also had the unordinary woven into the fabric of his days, and did not need to boast about it, neither pretend that it was not there.

We walked arm in arm through the park singing "Wagon Wheel" at the top of our lungs. "If I die in Raleigh/least I will die freeeee." He was twenty-eight and I was twenty-nine and neither of us had a cent in our bank accounts, and in the eyes of the world and sometimes ourselves we were failing miserably at being alive, but who fucking cares, we had art, we were breathing, we had love. A girl at a bar said to us after watching us dance, "I feel like punching you guys in the face." We smiled benevolently at her but did not contradict. Yes, we are truly happy, I'm sorry you are not. We kissed so much I began to feel like I'd kissed him more minutes than I'd been alive. We danced all night barefoot to the local bluegrass band in a parking lot at sunset and then he tied a peach thread around my left finger, speaking forever with each wrapping, the sky all stars, and we were in a field. He said "I'm wrapping it cause a ring should be something you can always change, rather than a knot which is just an illusion about forever." He kissed me long and then smiled into my eyes. "May we never stop laughing," he said.

Then I drove him three hours north to the sailboat where he lived, and wished him good luck and goodbye on our last night together, for he was leaving the next morning to sail around the world.

Except for then he said, "Please. Come with me."

And I realized with great astonishment that no amount of those horrific, heart-death breakups where you realize you've been wrong about everything—Togetherness, full-body Certainty, Attraction, Need—no amount of those had managed to weaken in any way my complete soul-following of this illusive concept of LOVE when it crashed into my course like a wayward unicorn and beckoned me to climb on.

For no matter how many times I have fallen off the back of that unicorn, burning and bruising and breaking myself,

I seemed to be incapable of refusing the wilderness of the offered ride.

"There is no remedy for love but to love more," Thoreau said.

So that September I let my plane ticket go, apologized to the dance program in Israel, and climbed aboard a forty-nine-foot sailboat, headed an indefinite due west.

On Labor Day we set sail. It was early morning, the sun just over the horizon and hanging. Pink light on the water. Marina silent. A scarf of fog around the islands. When they pulled the sails up and the wind caught, my heart shuddered, and lifted. I thought: Finally. Free.

It was the water, and the rocking of the boat. The leaving so much behind and blending into what was quiet, and more true. I thought *this is it*, from now on my only job is to say yes to the heart, this is all there is, and *yes* I want to be more everything in the fiber of the world. May I do nothing but live the life of an artist now, I decided, and should I burn up there, then so be it, but god forbid I leave this earth doing what so many others seemed to be doing—feeling half, being half, doing should, trying wrong.

And indeed most everyone agreed with my decision to sail around the world with two men I had just met, even my own mother, despite her real panic that I'd also die. Everyone agreed—with bells and stars!—because people will just eat up that romantic bullshit. Because as much as it is bullshit, so is it the food we survive on. There MUST be another option than the way we are normally living, and we MUST believe that some brave few will find that option, and tell us about it—the swish and the glory of True Love. The relief of being, at last, in the comfort and safety of Following Your Heart with your One.

\*   \*   \*

The captain had agreed to take me on board in exchange for my services as a movement educator. When the captain had first had his stroke, the doctors told him one third of his brain was toast, and that he should plan on never walking, talking, or reading again. He couldn't talk yet when they told him that, but he said he laughed. Don't tell me what I can't do. He learned it all back, enough to walk, read, and even sail, though he did still struggle with speaking and finding words, and he wanted my help going deeper into the work with his body. "You can't *hurt* anything in me," he assured me when I told him I'd never worked with a stroke patient. "There's nowhere to go but up."

I tried to believe him. I took my appointed job very seriously. I gripped my anatomy books aloft and explained developmental movement exercises to him with my knee wedged into the corner of the bench, my other foot stabilizing against the toolbox as the boat bucked and he steered. I balanced above him as he lay in a nest of ropes, and I unwound the tension in his neck with one hand while I held on to the rigging with the other hand. My biggest fear was that something would happen to him. It was quickly becoming apparent that my One was as incompetent as me in the sailing department. Every time he was left on watch, it was inevitable that the boat would start spinning in circles or else heading in the completely wrong direction. If the captain went out to check on the fishing pole or tie a line I'd watch him with knife-eyed attention, as though my stare could pin him to the boat. If he fell over I knew that neither my One or I had the ability to turn the boat around to get him. I worried about his sleeping, if he was getting enough, about him stroking out again, or his elbow wound getting infected. I begged him to wash his hands after touching the raw chicken. "Salmonelli, is that you?" he taunted me, mocking a kiss to the raw, pink flesh, but let me spray his hands with antibacterial wash and wiped

them on the paper towel I handed him, smiling at me out of
the side of his mouth. "Well for a goddamn piece of chicken
you're bout ready to die for it, it ain't worth it, right?"

And thus the days and the nights passed. A roll of blue
wind and water and moments together. Our bodies moving
always with the crash of the waves. Learning how to balance
on the ocean's constant change. Dishwashing, peeling potatoes, cooking meals for each other, all became a dance—an
ever present awareness of our connection to both gravity and
sky. In the mornings, as we drank coffee together, we marveled at our hand's intelligence, the way, when you left it to
its own device, it knew how to constantly adjust the angle of
the cup to the shifting floor of the boat in order to keep the
scalding liquid from spilling out. "How does it know? I mean
really, how does it know how to do that?" We'd shake our
heads, watching our hands, our full cups, utterly entertained.

We discussed, told stories, were silent often, and laughed
more than anything else. We laughed about my One's multiple douses of the kitchen in coffee, then the Captain's early
morning spill of the same. The kitchen a wasteland of egg-
shells, coffee grounds, banana peels, bruised apples and soggy
paper towels. My One attempted banana bread, and it ended
up in three different piles on the floor. We ate the remains—a
half-cooked pancake sized slab that was raw in the middle
and burnt on the outside. "Enough of the yellow shit and its all
good," said the captain, applying another spoonful of butter.

We listened to Sirius radio for company, the songs like
people we invited over to play. The Captain would put it on
the seventies Rock station, my One on Classic Country, me on
the Love station, where they played all the love songs from my
middle school years—Baby Face "Missing You" and Journey
"Faithfully." We counted how many songs, on all of the stations, made references to sailing—it was about one in three.
My One, an extremely talented writer, said "What if, when

we get out of here and try to write, the only metaphors we'll be able to use are ones having to do with the sea?" This, after I'd said of my headache, "The pain comes in waves." I was singing along with the Love station. "This guy was my favorite singer in elementary school," I told him at a break in the chorus.

"What's his name?"

"Billy Ocean."

We met eyes and cracked into hysterics for the fifth time that morning. Our eyes streaming from the giggles, until the captain told us to go drink water—"People only laugh like that about nothing if they're stoned or dehydrated or both," he said.

All this, and the ever-changing landscape of the sea. At once caring so much and caring so little of us. Every day we rode onward, and when I closed my eyes, or at night too, it was as though we were also on land, being carried on the back of some slow dancing elephant, waltzing so tirelessly through the endless, shifting sand. And there was no Time, and I was no longer Dayna, failing at growing up, or failing at making money, failing at getting married or making a life that I thought I should make—no, there was just every day the water, and love, and the sweet Unknown.

The sun was setting, and I was just preparing to start a therapy session with the Captain, when the wind came up. My One said his stomach hurt, and he went to bed early, skipping his watch duty. The captain hadn't slept in days but he didn't complain; he climbed into his negative-thirty-degree jumpsuit and hunkered down behind the wheel—"Whatever, I've only been doing it all of my life," he said in response to my concern. I had drunk too much coffee earlier in the day and my nerves felt shot, also my stomach hurt. In the forward cabin my One and I fell into thick sleep and woke feeling battered and angry in the mouth of a terrific storm.

It was almost impossible to stand. Impossible to walk. I felt sick and scared, and he found me later lying on the prow, where I was gripping onto the line and sucking slow breath from the crashing wind. With high, glassy eyes and a sick-sweet smile he said, "Why didn't you clean the kitchen?"

All the hairs stood up on my neck. I'd never heard that voice from him, and I couldn't place whatever tone I was hearing. It sounded like . . . hatred. "What do you mean why didn't I clean the kitchen? No one can clean the kitchen. No one can even stand up right now."

His wide, stretched-mouth smile didn't shift an inch as he held on to the mast of the thrashing boat. "I just realized you are a selfish princess, that's all. I can't believe I didn't see it before. You're just lying there. It's a metaphor for everything. You give nothing, absolutely nothing."

I'd never heard a cruel word from him before. But what was more shocking was that I'd just, the day before, confessed tearfully to him that my deepest fear sometimes was that I wasn't giving enough to the world, that perhaps my choices to live the life of an artist were merely choices of a selfish, self-centered princess. He'd held me and assured me that my presence on the planet had immeasurable worth, no matter what I did, and he'd been sweet, and comforting, as one would wish any boyfriend to be. But now he was standing above me, somewhat gleefully and systematically twisting the words I'd said to him earlier, a look of terrible scorn in his sea-glass eyes. I gaped at him as the prow crashed down the slope of another forty-foot swell.

I can't say that he hadn't warned me. Sometime between taking him to my best friend's wedding and falling madly in love with him he *had* warned me—that he was "fucked up," that he'd been given a sociopath psychological test and showed a 95-percent chance of being one, that he had a bit of a split in his personality, and sometimes he flipped into this snake, and he knew it, and he loved it, because it was his power and he could use it against other people, to manipulate bad people, but he'd never use it against me. Something to that effect. Obviously I hadn't really been too concerned.

But as the storm gathered in volume, as I looked up into the dull, flat malevolence of his face, I realized I'd made a mistake, again. That I'd lost my own course for another man who turned out to be, for an entirely different reason, but still—*again*—a total flop. That our hours of play, lovemaking, and laughter in the end were no match for this gaping hole of a man who was now, in a smooth, velvet-lined voice saying, "You'll never succeed at what you want to do. It's just all ideas in your head that will never become real, because you're too selfish to really love, and you're not talented enough to make good art." I didn't move, or breathe, or look at him, so terrified at this shift in someone who I had just, hours earlier, felt so close to. "I'm sorry, I don't know what you're talking about, but I'm really sorry," I said finally. Thinking that if I was sweet enough he would snap out of it, come back to me. I didn't know yet that I was just becoming the ultimate dream of the sociopath: a willing victim.

The storm grew around us. He held onto the ropes, and his voice so thankfully got lost in the wind as I gripped hold of the side of the boat. The waves crashed over the prow, drenching our clothes. From the bowels of the ship came a long, drawn out moan. The autopilot had broken. The captain, at the wheel, cursed. I clambered my way to where he was, and my One followed me. The Captain wrestled with the wheel, turning us further west, into the swells. The navigation system showed us as a tiny red boat bumbling out farther and farther into white space. No land. I was suddenly so scared I could barely hold on to the rope. My eyes locked on the darkness where the wind was slamming us, my chest like ice was on the inside, and growing, as my One tried to get to me across the space between port and starboard benches—he wanted to hold me. "I've got you, I'm here," he was trying to say to me, like a sadist who wants to bandage the wounds he himself has just cut. In wild-eyed panic I looked to the Captain, whose white-blue eyes were so steady on me I felt I could have physically held on to his stare. "Trust the boat," he said.

In the morning the storm had barely died down, but at least we could see the way the waves were hitting us and the steadiness of the boat, righting herself again and again, regardless of what this motion was doing to our stomachs.

"You'll be fine out here, Dayna," the Captain said. "I knew that the first day I met you." The water lifted and tossed us forward. The wind whipping at the plastic sheeting around the cabin as I held tight to the rope and fought down nausea. "Because there's nothing like it. People can talk about it, or think about it, or sing about it, but you don't know until you're out here. There's something you can't know unless you're here. And I know you want to know it."

I wanted to know it.

What the sea knew.

So I gripped on to that boat and listened through the roar of my fear, as our moods, our sleep, dreams, meals, words blended into the storm's song; complicated, eternal, battered, day after day after day.

My One got worse—tearing through any intimate vulnerability I had ever shared with him and prodding me with twisted versions of it to see if he could hurt me. He'd tell the Captain I was doubting the Captain's abilities, then me that the Captain regretted me coming on the boat. We both ignored him. He accused us of having a "weird, sick, older man, little girl relationship." We ignored him. "This is what

I do, I fuck with people's heads," he told me one night. "I'm very good at it. You'll never even be able to pinpoint what it is I'm doing, you'll just feel like shit about yourself and then I can control you." Even he was unraveling. Admitting his methods. I felt nauseous and cried often. The storm heaved and pushed us on.

Then one evening, while explaining nerve regeneration to the Captain as he wrestled the wheel, the wind simply dropped away. The Captain pointed, and I saw a pod of dolphins had surrounded us, jumping four abroad beside the boat, out of the dark, choppy water. I gasped and dashed to the side to reach my arms towards them.

You think you're alone. And then.

Their bellies iridescent turquoise under the dark water, and they jumped and they jumped, the ocean parting with little pleasure hisses as they leapt up—to me, not to me, to the sky. I was delighted and shy also. I didn't know how to talk to them. They raced beside us and smiled at me anyway.

At the helm, the captain had rigged the spinning wheel steady with ropes, and he and my One were eating fried bread with peanut butter and jelly, as the ocean around us went crashing on and on and on. Here we are together I thought suddenly. Hating each other, loving each other, fearing each other as we drank tea and ate bread and talked and laughed anyway. The Captain brought a cup of tea to where I sat at the edge of the boat. His hand, and then my own, automatically adjusting the angle of the cup to keep the liquid from spilling. We just do that. Our hand just knows how to do that.

And I thought, maybe *this* is the only thing I need to learn in this lifetime. Not how to be an artist, not how to make anything of myself, neither to fall in love, have children, get married. But rather simply how to eat and drink and laugh when the world is shaking and shows no sign of stopping. How to take comfort in the things you have, even if it's only your hand's inherent intelligence, which saves you, again and again, from pouring scalding liquid into your own lap.

I draped one arm over the boat and let the sea wrap itself around me. Her depth endless. The dolphins untouchable and everywhere close, watching. I begged them to stay, but when they felt like leaving, they did. And I felt terror for my utter and complete lack of control. And such sweet relief for the exact same reason.

At last, the hazed line of something solid appeared on the horizon. My One stood at my shoulder as we sailed toward that green coastline. There had been some lulls of peace in the last days, but sometime earlier that morning he had flipped again, and had been following me around the boat all day like my own personal demon, whispering my blackest fears as he waited for me to break.

"You know that it was you who destroyed our relationship, don't you?" He was smiling a soft, condescending smile. His once-beautiful eyes now looked sick and terrifying as he stared at me with false sympathy. "I'm so sorry for you that you do this."

I looked away with a shudder, out at the lit blue water of the bay, flat in the morning sun. I was still as scared as I was in that storm. Like if I couldn't make things work with him, I wouldn't be able to make things work with anyone. That I would never trust anyone, or love anyone again. My mind told me such thoughts were ludicrous, but at the sound of his words my body felt all the sensations of panic all the same. And what could I do? The body is a boat we can only escape from at the very end. The only remedy for feeling is to feel more. So I cried and stared at the water and waited for the Captain to take us into land.

And when we did—nosing gently into the dock—I leapt to her and ran on gooey legs, to collapse under the pine trees and press my ear to the ground; the great, quiet, unchanging mass of her. Whispering, *Thank God that this, too, is here. The ground.*

The captain hugged me brusquely goodbye in the doorway to his cabin, and then, again, pulling me closer, he kissed my cheek. "No one knows what any of this living is and so we just try to fill it," he said in my ear. He nodded his chin at my One, who was waiting for me on the prow in the spotty afternoon sunshine. "And then what happens? We get all this crap between the Love and Us."

I nodded. "Thank you. For taking me out there."

He squeezed my hand in his giant, weathered one. "Where will you go now?"

"I don't know. North Carolina, I guess."

"Can I sail there?"

"Yeah."

"Then I'll see you again."

My One carried my bag from the boat to the cab, huffing with the weight, and then, crashing it down at my feet he said, "In the story you write about this you'll have to include the symbolism of me carrying that bag for you, Princess."

So here it is: You're so vain.

But it will be a while before I know that this whole song is not about you.

It will be a while before he will stop calling me. He will leave me messages, "Last night I slept with another woman. I wasn't drunk and I don't regret it. She wasn't a princess like you. She made me feel good like you never could."

It will be a while before I stop crying every night over my lost dance opportunity in Israel, my poor judgment in all matters romantic, and anything else I can dig up in the moment to feel helpless about. The state of the economy. The amount of sociopaths in high government offices.

It will be a while, but eventually I do, drive myself across the country and find myself a house, begin work, and continue on with my dancing. And sooner than I am ready for it, and definitely when I have given up looking, I meet another One.

And we're sitting together in a seaside bar in the evening eating Reubens stacked fist high with meat when he says, "But what happens if you're not The One?"

We'd been discussing moving in together. I pause with open mouth, sandwich halfway there.

He tells me about a moment in childhood, when he cried in his bed alone after realizing that the sun would eventually explode and consume the Earth; that our existence here was a humble one, a short-term one, and an Unknown-Why one. "What's the POINT?" his six-year-old brain lamented, and this question was the same he revisited upon meeting me. "I love you, of course, but if you're not THE one—my life partner, the one I'll raise my children with, buy those forty acres with, grow old happy with—what's the point of being together at all?"

We both stop eating for a while to think about that.

Why do we need our partners to be The One?

Nobody knows what this living is, and so we just try to fill it.

The harder thing being to let our loves be wild. To let our loves be unknown at the same time as they carry you, direct you, change you. As the ocean carries the boat, let ourselves be tossed by the sacredness of whatever it is we might feel— about others, ourselves, our lives that we are failing or not failing at. Trusting the boat to handle the storm and the sea to eventually deliver us.

I stare at my new One. The tousle of his blond hair, his blue eyes serious and scared and a little sad. I know without a doubt that he is not a sociopath. I also know that he is not The One in the way I want The One to be. I know that he is the opposite of all the things he thinks he is, as is true of me, as is true of all of us. I know that as he's strong, he's also equally weak, and he'll probably never want to admit that, the way none of us do. And I know that there will be times in the course of our relationship in which we'll tear at each other, wanting the other to be stronger, bigger, better, until maybe we part ways furious, communicating via three- or four-word texts in regard to some beloved pair of socks I left at his house or a book he took that needs to be returned to my mother. I held and loved and laughed and shared everything with my first ex-One every single day for years, and now I don't know where he is, and he doesn't know where I am and neither of us know what it means, what we went through, other than that it got us to where we each are now—Here.

I want to tell this New One, sitting across the table from me, his sweet lips pressed with worry, "If we don't think we'll be together forever then we should quit right now," but I wouldn't even be able to get through that sentence without laughing, because, hell, this is just the way things GO. We love, we want, we shut down, we replace, we do it again, in the same order maybe, and the truth is I probably won't ever give up this unicorn ride. I'll go to the center of the sea for it, with all the hypocrisy and the fantasy and the foolishness, calling out the Ocean's name, "It's for failure that I'm calling you," and the many that are She will laugh their one voice and say:

"All I want is for you to sing that one back to me. With that useless word, failure, make me something beautiful."

❧ ❧ ❧

*Dayna Brayshaw is a somatic educator in Asheville, North Carolina, when she's not somewhere else doing something else. daynabrayshaw.com*

❧ ❧ ❧

# Neil and I

Looking back in time and space,
a relationship comes full circle.

Neil Armstrong did me two favors—one as big as the
moon, another as small as a footprint—neither of
which he knew about. We didn't know each other, but we
did; we knew each other, but we didn't.

In 1969, my buddy Willy and I, fresh college graduates, took
a summer-long trip to Europe. We didn't have much money,
but we planned carefully. Or, rather, I planned carefully, for
Will was a free spirit, whereas I had OCD before they invented
the term. I calculated exactly how much I could spend each day
for the projected time span—meals, Cokes, hotels. Willy didn't
give a shit. He figured one way or another he'd survive. That
should have been my first clue. Still, we had been friends a long
time, and if not for his adventurism, I probably wouldn't have
gone in the first place.

Mostly, I cursed that I had.

Willy papoosed a backpack; I schlepped two of my parents'
plaid suitcases. Neither of us had ever been far from home,
let alone out of the country, yet he was savvy enough to know
that if you're twenty-one and traveling through Europe, you
don't pack a steamer trunk. Today everyone, young and old,

travels by backpack. But in 1969, some of us (Willy) were ahead of the curve, some (Gary) way behind. No one from the Midwest was actually on the curve. And so Willy wore the same tank top for the entire summer, whereas I donned a sport jacket and tie, changing them often. Looking back, Willy should have ditched me sooner than he did.

It was the Day of the Hippie. I had never been one. I liked hot showers and haircuts and privacy, and I liked my country. I had considered smoking grass once, just to see what all the fuss was about. But then, the observant writer I hoped to be, I noticed that nature had given me two of almost everything—arms, hands, feet, kidneys, lungs—any of which I could, in a pinch, substitute with its twin. But for some reason known only to itself, that same nature had dished me only one brain—the organ of which, ironically, I was most in need of two. Getting stoned, falling asleep on Amsterdam's interurban trolley tracks, and getting a leg sliced off might be embarrassing but, given Holland's excellent health-care system, probably wouldn't be fatal, literally or creatively. But getting stoned and falling asleep on London's Carnaby Street and getting my head smashed by a double-decker bus would be (sorry) a no-brainer. You see what I'm getting at? No more writing (keep your snide comments to yourself).

Like travel budgeting, I tend to think these things out in advance.

Willy, on the other hand, was fully wasted for the width and breadth of our trip. It was hard not to be. So many American long-hairs descended on Europe that summer—the dollar was strong, air fare low, and since they'd soon be getting their asses blown off in Southeast Asia, the guys figured they may as well breathe happy while they still had breath—that to inhale was to get high. Train cars were marijuana dens, stations hazy with giddy smoke. All the famous gathering spots—Piccadilly Circus, Trevi Fountain, Ponte Vecchio,

Place de la Bastille—billowed bell bottoms, beads, and bam. It was impossible to walk from one neighborhood to another and arrive in your right mind.

Willy always managed to find a source. He'd peace sign the right dudes, black-power fist the right brothers, surfs-up signal the right chicks and land somewhere to freak that night. Public squares and youth hostels were the crash venues of choice. Me, I preferred bathrooms with locks. So Willy and I would compromise with *Europe on $5 a Day*-recommended *pensiones*, but he wouldn't show up anyhow. In the morning he'd leave word at the desk that he was still alive and would meet me for dinner, if he remembered. Sometimes we'd link up for an afternoon of sightseeing, but more often than not I'd wind up waiting for him in vain, and when, two nights later, he'd finally poke his head into our *pensione*, he couldn't seem to recall my name or where he'd been.

In short, I was a complete killjoy. I'm an introvert. I kept to myself. I didn't want to sleep with strangers in the same longitude, let alone the same room. At night I would curl up and write in my journal or letters back home, like a real writer but not quite. I had a sort-of girlfriend in Chicago—a convenient excuse for not, like Willy, picking up any glaze-eyed chick prowling for a hit. The problem being, what with Willy out having a great time, living life, loving life, and I perfecting the art of being a Republican, I was miserably lonely. That years later Willy would have absolutely no recollection of our entire European summer, not a single moment, was for me, then, of little consolation. The truth was, I was as forlorn as a wet cat.

Unhappy people write. Happy people bowl.

In desperation, I confronted my freaked-out friend. "This isn't what I signed up for!" I bellowed. He did not seem sympathetic. He called me antisocial and told me to fuck off. "We're gonna get drafted soon and die in a fucking rice paddy!" We squared off, but through his grassy stupor, his reason, such as it was, prevailed. He was taller and heftier, but I had been the college boxer.

Still, he had won the reality match. Yes, we knew—we all knew, all of us clinging to Europe that summer—that this great fling might well be our last. Vietnam was lurking, licking its chops, and for newly graduated dudes, the odds of getting impaled on a *punji* stick were higher than scoring an Amsterdam spliff. So in his own incoherent way, Willy had left-hooked me a fistful of truth.

If I was afraid of lockless toilet doors now, how would it be when I had to poop in front of fifty other GIs? If I was so homesick now, how would it be when a platoon of Viet Cong were trying to shoot my testicles to kingdom come?

Beating up Willy wouldn't change the truth.

And so he went his way—to Greece and Israel, I learned later—and I mine, according to our original itinerary and budget, tearing out Frommer's chapters as I dragged along myself and my plaid. If I was lonely before, now I was wretched. I kept reminding myself that, as Emerson had said, "We all walk alone"—and so learned to despise philosophy. In Copenhagen I wandered through Tivoli Gardens, watching young couples snuggle under twinkling lights. Eurail-Passing Switzerland, I marveled at the Alps and charming mountain villages, but writing home about them wasn't the same as seeing them with someone you love.

One night in Genoa I went to a bar (a couple of cuties sat nearby, but I didn't have the courage to introduce myself) and listened to an American duet sing Simon and Garfunkel, which made me dissolve in homesickness.

On the ride to Rome, the train stopped at a platform. A rumor rumbled through the cars that we were all supposed to change trains. Hundreds of bell bottoms got off and crowded on the planks, looking for, waiting for . . . what? Having not personally heard any conductor tell us to change trains, I remained in my compartment, watching the backpacks mash together on the platform like migrating wildebeest on a river-bank. And I watched the herd shrink behind me as my train continued to Rome. Where the antelopes wound up, I have no idea.

So I felt smarter than the rest of the world but more alone than ever.

In Rome I checked into one of Frommer's recommended *pensiones*, Splendide. I had a private room with bath and a clean, solid bed for only two bucks. In the lobby the manager, Maria, worked her counter, and on a table were an aluminum coffee urn, chipped cups, and cascading packets of Nescafé. There was an old sofa, three stuffed chairs, a floor-console TV, a sunlit Oriental rug, and it was all comfy and nice. But the cozy furnishings only reminded me of my own living room in Illinois, and I missed my family even more. I wanted to go home.

The problem being, if I gave up, I'd always know I was a quitter. I was a boxer. To quit was to lose. Oh, I would bullshit my friends about some good reason I came home early, but I'd always know I hadn't answered the bell. If I couldn't stick it out in Europe for a few more weeks, how would I stick it out in the army?

So it wasn't Europe. It was Vietnam. That's all the whole damn thing was—all of it to all of us: son-of-a-bitching Vietnam.

Maybe I was a quitter. Maybe that was the truth. But, I rationalized, maybe it's not bad being who you are. Maybe the bravado is what's bullshit. Maybe "peace with honor" meant getting your legs blown off for no damn good reason. Maybe you had to live to fight another day.

Maria recommended a nearby cafeteria and drew directions to the Forum and Colosseum. It was deep dusk, and nighthawks bruised the sky. The restaurant's fluorescent glare made it easy to find. I bought a piece of chicken, some roasted potatoes, and a Coke. At about eight-thirty I made my way to the Colosseum. Oddly, the streets were almost empty. It was July 20 under a hooked moon. I had not been home for six weeks, and I had lost touch with the news.

The Colosseum was dark except for the slivered moonlight. I was the only one there. A cat's shadow swept across the ancient stones. Inside, it was dangerous. There were no barriers. I could easily slip off a dewy ledge into the subterranean corrals. I squinted into the darkness and moved carefully. The pits were inky and deep.

I had a weird sensation. It felt haunting, standing there alone in that ancient place of depravity. Was it a death omen? Would my draft letter be waiting for me when I got home?

*I, who am about to die.*

Yes, I decided, this was an omen. So, if I was going to get blown up in a rice paddy and break my parents' hearts, to stay away from my family any longer would be inexcusably selfish.

I would go home.

Walking back to the Splendide, I felt giddy with relief. I was going home. It was the omen's decision, not mine. If I did get drafted, as I was sure I would, why should I continue to suffer now? If partying in Europe was Willy's final wish, mine was to be in my own bedroom, clacking on my typewriter, eating my last meals with my loved ones.

Why were the streets so empty?

When I walked into Splendide's lobby, I got my answer. A dozen people—Maria, her friends, other guests—crowded on and spilled over the sofa and chairs, all bent toward the TV, watching the *Eagle* lander lower itself in a dusty billow. When they saw me they jumped to their feet and applauded, as if it were me, personally, touching the moon. "America!" they shouted, pumping my hand, slapping my back. "America!"

In my self-pity wallowing, I had forgotten about the great mission. Now I sat with my new friends and, as they hugged me and cheered, we watched it unfold.

I liked being hugged and cheered. I liked it a lot.

That night, basking in my vicarious celebrity, I considered. What if the Colosseum omen had been something else, not death? How many people would ever be able to say they stood alone in that ancient monument, gazing at the moon at the very moment man first set pads there? One, that's how many. Only one. Only me. And I thought, fate has meant it to be a great story, meant for one person to write—the only person who was actually there.

And I decided that, no, I wasn't going to die in Vietnam. I was going to live and write that story and many more great stories, and that was my destiny.

I liked being hugged and cheered.

And I'll tell you what else. I thought if those guys could go to the moon, could face the prospect of dying alone so far from Earth, I could tough out one crummy summer in Europe. I knew that if I went home now, if I quit, I'd never be able to write about Europe, about the Colosseum in the moonlight, or maybe about anything else. The memory of failure would chain my creativity like a lion to stone.

So I stayed. And for the rest of the summer, whenever I got so lonely I couldn't stand it, I looked up at the moon and thought of *Eagle*, and I kept going.

I, too, returned home on schedule.

I waited for my draft notice, but it never came. I knew with absolute certainty, though, that I wouldn't have sat out the war in Canada, as did Willy.

That is the big thing I owe Neil.

And I waited for my story to come, but, like the draft notice, it never did. Years went by, and, strangely, I wasn't able to write about my experience in Rome. I'd think and think about my having stood alone in the Colosseum at that moment in history and rack my brain trying to make it a story, but nothing came. No story came. The years passed, and every time I tried to forge a plot, find a theme, create a drama, nothing came.

Any other writer would have begged for the chance to have had that unique experience and would have written something fine. But for me, the only person who was actually there—nothing. Over the years I kept coming back to the effort, assuming, hoping, that distance, experience, and maturity would reveal something, but I was wrong. Nothing came.

Stories travel on their own schedule. Our creative brains are vast and unfathomable, our conscious craft tiny and brittle. For a while we believe we are steering, for a minute we shine. But the cosmos will let them come or not, at its will and when.

Or we just run out of time.

On July 23, 1969, the last night before splashdown on Earth, the three astronauts made a television broadcast in which Commander Armstrong said, "To those people tonight, we give a special thank you, and to all the other people that are listening and watching tonight, God bless you. Good night from Apollo 11."

Neil Armstrong died yesterday. And, finally, finally, my story comes.

This is the footprint he has left me, the smaller thing.

Good night to you, too, old friend.

✺ ✺ ✺

*Gary Buslik writes short stories, essays, and books, among them the comic novel* Akhmed and the Atomic Matzo Balls. *He is also the author of the hyperbolic non-fiction romp,* A Rotten Person Travels the Caribbean. *He lives and teaches near Chicago.*

JAMES MICHAEL DORSEY

~ ~ ~

# From the Ashes

The life of Pan revealed.

The smoke of wood fires dulls the sunrise, silhouetting the spires of Angkor Wat as hazy apparitions.

The incomparable beauty of these temples, the soul of the Khmer nation, are a surreal backdrop for the tale of horror I have come to record.

I see Pan approaching, fingering his prayer beads, his saffron robes seemingly ablaze in the yellow mist. He walks as though he is not really there, feet barely touching the ground, a saint incarnate to the world at large but in his own eyes, a simple, humble, monk. He carries a quality I cannot assign to words, but people sense this as I notice heads turn with slight bows as he glides past.

He is bent from time and suffering, having lived through and seen more than anyone should, and I know through mutual friends he wishes nothing more than to spend his remaining time in secluded meditation, but upon hearing of my book project he readily agreed to speak with me in the hopes that no one should have to relive it.

Pan is a Theravada monk, one of about 350,000 throughout Cambodia prior to the Khmer Rouge, and now one of but 30 to have outlived their regime. Besides surviving personal atrocities, he bears the weight of trying to re-establish a religious order dragged to the brink of extinction under a barbaric reign.

Theravada means "Teaching of the Elders." It is one of three main branches of Buddhism that originated in northern India and Nepal in the sixth century B.C. and rapidly spread throughout Southeast Asia until it was introduced to Cambodia in the thirteenth century via monks from Sri Lanka. It is a personal religion that worships no deity but rather teaches self-control in order to release all attachment to the material world and achieve personal enlightenment. Most Khmer men spend time as a novice before deciding to take the saffron robes or return to a secular life. For many it is the only escape from an existence of dire poverty and only hope for at least a minimal education. For Pan, it was a calling that almost killed hm.

It is hard to understand how university educated people could evolve into the senseless butchers that were the cadre of the Khmer Rouge, and yet their reign has become just one more footnote in a long litany of genocide that is the history of man. Whatever the base reasons for a government slaughtering a quarter of its own population for a political agenda, it was the Buddhist monks who bore the brunt of the assault here in Cambodia.

Their modest education made them a threat to the powers that wanted to return the nation to a Stone-Age agrarian commune of illiterate peasants, and since they do not work in the traditional sense of the word, they were easily made into the national whipping boy, publicly declared useless and a drain on society to be removed. Under the Khmer Rouge, the saffron robes were turned red.

Pan sits next to me on the stone railing of the Angkor moat bridge, lightly as a butterfly, radiating peace. From under his robes he produces an old oil cloth to reveal a small, shiny bowl; his rice bowl as he calls it.

In a matter-of-fact voice he tells me it is the top of his brother's skull, killed by the Khmer Rouge, and in true Buddhist fashion, he has kept it as a daily reminder of his own frailty and impermanence. After my initial shock, I decide it is a fitting prop to begin telling his tale. He stares at his dangling, sandaled feet, too short to reach the ground, as he speaks.

His story begins with the first night, when he was still a novice and lighting candles around the monastery when the door burst in and everyone was herded outdoors at gunpoint. Outside, in a huddled mass, the Abbott and all elders were singled out and summarily shot with a single bullet to the back of the head. By now, the attendant nuns were being stripped by the soldiers, intent on a long night of debauchery.

Next he tells me several monks were hung in the trees by their thumbs with small fires built underneath them, not enough to kill but just large enough to singe the skin. One of the nuns, now hysterical, was stripped, held down, and a monk was made to kneel between her knees. A pistol was put to his head, and he was ordered to copulate with her in front of all present. When he refused, a single shot rang out to the applause and cheers of the "soldiers" and another monk was brought forward. According to Pan, this went on for quite a while, until several monks had done the deed while several more had died in refusal. The fate of the nun was left unspoken

I search his face at this point for some sign, some emotional reaction, but see only tranquility. He has removed himself from this physical world and now occupies a separate reality. His roadmap face is a spider web of creases but his eyes burn bright. I pray his religious advancement had brought him true peace and that he is not simply numb in relating such unspeakable events. He returns my stare with a slight smile and says, "Tell this story once so it might never be told a second time."

There is no self-pity or regret in his voice. To him it is karma, and all that surrounds him now is Maya, an illusion to wander through until he reaches true enlightenment. The realization of his unshakable faith hits me like a fist, and at that moment I yearn to find that level of peace.

We begin to walk into the main courtyard of Angkor, and though surrounded by thousands of tourists, I hear only Pan as he continues in his soft voice.

He was sent to the countryside and made to rip up railroad tracks, brutally physical work under a blazing sun while enduring non-stop blows from the fists and whips of his overseers. Soon, slowly starving, and with only putrid river water to drink, he was near death, the final plan for him from the beginning. In the end, his will to live overcame his belief in karma as he crawled away one night, into the jungle, and there, lost all track of time.

He recalled his first morning of this illusionistic freedom, waking in the crook of a tree, sucking the dew from leaves to ease his parched tongue, covered with ant bites. Dropping to the ground, his weakened legs would barely support him as he made his way into the bush, surrendering to the most basic human instinct, survival.

He was not sure how long he stayed in the jungle, but once there he soon found others like himself, survivors, all with an unspeakable story, all wishing to live. Everyone had a talent, some could fish, others snared small animals; Pan knew a lot about medicinal plants and soon became a gypsy doctor, moving every few days, avoiding roads and villages, helping the more needy for a handful of rice, defying the odds at the bottom of the food chain.

One day, while foraging near a village he spotted a saffron robe and, not believing his eyes, knew he had to talk with this brother. The Khmer Rouge were gone, but the damage had been done. Pan listened to the monk's litany of atrocities all day, but told me he fell asleep while doing so and the next morning, he woke up under a roof, on a cot, for the first time in months if not years.

When he revealed his identity, he was called to the capitol of Phnom Penh, where he was received as a revered elder and met a delegation of Theravada monks from Vietnam who had come to help re-establish the religion. Only then did he realize the extent of the genocide, the monasteries destroyed, the sacred texts burned, countless brother monks slaughtered, and for the only time in our conversations, I saw a single tear roll down his cheek.

Two subsequent visits with Pan were deliberately kept light-hearted and fun, and I learned that he loved shave ice and to laugh, but it is more of a sustained giggle than a laugh that spares no part of his face. His joy in all that surrounds him reminds me of a small child, and though I could not see it, I often felt his aura.

When I left, Pan was in great demand, traveling around to various monasteries, imparting the old ways, "The Teaching of the Elders," to a new generation of monks who now use the internet, have cell phones and iPods, and ride motorbikes, but this does not seem to bother him in the least; how could it? Karma.

His goal has always been to spend his life in meditation, and I am sure that since our time together he has merged with the cosmos. I allow myself the fantasy to think he has been looking over my shoulder as I write this and knows that his story has been told, one more time, for the last time.

Today there are close to 60,000 Theravada monks throughout the country and almost 5,000 monasteries, all because men like Pan refused to give up their faith, and though he would laugh and shake his head at the thought, he is one who made a difference.

～ ～ ～

*James Michael Dorsey is an explorer, award-winning author, artist, and photographer who has traveled extensively in forty-five countries. His principal interest is documenting remote cultures in Africa and Asia. He is a seven-time SOLAS category award winner for best travel writing from Travelers' Tales and has written for* Colliers, Christian Science Monitor, Los Angeles Times, Natural History, Sea Kayaker, Perceptive Travel, Seattle Times, Orlando Sentinel, *and the* Chicago Tribune. *His latest book is entitled* Vanishing Tales from Ancient Trails. *His photography is represented by the National Wildlife Federation, Shutterstock, and Camerapix International. He is a Fellow of the Explorers Club and a former director of the Los Angeles Adventurer's Club. www.Jamesdorsey.com*

V. HANSMANN

~~ ~~ ~~

# Ohio House Tour

The simplest journeys are often the best.

*S*ome people say the most splendid thing about a road
trip to Ohio is the road trip from Ohio. I might have
agreed; benighted Rust Belt, flyover, swing state that it is. But
follow this simple itinerary and you may come away with
affection for Ohio. Spring is a good time to travel.

I had signed up for a nonfiction conference at a small
university in a small university town in the middle of Ohio.
The keynote speaker, Scott Russell Sanders, was someone
whose work I respected, who had written a wrenching essay
I could not get out of my head. Once I decided to drive, I
started examining the road atlas for possible routes. There
is no getting around Pennsylvania if you want to drive to
Ohio from New York City. Two basic corridors exist—
Interstate 80 to the north and the Pennsylvania Turnpike
to the south. Driving the full distance would be more than
a day's work: so, to break up the trip, where to stop? What's
beyond Harrisburg?

Fallingwater.

I could visit Fallingwater—Frank Lloyd Wright's masterpiece that sits astride a stream in a tiny western Pennsylvania
town. I have been an architecture nerd since a college survey

course, and I believe no structure, big or small, exerts such exquisite tension on its setting as Fallingwater. So I went.

I dropped my things at a B&B nearby, then found some startlingly good sushi, and ultimately wound up at the multiplex in time to be disappointed by *Star Trek Into Darkness*. Early the next morning I wound through hollows pillowed with ground fog to the invisible town of Mill Run, Pennsylvania.

Wright built Fallingwater as a weekend home for department store magnates from Pittsburgh. They gave him free rein, and what they got was a glory, a stack of cantilevered terraces that stunningly recapitulates the waterfall below. The rugged watercourse adds music to the breathtaking geometries, while the yellow-green leaves of spring cast a dazzling play of light. It feels like there is a breeze. The terraces levitate, suspended from a supple column of stone and glass by good fortune alone. The boundaries of inside and outside dissolve. Somehow, gravity doesn't operate. Within, the sensation is almost Cubist in that sights and sounds and smells and textures shift and overlap in a wondrous, kaleidoscopic way. Instantly, I knew I could live here, not intellectually or from vanity, but the house could effortlessly fit into my life and my life into it. Setting foot in Fallingwater fulfilled an ageless daydream. I will forever know it in all four dimensions.

Abuzz with satisfaction, I pushed on to Ashland, Ohio, site of the conference. Tedious interstate unspooled before me as I scanned my efficient directions. Ashland lay between Columbus and Akron, and I imagined it as the Ohio equivalent of those moribund New England mill towns, a hodgepodge of seen-better-days, a hollowed-out downtown and weary streets of unhappy houses.

I picked up my room number and key and my sheets and towels. My dorm was a three-story, motel-style slab at a right angle to a busy intersection. The rest of the university sprawled across the street, in a mid-twentieth-century industrial park sort of way. Lavish flowerbeds, generous swaths of color, softened the utilitarianism. Remarkably for a 125-year-old institution, no building predates World War II. What might the campus look like filled with undergrads? Corporate on a very casual Friday.

Perhaps the most striking feature of Ashland University was its rococo fetishizing of memorabilia. Every possible vertical surface was covered with framed and captioned photos, documents, posters, and tchotchkes, as well as trophies, beanies, balls, and plaques. Every corridor was a walk down somebody's memory lane or a stumble down a gauntlet of arcana to an end so trivial that all you noticed were the bouffants and bell bottoms. One could not help but observe a dismaying partiality for magicians and Republicans. Astonishingly, Ash U has nurtured a fine nonfiction literary magazine called *River Teeth*.

Back in the wintertime, I had submitted my "manuscript," a swiped-together selection of discontinuous personal essays, for an "assessment." No one had seen the thing since its days as a master's thesis. I discarded about 40 percent of it in favor of current writing. In addition to the many other stimulating aspects of a gathering of like-minded writers, the opportunity for someone of reputation to read my writing and proffer their opinion had me vibrating with apprehension. While I'm not shy about letting other people see my work, I sometimes play a very self-manipulative game with fantasy outcomes.

We sit at a picnic table in the quad in the afternoon sun. Kate, my reader, says I have a book here. She points out areas that need expansion and whole pieces that should be set aside. But I have a book, if I want. How about that.

The conference did not provide breakfast on departure day, so I tracked down some to-go coffee, gassed up the vehicle, consulted the next page of the directions, and pointed the car's nose toward Kidron, Ohio. My friend Becca and her husband

Michael had offered to show me around the Amish counties of eastern Ohio. She had grown up there on the family farm. Ohio is home to more Amish and Mennonite families than Pennsylvania. The highlight of the tour would be lunch with her grandma, Ruth Amstutz, who lives in the farmhouse built after the family emigrated from Switzerland in 1840.

I pulled into the yard on the dot of ten A.M. It was a damp, soft-focus morning, somewhere between overcast and foggy. From the looks of it, there didn't seem to be anyone home. I double-checked the address. Despite a smidgen of doubt, I maintain a steadfast, manly faith in printed directions. I rang the bell. Becca answered. She stood in the doorway, always taller than I remember, her strawberry blond hair pulled back, and a big, sweet smile on her face.

She tilted her head just a bit to the left and said, "V."

"Becca."

We embraced.

Michael stood behind her and Grandma behind him. With a flurry of pleasantries, I was ushered into the fine old house, spotless and modest. Did I want lemonade or iced tea? Grandma Amstutz carried a pitcher of lemonade and four glasses onto the back porch, and we fumbled joyfully through small talk. The voluble dachshund seemed to like me.

After draining our glasses, we departed for a prelunch exploration of the rectilinear byways of the Ohio countryside. The infinite farmland was either still bare or covered with new green. Proud barns with acolyte silos lorded over congregations of dusty outbuildings and cast nets of white fence everywhere. In the fields, mighty horses pulled plows, and in the yards, wash hung limply on lines. The farm folk always waved as we passed by. Kids were dressed exactly as their parents. A man in overalls, navy blue long-sleeved shirt, and straight-brimmed straw hat walked beside the road holding the hand of a tiny, perfect version of himself.

They brought me to a rambling emporium called Lehman's, which strived to meet all the simple requirements of the farm communities, while anticipating summer tourists' insatiable need for stuff. The hokey practicality and impracticality of the abundance extended to fifty different types of hatchet, psychedelic displays of seed packets, stiff, tubular denim trousers in every imaginable size except for "fat," and Amish romance novels.

I guess we had been working up an appetite. By the time we got back to the farm, Grandma Amstutz had laid out an epic lunch—a plump breast of chicken accompanied by egg noodles, mashed potatoes, stuffing, crescent rolls, and asparagus. And a mountainous apple pie and coffee. If I were heading back to the fields, I'd have energy to burn, but after such a painfully hearty lunch, I was predisposed to snooze. Michael and Becca had other plans for me, but first she beckoned, "Come to the springhouse, V."

Behind and below the farmhouse sat the whitewashed springhouse, two stories, two rooms. Two, small, square windows in its wattle-and-daub walls flanked the thick door, which opened noiselessly. In the half light hung a rich, chill dampness. A long stone trough stretched against the back wall, filled with cold water of unearthly transparency. Opposite was a great fireplace with a heavy kettle suspended above the swept hearth. "Everything happened in the springhouse," said Becca. "It was the center of existence."

"I see," I said, really seeing.

We stepped out into the now bright May air.

More hill-and-dale driving, in search of authentic Amish baskets. Becca knew of a gentleman who set out his excellent wares in the parking lot of Shisler's Cheese House on weekends. We stopped by, got his address, and then lit out on a GPS adventure. A half hour later, we beheld a hand-painted sign, red baskets on a white section of corrugated metal nailed to a fence post. Abruptly, we turned left. I was in the back seat, my view compromised, as we bucked down a dirt road. A pair of curious sheep paced us from behind a fence. We stopped short of the house, and chickens ran across our bow. Again, no sign of human life.

I strode onto the porch and announced, with some self-conscious bravado, "Hello?" through the screen door. The interior of the farmhouse lay deep in shadow. No response. I turned to my friends with a shrug. Then, behind me, the screen door creaked.

"You woke me from my nap."

"Oh, hello there. Your nap?"

"After the noon meal. My nap."

"We got your name from Shisler's," Becca said. "We'd like to see your baskets."

"Baskets, yes. In the shed."

He stepped off the porch, and we followed him quietly across the hardpack yard and through the Dutch door of a red, weathered building. In a corner, spilling off a workbench and piled underneath, every conceivable form of woven container—breadbaskets, wastepaper baskets, pie carriers with leather handles (one-, two-, and three-pie), baskets that fit baking dishes of all sizes, and hampers with and without lids. The sharp smell of linseed oil cut through the dusty gloom. The basket man grew increasingly animated as he displayed his handiwork, which was very handsome and not without some quirky flaws. Before we knew it, he had disassembled the great pile basket by basket, and I had selected four different ones for Christmas purposes. Well, three. The two-pie basket was for me.

The joy of beautiful, simple things, of found art, and of a peculiar, almost mystic, encounter way outside the bounds of my customary experience, made for a chesty exhilaration, a core happiness shared with friends. Back at the farmhouse,

I stowed my finds in the trunk of the car and bid Becca and Michael good-bye. The music of Cleveland beckoned.

From the south, I arrived at Cleveland via a boxed-in interstate that gave way to a tumble of squat, banged-up industrial buildings. All of a sudden, a Mylar-shiny baseball stadium ballooned into view on the left. An afternoon game would be getting underway. A beefy crowd clotted at the crosswalk, then streamed across, more likely to aggravate a melanoma than see the Indians win. After driving just fifteen more blocks, I could see the lake and, Jesus, another stupendous stadium. Cleveland—city of light, city of magic. Thank God its streets were numbered.

The Hyatt Regency hotel had been retrofitted into and out of a grand nineteenth-century structure called The Arcade. In its original configuration, the five-story atrium was surrounded by lower floors of retail and, on the upper ones, offices. Now it was all hotel. The atrium ran the length of a city block beneath a glass canopy, so that the space flooded with soft, saturated light. Cast-metal gargoyles circled the fourth floor, leaning balefully into the vast space every twenty or thirty feet, each with a small incandescent bulb in its mouth. It's a breathtaking interior. I was to meet my friend, Chet, there. He had driven up from Dayton to join me at the Rock and Roll Hall of Fame.

A couple of phone calls and a knock on the door, and there he was, lanky and gnomic, wearing jeans and a blue Indian-style shirt. Chet had flyaway white hair and a white beard that he tucked into his shirt for some mystifying reason, which he eventually explained to no avail. His features were large and well-formed; the giant ears had been pinned back many years ago to discourage involuntary tacking in high winds, so it was up to his noble nose to give focus and gravity to the entire facial conglomeration. He carried himself with the quiet aplomb of the professional actor. Chet was fond of me and I him. I offered him a seat, and we proceeded to catch up—the comings and goings of our children, his search for community among the far-flung and long-lost, my writing process.

We adjourned for a dinner reservation nearby. A quick stroll along the ground floor of the Arcade, out the back door, and soon we were seated in the noisy frat bar front room of a highly regarded tavern. Though the decibels peaked and troughed relentlessly, we gabbed with enthusiasm. Chet described his curious method of decision making, which involved a rubber cork on a length of chain that, held aloft, waggled one way for "yes" and the opposite for "no." His divination technique had a friendly name I immediately forgot.

It developed that Chet had decided to forego the Federal Reserve Bank of Rock 'n Roll in favor of visiting an old friend from his days in the copy department of a greeting card company. His little rubber stopper jobber had advised him to alter his plans. I felt a twinge of abandonment, but quickly adjusted to the new normal. We agreed to meet for breakfast in the hotel and then proceed on with what the cosmos had in store.

The Rock and Roll Hall of Fame has affixed itself to the shore of Lake Erie, a striking prism of glass, a bell jar of nostalgia and hype. A banner across the marquee announced THE ROLLING STONES. The ticket guy proposed that I take advantage of the opportunity to pose against a blue screen holding a red electric guitar with rocker intention. At the end of the visit, a 4x6 print would be available for purchase. *Oh, no thank you, not this time.* I've posed as Elliot on his bicycle with ET in the front basket, and nothing could possibly ever come close to the stupid magnificence of that.

Holy Shit! The Rock and Roll Hall of Fame was a ridiculous, entertaining, exhausting place, crammed to the gills with minutiae, a lot like Ash U, but without the Republicans. In addition to the tsunami of ephemera, small print to squint at and presumably read, there was treasure—you could find pieces of the plane that took Otis Redding down, an "Otis" fragment and a "Redding" one; Jimi Hendrix's sofa, an uncomfortable-looking section of a sectional; Michael Jackson's glove revolving on a plexiglass pedestal, pinned by a spotlight, resplendent and dead as a butterfly; and CBGB's awning that I used to see from my New York window until a couple of years ago. It sometimes had the feel of uniquely glamorous, museum-quality episode of *Hoarders*. The exhibit hall in the basement was pitch dark, with labyrinthine, chronology-averse catwalks and cul-de-sacs that shunt you from Metal to Doo-Wop to Disco in an eyeblink. The whole thing was claustrophobic, overreaching, and spectacular, like Aretha Franklin being squeezed into one of Diana Ross' gowns.

On a higher floor, I ducked into a dark theater, stood in the back, and watched a compilation film of the famous inductees, beginning at the museum's inception in 1986 with this bunch: Fats Domino, Buddy Holly, Chuck Berry, Little Richard, the Everly Brothers, Ray Charles, Sam Cooke, and Elvis. It played the soundtrack to my life. When it came The Band's turn, Levon Helm sang a snippet from "The Night They Drove Old Dixie Down." Just a fraction of a second, it seemed. Those seven words was the entire length of the segment, but my breath caught and my eyes filled. This crazy place was too rich for me.

My final stop was the city of Akron and the house where Bill Wilson and Bob Smith, two drunken Vermonters, met, and where, on June 10, 1935, Dr. Bob Smith took his last drink. From that date, Alcoholics Anonymous marks its beginning. The modest house was built in 1915 and Bob Smith was its first owner, living there until he died in 1950.

I am sober since 1985. For me and many, the story of how Bill W. met Dr. Bob carries the resonance of creation myth. The principles and history of AA all depend upon the simple practice of two alcoholics sharing an honest conversation. Only that kind of intimacy can keep us from drinking. I believe this in the very center of my being.

Swooping over the swells and dips and swells of the red brick streets of the old suburban neighborhood, a fluttery anticipation tussled with the real concern I might get hopelessly lost. My directions had me slowing down to make a turn every three or four blocks. It felt like it took hours to find 855 Ardmore Avenue, and I knew the house was going to close at three o'clock. And then, there I was, parked at the curb of a leafy street like any other. The house sat high on a corner lot, white with yellow trim and a wide front porch.

I couldn't help feeling just a little self-conscious, climbing the twelve steps (yes, the twelve steps) to the front door. Once inside, that sensation dropped away: the house enveloped me. Standing in the front hall, one could see, or certainly sense, the four exterior walls of the house; it was that small. This also meant the house was full of light. First thing, I signed the guest book. A half dozen people milled around in the entry and living room; coming or going, it was impossible to tell.

A stocky, open-faced guy in blue coveralls approached and asked if it was my first time. I chuckled, and he chuckled back. The name embroidered above his pocket said "Doug."

"My name is Doug. I can give you a tour, if you like. We're all volunteers here," he said.

"I'd like that," I said. "This is my last stop in Ohio. I'm here on purpose. I guess we all are. On purpose, I mean, Dr. Bob and all . . . Doug."

"Uh-huh. Yeah. Let's start upstairs then."

I poked my head into the three bedrooms that had provided respite for countless drunks, often forcing the two Smith kids to bunk in the third floor attic. This must have been a lively place; both before and after Bob Smith stopped drinking.

On the ground floor, what struck me was the kitchen table, around which Bob and Bill had their life-changing conversation. In addition to two half-full coffee cups, I saw a plate of Windmill cookies, the kind I see all the time at meetings in New York. The only spot on the globe where I've felt the presence of such quietly turbulent spirits was Delphi in Greece in the early morning. Maybe that's a reach, but the restorative legacy of 855 Ardmore Avenue is unquestionable.

Eventually, Doug and I made our way down to the cellar, a whitewashed room remarkable for nothing in particular. For the Smiths, being on a corner lot allowed the basement to have a set of double doors that permitted off-street parking. Photographs of Dr. Bob's automobiles lined the walls.

"How much time do you have, Doug?"

"Seven years clean and dry in a month."

"That's impressive. It sorta rolls along after a while, the not drinking and going to meetings," I said. "This commitment must help. How often do you take people around?"

"Only once a week."

"Only? How come?"

"There's a demand. Some people say it's the best job in Akron."

"And you've got the Tuesday afternoon commitment. Lucky me."

The two of us continued the conversation in this abbreviated vein—questions, simple answers, fencing, sideways admissions.

It's all in the eyes. "AA eyes," as my friend, Brigid, says. What Dr. Bob called "the language of the heart." Doug and I struck a chord of commonality in half an hour. We didn't have much in common in the specifics of our lives, but we weren't drinking, and that took care of just about everything. I couldn't have been happier, what they meant when they talked about the joy of living.

For you, the pleasures of Ohio are there to be discovered.

❧ ❧ ❧

*V was raised by wealthy people in suburban New Jersey and grew up to be neurotic, alcoholic, homosexual, and old. For thirty years he worked on Wall Street managing other people's money until the office closed in 2008, when he decided to try his hand at poetry and nonfiction. V completed an M.F.A. in creative writing from the Bennington Writing Seminars in June 2011. His publishing credits consist of an anecdote in the Metropolitan Diary section of* The New York Times *about shopping for styrofoam with a nickel stuck to his forehead and an essay in* The Common *about therapeutic spelunking.*

STEPHANIE GLASER

≈ ≈ ≈

# I Have a Problem with the Blood of a Woman

A certain bonding happens over biology.

Stationing myself next to Ba-Ba-Reeba's restroom, I stopped every woman who entered and asked, *"Perdon, tiene usted un Tampon? TamPONE? Tampax? Playtex? Kotex?"*

Just moments earlier while enjoying a beer and tapas at the Barcelona bar with some Americans I had met on a train from Madrid, I discovered the added company of my period. *Yikes*—my supplies were a few miles away back at a pension off Las Ramblas. I asked my new friend Allie if she had a tampon. Nope.

Back in the bathroom, there was no dispenser in sight, and no one who came in seemed to have any spare tampons or pads. Didn't anyone carry backups? It was time to act since I didn't want my only pair of jeans to be ruined. Leaving Ba-Ba-Reeba, I searched the streets near Plaça de Catalunya. Surely, Walmart had invaded Catalunya.

It was siesta time, and the nearby shops and stores were closed while shopkeepers observed the afternoon break. It seemed inevitable. I would have to approach the intimidating women of Iberia on the streets.

## AFTER ARRIVING IN SPAIN . . .

For the past few days, I had lumbered past elegant Spanish women who sauntered with precision in the highest and thinnest of heels along the city streets, avenues and cobblestoned alleyways of Barcelona.

It began the day I emerged from the train station, Estacio Sants, and tied my rumpled denim jacket around my waist, hurled my dusty duffel bag over my shoulder and trudged forth in my burly velcro-adhesive sports sandals. I felt large. *Grande. Muy grande.*

Spanish women, generally speaking, can make you feel like you have a permanent personal flotation device secured around your waist, and not just junk in the trunk but the whole junkyard back there. Think of standing next to Penelope Cruz — many Penelope Cruzes.

Clad in posh tailored jackets and short skirts that never appeared to crease, wrinkle, or ride up to expose cellulite, the young women of Barcelona looked like they were constantly working a Catalan catwalk. Their polished appearance included the perfect application of makeup, too. Long ago, I accepted my "dewy" complexion. I never once, however, saw shine glistening on a Spanish woman's T-zone.

As an American woman and solo traveler, I had assumed that I was stronger and more independent than most European women. In a troubling development, strength and independence took a back seat to beauty. But, seriously, despite navigating in precariously high heels, what made these Spanish women strong and independent?

Meanwhile, clodhopping my way along the famous street, Las Ramblas, I looked for a place to stay. Fortunately, the owner of the pension I finally found was a dowdy woman who definitely had settled for sensible rubber soles. She was, according to my brief observations, the only woman in Barcelona with orthopedic shoes.

## BACK TO THE TAMPON
## SEARCH SCENE . . .

I stood waiting for some younger women to pass by. Soon, two Penelopes came into view. It was worse than I expected. They both wore the uniform—the tailored jacket/miniskirt combo and strappy heels. Bright red lips and long dark hair that was so glossy I could practically see my desperate reflection within it completed their look. No doubt they were fashion muses. One for Dolce and one for Gabbana.

Did I dare ask *them?* Would they recoil at the sight of me? Would I be shunned like a pair of underwear at a young Hollywood starlet's debut in front of the paparazzi? More importantly, would they have a tampon between the two of them in one of the designer reptile-skin bags they each carried? I approached slowly, stopped them and then told the muses my situation.

*"Perdon, tengo un problema con la sangre de una mujer."*

There. I said it. Because I couldn't recall learning verbs such as "bleed," "stain," or "spot" let alone "menstruate" in my high school Spanish class, I settled for the primitive, yet direct, statement that translated into:

*"Excuse me, I have a problem with the blood of a woman."*

The muses looked at each other and then back at me. I was ready for the bitchy blow off. Instead, one muse took my hand, and the other hustled us down the street in the opposite direction they were traveling. We stopped at a pharmacy that was closed. The two women halted, consulted each other and then pointed to a large distant department store, El Corte Inglés. As they assured me I would find what I needed, I had the feeling the muses would have taken me to Spain's manufacturing plant of Tampax if they had the transportation.

I hurried to El Corte Inglés, which wasn't closed for siesta. Entering the expansive store, I repeated my *blood-of-a-woman* saga to a clerk who was working at the cosmetics counter. She

immediately took me by the hand. I towered over this wisp
of a thing who, despite her youth, looked like a professional
chemist in her white lab coat.

I must have looked like a trained circus bear following
behind her while we weaved through perfume counters and
hosiery aisles to the department drugstore. Taking me directly
to the attending clerk, who was with customers at the time, the
cosmetics chemist explained my dire situation. In an instant,
the pharmacy clerk turned away from her customers and took
me to the sanitary products aisle.

I figured then I could take control of the situation, but the
clerk took one box after another describing the strength of
each one. "*Aqui*, SOOPER PLOOSE," she said turning to
me and letting me inspect the product. I pointed to the Super
Plus box and nodded. Back we went to the register. Ignoring the women who were still waiting, the clerk rang up my
purchase, and then she took my hand and steered me in the
direction of a restroom.

After the threat of major leakage had passed, I wanted to
celebrate the recent show of sisterhood somehow. Surely there
was a Catalan karaoke bar where I could meet up with the
helpful Penelopes from El Corte Inglés. We could swill beers
and sing Helen Reddy's "I Am Woman Hear Me Roar" or do
something along those lines. I would just have to overlook all
the fashionable footwear, and that, essentially, in comparison,
my feet appeared to be strapped to discarded tire remnants.

꤫ ꤫ ꤫

*Stephanie Glaser is a teacher and freelance writer. Enjoying the
humor in life, she writes about travel mishaps (mostly her own)
for her blog, Travel Oops. She lives in Salida, Colorado with her
family and teaches English composition and public speaking at a
local community college.*

❧ ❧ ❧

# Surfing the Millennia

Arizona's remote stone wave crashes
into memory, where it will return again and again.

The afternoon before visiting the Wave, we watched a
madman stagger out of the desert.

My friends and I were hiking back from Buckskin Gulch,
part of the surreal Vermillion Cliffs National Monument on
the Utah/Arizona border. Our permit for the Wave was for
the next day—but this poor soul had just been out there. He'd
lost his way coming back. His eyes were wild, and his broad-
brimmed hat askew.

"I went up the wrong wash," he gasped, visibly calmed as
we showed him the path back to the parking lot. "There's no
trail . . . the maps they give you are !@$#% worthless . . . I've
been lost for an hour and a half."

At least he didn't die out there. Some people do. The Wave
may be one of the most visually stunning, ardently photo-
graphed features in the Southwest desert, but the Bureau of
Land Management doesn't make it easy to find (or to find
your way back).

"People come to the Wave and expect to have that
'National Park' experience," says BLM Monument Manager
Kevin Wright, who administers the area from his office in

St. George, Utah. "But there's no formal trail out there. Or potable water. And in the summer, it gets over 100 degrees."

All of which, of course, is part of the appeal.

The Wave is a tangible hallucination, a convoluted corridor of multicolored, brilliantly striped sandstone. Its history dates back to Pangaea: the single, giant continent that once covered the Earth.

Back then, about 170 million years ago, the North American and African plates were splitting at the hem, forming the Atlantic Ocean. But dinosaurs roamed freely across the enormous, sandy desert that covered the Southwest: land we now call Utah, Arizona, New Mexico, and Colorado.

"The dunes marched along, leaving layer after layer," says Ron Blakey, author of *Ancient Landscapes of the Colorado Plateau*. "The dune that makes up the Wave may have thousands of layers in it—and it's part of other dunes that also have thousands of layers. So the cross-bedding we see today may have *billions* of layers—each one representing the advance of a sand dune."

For more than 100 million years those dunes were buried miles underground, where they hardened into a layer of rock called Navajo Sandstone. Slowly, those layers were uplifted— until, a mere 4–5 million years ago, they breached through the ground. Water and minerals seeped into the now exposed sandstone; the wind sculpted its surface. Over many millennia it was painted and carved, creating the fantastic shapes and rainbow-hued stripes (called Liesegang bands) that now enliven desktop screen savers everywhere.

The Wave sneaked onto every landscape photographer's wish list in 2004, when it was featured in a German documentary called *Faszination Natur Seven Seasons*. Today, about a third of the visitors are from Europe (and, more recently, China and Japan).

But seeing the Wave *in situ* requires luck and planning. The BLM, which administers Vermillion Cliffs, uses a strict permit system to protect the fragile area from overuse. Only twenty people are allowed in each day. Ten permits are issued online, four months in advance; the rest are awarded by lottery at the National Monument office in Kanab, Utah, at 8:30 A.M. (the permits, $6, are valid the following day). During high season, March-November, as many as 120 hopefuls show up each day. All but ten will leave disappointed.

Bribes don't work.

Tom Reep, thirty-two, is a nine-year Army Veteran who served two tours in Iraq. He's currently the point man for Wave permit requests. Reep has an open flame tattooed on his arm and a deep affinity for the desert. But he has little patience for people trying to buy their way into the Wave.

"The monetary record is $2,000," Reep remarks as he, Wright, and my small group hike from the Wire Pass parking area and trailhead toward the Wave. "I've even had a lady on the phone ask, 'Well, what if I take you to dinner and a movie, and we'll see what happens afterward?'"

Kevin Wright has also turned down multiple requests—from the *Sports Illustrated* swimsuit edition to representatives of the Occupy movement (who wanted to hold a candlelight vigil at the Wave). "Even *National Geographic* had to get a permit," he says reverently. "We do give permission for research: science in the public interest. Otherwise, we never make an exception. I can't think of a single case."

"Come on," I nudge. "Not even the President?"

"If the President wants a permit," Wright pronounces dryly, "he will get one."

We cover about three unmarked miles, meandering through a landscape pocked with vivid red and orange bumps and valleys—like acne writ large. The land is sparse, but not bare; we pass sagebrush, twisted junipers, and hills bristling with Indian rice grass.

After ninety minutes of rugged walking, a short, sandy hill leads us up to the Wave itself. It's a weird feeling, to be approaching a rock formation with the same anticipation one might feel at Angkor, or the Taj Mahal.

"This whole area is amazing," I remark. "Will I even know the Wave when I see it?"

"You'll know it," Wright says.

He's right, of course. So much of the Southwest is wild and magical that it's hard to think "Best of Show." But the Wave is a contender. I stare at the layers of whorled stone, trying to come up with a good visual metaphor. The sandstone ribbons range in color from beet to pumpkin, cayenne to saffron. Farsi finger painting? Tutti-Frutti taffy? A stretched-out sand mandala? One friend comes even closer: "Stacked Pringles."

We pass between the undulating Wave walls. It's only 10 A.M., and the sun hasn't penetrated the interior; it's cool and mysterious in the "tube." After a few yards, the wall opens up to our left. A dozen other visitors are sitting on a saddle above us, capturing the postcard view of the Wave. They wait gamely as we pass through their viewfinders.

"We'll come back later," Reep says. "There's lots to see."

Our little group continues walking, emerging from the Wave onto an exposed outcrop. The view beyond is alien, fantastic, a scene from Dr. Seuss. Reep leads us on a long loop behind the Wave, pointing out some of the area's lesser-known dreamscapes. We stop at a viewpoint over the "Second Wave"; to the east stands a group of tall, cauliflower-topped hoodoos called "Brain Rocks." A 200-foot scramble up to a harrowing ledge ("Don't look to your left . . . or to your right," Reep grins) leads to Top Rock, our lunch spot: a wind-carved arch with a staggering view across the landscape below.

My favorite site, though, is a simple pool of rainwater, filling a sandstone dip just a few steps from the Wave itself. Reep reaches into the water, and shows us a black creature that looks like a fat tadpole. "A horseshoe shrimp," he explains. "The oldest living species on Earth." Exquisitely adapted, her eggs can survive up to twenty years between rains.

At about 2:30, Tom and Kevin head back to their truck. The other visitors have left, too. I'm left blissfully alone with a few good friends, the Wave, and the oldest shrimp on Earth. Good company.

My fantasy is to head toward our car at dusk, but the group's greater wisdom prevails. We start back at 4:30 P.M. It's a good thing; the BLM's route-finding map has you navigate using a half-dozen small photographs of the local landmarks you see (or don't) around you. It's hard enough to follow the path in the late afternoon; it would be nearly impossible in the dark. Even now, we almost take a wrong turn up what seems to be a trail, but is only a wash between two tall hoodoos.

Getting lost here would be easy—and possibly fatal, as it was for an unlucky exchange student in 2011. He'd arrived at sunrise, and stayed until sunset. Dehydrated and disoriented, he took a wrong turn toward Buckskin Gulch—and fell into a slot canyon.

With a collective sigh of relief, we find our way out. As the dark, weird shapes of the buttes loom against the moonlit sky, the desert seems eternal. But even that view—like the false trail that snaked off into the sagebrush—is an illusion.

"This landscape is ever-evolving," *Colorado Plateau* author Ron Blakey points out. "The Wave you can touch with your hand is probably less than 1,000 years old. It's constantly changing, constantly eroding, grain by grain, layer by layer. What you see today is not going to be there 5,000 years from now."

The Earth is a living planet. Even the Wave, one day, will collapse.

✤ ✤ ✤

*Oakland-based Jeff Greenwald is the author of six books, including* Shopping for Buddhas, The Size of the World *(for which he created the first international blog), and most recently* Snake Lake, *a novel set in Nepal during the 1990 democracy revolution. His stories and essays have appeared in* Smithsonian, Afar, Wired, National Geographic Adventure *and* Salon. *Jeff also serves as Executive Director of Ethical Traveler, a global alliance of travelers dedicated to human rights and environmental protection (www.ethicaltraveler.org).* Shopping for Buddhas *has been re-released in a new, up-to-date edition for its 25th anniversary.*

~~ ~~ ~~

# *Feliz Cumpleaños*

Youth is wasted on the young. —Oscar Wilde

It's late afternoon, and Erin and I have occupied the sunny courtyard of La Canchanchara for hours, drinking *cervezas* and taking turns dancing with José Luis. Now he's tutoring Erin on the *güiro*, a traditional Cuban instrument made from a hollow gourd. He leans close as he teaches her the rhythm, locking eyes with her, and in unison they scrape thin sticks over the carved ridges of their instruments: *cha, cha, chachacha, cha, cha, chachacha.* The band plays *son*, and the sweet smoke from his hand-rolled cigar encircles our heads. As the sun crosses the sky and we order another round, José Luis takes my hand and begins serenading me in Spanish, soft and low. I sing back. Across the table Erin grins: mission accomplished.

Four days ago she picked me up at the Calgary airport. "I've been in a foul mood for months," she said, backing her car out of the snowy airport parking spot. "I promised Drew I'd come back with an attitude adjustment."

Erin is my best friend, and Drew is her Canadian husband. We met him in an Australian backpacker bar ten years ago and shared a pitcher of beer, and within minutes I knew he would marry her. What I didn't realize was that he'd whisk her away to the cold plains of Canada, after which the only way I'd ever see her would be to bribe her with sunshine.

"I'm sick of my job," she said, driving us toward the spray-tan salon where we had appointments to turn our grayish skin bikini-ready. "And this weather isn't helping."

She looked sideways at me, apologetically, as if I might judge her. Erin and I had been friends for twenty-five years; if I didn't judge her when she was our high school's head cheer-leader, it was unlikely to happen now.

"Don't worry," I said. "We'll find you a new attitude."

The last time we traveled together I drank so much Tecate with two guys named Miguel that at the end of the night I decided to sleep in my Subaru outside our rented casita. "Are you crazy?" she'd hissed, holding the car door open. "I am *not* letting you sleep in a car, alone, in the middle of Mexico." Now, three years later, we were off to Cuba—Erin in search of a new attitude, me in search of a cure for the insult of turn-ing forty. At least if we failed, we failed together.

Our flight to Cuba kicks off with two complimentary glasses of champagne, and following Erin's announcement that it's my birthday, two more appear. While she reads a guidebook, I study *See It and Say It in Spanish*, enlightening her occasionally with useful phrases like *Caramba! Eso es ridiculo. No tengo un gorilla en casa*. Inexplicably—alarmingly—she appoints me our official translator.

I have never in my life taken a Spanish lesson, and even if I had, my brain isn't as absorbent as it once was. But I did bring this handy kindergarten-level language book, along with several Lonely Planet and Rough Guides, whose glos-saries should at least add some practical vocabulary to supple-ment *See It and Say It in Spanish* gorillas, geraniums, radishes, and accordions.

In addition to the dried-up sponge in my head and other obvious indicators of age—gray hair, wrinkles, sunspots, flabby waistline, unforgiving hangovers—one area in which it's clear that forty is old is when packing for a trip. Between the ever-expanding first-aid kit, ugly-but-comfy shoes, just-in-case jackets, healthy snacks and emergency provisions, guidebooks and back-up documents, packing has turned complicated. In my twenties I could squeeze three weeks in Vietnam and Cambodia into a tiny zip-on daypack. Now I feel chastened each time I lift an overstuffed pack onto my shoulders or—so very much worse—admit defeat by opting for the expandable rolling bag. But this time was easy. My boyfriend Dan had just returned from Cuba (his guys' trip to my girlcation) and called to offer advice. "Cuban women wear skin-tight spandex and low-cut shirts," he said, "but if you don't want to get whistled at and have men following you around making kissing noises, dress modestly. Wear jeans."

"Right," I said, tossing tiny tank tops, skimpy sundresses, skirts, bikinis, and shorts into my pack—and leaving the jeans on my closet floor. I was turning forty: damn straight I wanted men following me around making kissing noises.

Dan offered other helpful advice: bring Imodium; change dollars to euros first; go to Staples and buy a new memory card for your camera; bring your iPhone but keep it on air- plane mode; pack light. When I shared his suggestions with Erin, she said, "Does he know this isn't our first rodeo?"

It really wasn't. Our friendship was founded on movement and adventure, and sustained by both. It began in high school: bored with the entertainment offerings of our small town of Flagstaff, Arizona, we spent nights driving the highway, through the desert or mountains, in search of little more than an elsewhere. We drove to Prescott late one night to see if their Jack in the Box burgers tasted different from ours. We drove to Sedona and peered into darkened shop windows filled with incense and dream catchers. We drove to the north rim of the Grand Canyon and sat on the side with our feet dangling over, talking about the boys we loved. We drove to Phoenix, gassed up, and drove home. We drove to see how far we could go and make it back before anyone noticed we were gone.

Freshman year in college we crossed the border into Nogales, Mexico, on Friday nights to do tequila shots. Sophomore year we scribbled the names of ten cities on scraps of paper, threw them in a mixing bowl, and spent our summer in the one we'd blindly chosen, Seattle. Senior year we backpacked through Europe. After university, we lived in South Korea, vacationed in Bali and Saipan and Thailand, went scuba diving and hang gliding in Australia. And eventually we married her off on a beach in Costa Rica. We fell in love with the world together, and our lives were stitched together with the threads of a thousand overlapping stories. And now we were turning forty and crossing destination *numero uno* off our list: Cuba. It offered art and history museums and salsa dancing for Erin, guitar concerts and food and confusing politics for me. But mostly, it offered a place we weren't actually, technically, allowed to go. *Sí, por favor.*

When we land in Varadero, Erin and I are immediately singled out as Americans. Standing in the center of a one-room airport while all eyes watch with interest, a trio of immigration officials question us. We entertain them with feeble, comical attempts at Spanish until their concern finally turns to laughter and they send us on our way with a *"feliz cumpleaños."* (Because Erin doesn't know how to say, "It's her birthday" in Spanish, she simply wishes everyone she meets a happy birthday, then points at me.)

A shuttle drops us at our hotel, which looks fine from the outside. But inside it's dark and dingy, like the foyer of a small-town prison. We wait nervously while the desk clerk looks up our reservation, and when after a few minutes he announces he can't locate our reservation, we both smile with relief. The only redeeming feature of the hotel is the patio bar, so we sip our first Cuban mojitos while we weigh our options. Do we walk around Varadero seeking alternate lodging? We're in this ritzy town for just one night, and only because hitching ourselves to the Canadian resort-goers' wagon was the cheapest flight from Calgary. In every other town on our itinerary we plan to stay at *casas particulares*—private homes of Cubans who have licenses to rent rooms to tourists. But we've read that in Varadero, *casas particulares* are not legal; all our guidebooks state it's impossible to find one. We are therefore tremendously pleased with ourselves when ten minutes later we've secured a lovely, reasonably priced room in a charming *casa particular*, after being approached by a man who asks in a whisper if we need a place to stay. As Erin and I perch on our double bed with the pink-and-yellow flowered quilt, our hostess sits between us with a town map, indicating sites of interest and miming.

"*Aquí*," she says, "*su casa*," pointing at the floor and marking it on our map with a star. "*Aquí comida*," making an X on the map and lifting an invisible fork to her mouth. She circles the market, beach, bus station. Then she becomes serious. "*Ahora*," she says, making sure we're listening intently. "*Muy, muy importante*." We wait for the warning about sketchy neighborhoods, or perhaps another plea to keep her *casa* a secret. Something about the government? A rule that we, as Americans cannot, should not break?

"*Aquí*," she says, carefully circling a spot and tapping it several times with her pen for emphasis, "*es casa de la música*." She mimes dancing, and we all laugh—but she's right. This *is muy, muy importante*. Later, we follow her map to a bar where professional dancers circle the floor. At one point there's a pseudo-Santería ritual featuring flashy dancing and fire.

Meanwhile, locals salsa in the street outside. While I drink my Cristal beer and laugh at the cheesy tourist show, Erin dances with a tall Cuban named René. He's handsome, with a gentle demeanor, and after twenty minutes tries to kiss her. "No," she says.

"Just one kiss," he insists.

"I'm married!" she says, showing him her ring.

"And you?" he asks, suddenly remembering I'm sharing their table.

"I have a boyfriend."

"So you," he says to Erin, "are dead, and you"—pointing to me—"are very sick." Then he tries to kiss her again. A few hours later, outside another bar, a friendly, corpulent gold-toothed CD seller approaches us. After Erin buys a disc from him, he too asks to kiss her. "I love you, Erin," he insists, calling after her as we head home.

I'm reminded of our summer in Europe. We were twenty-three, and everywhere we traveled—Greece, Spain, Italy, France—the men called Erin "Miss America." At a London hostel, an Australian named Troy climbed our fire escape and perched outside the window serenading her on the guitar as we drifted to sleep. In Greece two bronzed boys, Mikhal and Christophe, followed her around begging for attention. But Erin was faithful to her boyfriend back home and left them brokenhearted. One night at the end of our week on Corfu, as I danced with Mikhal, he whispered that he loved me.

"But Mikhal," I teased, "last night you loved Erin.'"

"Yes," he nodded earnestly. "But tonight . . . it is your turn."

As we walk home from *casa de la música*, Erin tells me she read in her guidebook that sex is the only thing not rationed in Cuba. And as our week on the island unfolds, we begin to see the effects of this. It doesn't feel seedy, though—there's something thick and sultry about it, yes, but equally playful.

It's in the way middle-aged men with unbuttoned shirts lean in doorways and watch women passersby; how they flirt—smiling, eyes sparkling—but it's also in the way those women look back, flirt, sparkle. It's in the way those same men smile and flirt with us. When we were younger, it would have made us squirm. Were we available for romance, it might make us nervous. But no—this attention is welcome and we let ourselves soak it in, absorb it like expensive wrinkle cream. Of course we've read about *jineteras* (women) and *jineteros* (men) who trade sex or love for money, favors, the remote possibility of a life lived elsewhere. This doesn't feel like that—this just feels like a place where joy and sexuality and music are celebrated, the way capitalism is celebrated in my country.

Still, there are rules. Later in the week we'll meet a woman traveling with her husband, and she'll tell us men don't even look at her here, much less speak to her. There's a code of respect: if you're already partnered you won't be spoken to or propositioned or invited to dance. And so we finally understand why Erin is always approached right away—within minutes of entering a bar or finding a table. Once someone establishes himself as her dance partner, no one will bother her for the remainder of the evening; she's off-limits. And since we don't care who we dance with—we only want to dance—we find this positively charming.

The next afternoon in the town of Cienfuegos we walk the Paseo del Prado, a long tree-lined boulevard, down to the pier, stopping to photograph the classic cars covered in house paint—shades of popsicle pink, orange, lime, grape—and the remarkably lifelike statue of Beny Moré, a native of Cienfuegos. Moré is Cuba's most beloved musician, known as the *barbaro de ritmo*—the barbarian of rhythm. The day is hot and humid, and we are dripping but determined to make it to Punta Gorda. As we finally near the pier, a young guy rides by on a bicycle, slows down, and—cupping one hand around his right man-breast—looks me square in the eye and announces loudly and reverently: "*Bueno.*"

"Did that just happen?" I ask.

"Oh how sweet!" Erin says. "But we should teach him how to say it in English. 'Hey!'" she calls after him. "It's 'nice rack!'"

That evening at another *casa de la música*, a lively salsa band plays and Erin dances nonstop. "Why does everyone ask you to dance?" I whine. "And never me?"

"Because I sit here chair-dancing till someone takes pity on me," she says. Then she stands up to be swung around by the translator who has claimed her for the evening. When we leave the club an hour later (fending off the translator's disappointment), we see the guitarist from the band crossing the street.

"I'm going to ask for his autograph," I say, suddenly fourteen.

On the liner notes of my CD he scrawls his name, Roberto, along with a long and involved inscription, the only words of which I understand are "*a las 2 chicas Americanas,*" and we chat for a few minutes—his English is practically perfect. Then his friend saunters up holding a guitar, and they serenade us on the sidewalk. After, they translate the lyrics: "When will I see you again? When the world turns over." The evening is warm, and people are out strolling on the *malecón*, so we join them. After a few minutes we pair off, and as I walk ahead with Roberto, I try to figure out how to broach the topic of his political situation—I want to ask everyone we meet about the "situation," and Erin teases me about this. If I comment that a little girl is cute, she asks, "Do you want to ask her about her *situación?*"

I do. I'm ignorant about Cuban politics, I know—I've done my share of reading but it's complicated and I want more.

I want to know things I cannot intuit or see in the streets. I want to know whether things are changing with Obama in office—how they are changing with Raul Castro in charge. I want to know about limitations and expectations, shortages, and to what lengths they go. I want to understand why everyone is so friendly to Americans while I feel, if not guilty exactly, genuinely sorry.

I'm too afraid to ask, though, so we talk music. But after some time, Roberto opens up. Every Cuban, he tells me, has a second source of income—selling cigars, helping tourists, hawking CDs. It's the only way, when you make the equivalent of $20 a month. "Can you imagine if Cuba changed?" Roberto asks at one point, his voice becoming higher. "Can you imagine?" Ninety percent of Cubans want it to change, he tells me—but most won't allow themselves to even hope for it. They live each day identical to the day before: without dreams, because there's no chance of dreams coming true. "We have nothing," he says at one point, stopping the conversation. "We have no freedom, we have no money, we have no food, we have no clothes, we have no instruments. We have no, we have no, *we have no.*"

Then he pauses beneath a tree, takes a breath and says, "If you and I got married, you could take me to Hollywood and introduce me to people."

As the moon shines down on us, as Erin and her guitarist approach, I fumble awkwardly, sadly, for the words to explain why I can't do that, why it won't ever happen. I have a boyfriend, I have no connections in Hollywood, I couldn't, I can't, I'm sorry. I'm genuinely sorry.

From Cienfuegos we take a bus south to Trinidad, where we've booked into the same *casa particular* where Dan and his friends stayed a week ago—in the same room. Our host shows me his name in the guest log, and as I set down my bag and lie

on top of the bed where he slept, I feel the loose filaments of
our new relationship tightening, strengthening. The last time
I saw him, before he left for his trip, he told me he loved me.
I haven't said it back yet.

On this, our first day in Trinidad, Erin is violently ill. I
sit with her through the afternoon and evening, writing in
my journal and conjugating Spanish verbs in my head. *Canto*,
I sing; *Canta*, you sing; *Cantamos*, we sing. But Erin finally
insists I go out—she'd rather be alone. And within sixty seconds I am at yet another *casa de la música*. This one is *al fresca*,
just off the Plaza Mayor. The steps of the staircase leading
up to the Iglesia Parroquial are filled with locals and tourists
drinking beer and watching the show in the square below.
Today is one of many Santería holidays, and the performers—
band members and dancers alike—are dressed in white from
head to toe. I lean against a crowded bar and wait to order
a beer, and before long I make friends: Torsten is German,
Angelica is Swiss, her husband Orlando is Cuban. Angelica
tells me that when she and Orlando were courting, he was
arrested for talking to her on the *malecón*. "There are cameras
everywhere," she tells me. "Be careful." (Later I'll learn that
none of these cameras actually work.) We dance, drink, and at
the end of the night Torsten asks if he can kiss me. Though I
say no—definitely not—I am beginning to see how this place
can change you, make you feel more desirable, more alive. It
turns you the way it wants to, gently, like a hand on the small
of your back as you dance.

The next day Erin wakes up with an appetite and some color
in her cheeks, so we strike out, hitting the lone Internet café
in town first, where she receives an email offering her a new,
better job. We celebrate that night at Casa de la Trova, a small
club with a warbling *trovador* who sings soppy ballads, the
kind Erin and I hate ourselves for loving. *"Besame,"* we sing

along, "*besame muuuuuuucho*." I'm asked to dance finally—
the first time in Cuba—by a nerdy boy named Leonardo
who's clearly looking to practice English (though he's already
quite proficient, having mastered lines like, "I have never in
my life met a woman like you"). But my feet are clumsy and
he leads me into the hallway, presumably to prevent me from
embarrassing him.

Casa de la Trova closes at eleven, but then La Cueva opens:
a thumping after-hours nightclub in an underground two-
story cave the size of a Walmart, complete with massive sta-
lagmites and stalactites, water running down the walls, disco
spotlights, and an animated DJ spurring an already-frenzied
crowd from a cage above the dance floor. We climb the steep
hill to the entrance of the grotto and enter to see the mob of
bodies—hundreds of Cubans—bouncing up and down on the
dance floor to the Black Eyed Peas. As we join in, Erin shouts
in my ear, "We've still got it!"

Walking down the street the next morning, our final day in
Trinidad, we pass two men who whistle, kiss the air, call after
us: *linda, linda*.

"When I get back to Canada," Erin says, "I'm telling Drew,
'You don't have to say I'm beautiful, but when I get up from
the couch to walk to the kitchen I'll need you to make kissing
noises, because I've been getting that all week and I'm used to
it now.'"

"I know," I say. "I'll miss this when I'm back in San Francisco, where all the men look at other men."

"Tell me about it. In Canada they just look at livestock."

I talk about Dan too much. *Dan says we should only eat at
private paladares. Dan says to make sure we catch this show. Dan
says there's a woman in town who gives private salsa lessons in
her house.* When I return I will tell him I love him too, and

Erin will say, "I knew in Cuba you loved him—nice of you to finally let him know."

Tomorrow we will leave Trinidad for Cienfuegos again, and then Havana, before heading back to the States. But today we follow Dan's advice and take salsa lessons in a cramped living room from a spirited older woman named Mireya. When we finish, it's late afternoon and we're hungry. Normally we'd check the guidebook for recommendations for a *paladar*—an in-home restaurant many Cubans run as a way to improve their "situation"—but today I decide we should wander. I want to escape the well-worn cobblestones and find a secret spot, a memorable meal, a languid afternoon. Erin is dubious; I'm not known for my sense of direction.

"Do you know where you're going?" she asks.

"Not really. But I think there are restaurants over here."

"O.K.," she says. "I just want to know that you know where you're going."

"I don't."

But then we turn a corner and hear live music—a traditional *son* band. We peek behind a lime green wall into a long cobblestone courtyard filled with dark wood tables and benches, wind chimes, potted palms, and people kicked back under umbrellas drinking, listening, and exhibiting an air of contentment. There is no kitchen and therefore no food, but we don't care—we'll fill up on beer. We claim a table and watch a wiry old man dancing in the space in front of the band. He wears a worn straw cowboy hat and plays the *güiro*—a hollowed-out gourd instrument—and a cigar the size of a small thermos dangles from his mouth. He looks eighty, dark and wizened, with bushy silver eyebrows and a constant grin. There's something inexplicably beautiful in his face. He's mesmerizing, and I can't stop photographing him—but I can tell he isn't one of the "professionally photogenic" old Cubans who troll for tourists with cameras, offering to pose for a fee.

When the song ends, I turn back to Erin. "I love that old man." And as if answering the call, within seconds he's at our table inviting me to dance. "Go!" Erin urges. I'm feeling only slightly more confident after the private lessons, but I obey. As he swings me, Erin takes photos. When it's her turn to dance I take video. Other tourists take pictures of us all, and I can't help but feel we're in the company of a star.

I buy José Luis a beer, and only then does he tell me today is his sixty-sixth birthday. I wonder over his life that has made him look fifteen years older than his age (especially when Cubans are known for looking younger than their years), his life that has made him so grateful for the cigar a friend bought him for his birthday, and for the cans of Cristal we share with him. For an hour, maybe two, he sits with us. Somehow we speak only Spanish (astonished by how useful *See It and Say It in Spanish* has become), and when Erin mentions she wants to learn to play the *güiro*, José Luis disappears and returns holding a second one to teach her. After Erin masters the instrument, he asks me where we're heading tomorrow.

"Cienfuegos," I say, "on our way to Havana."

José Luis immediately takes my hand and begins crooning to me, a song by Beny Moré. "*Cienfuegos es la ciudad que más me gusta a mí,*" he sings slowly, carefully enunciating every word. *Canto, canta, cantamos,* I remember. I learn and sing and clap while the band keeps playing and José Luis keeps pulling us to the dance floor. He is vibrant, joyful, smart and funny, wrinkled around the eyes and missing a tooth or two. He looks older than sixty-six, but he's undeniably younger than his years—and at last, at last, so are we.

࿗   ࿗   ࿗

*Lavinia Spalding is the editor of Travelers' Tales' The Best* Women's Travel Writing *annual compilations. She is author of* Writing Away: A Creative Guide to Awakening the Journal-Writing Traveler *and* With a Measure of Grace, the Story and Recipes of a Small Town Restaurant, *and she introduced the reissued e-book edition of Edith Wharton's classic travelogue,* A Motor-Flight Through France. *Her work has appeared in many print and online publications, including* Sunset, Yoga Journal, Tin House, *the* San Francisco Chronicle, San Francisco *magazine, and* The Guardian UK. *She lives in San Francisco, where she's a resident of the Writers' Grotto and co-founder of the award-winning monthly travel reading series* Weekday Wanderlust. *Visit her at* www.laviniaspalding.com

❧ ❧ ❧

# Biko

One man, many memories.

Steve Biko was my teacher and my guide. He led me, hand in hand, on a grand tour of political illumination that started in the ghetto of Maseru and ended in the white suburb of Westdene. For four months he was my companion, a quiet, incorporeal spirit subtly pushing me from one encounter to another, each one seemingly independent from the others. Yet when fused together they created an indelible impression of the realities of South Africa circa 1980, and a wake-up call that stays with me to this day.

At the time of the South African winter of 1980, Steve Biko had already been dead two and a half years. I, on the other hand, was very much alive and about to begin the second year of a "three-month" visit to Africa. I had settled into a comfortable life in the suburbs of Johannesburg. At that time Fourways was a quiet rural community of eclectic estates, folksy cabins, and hardscrabble farmland that was supported by a few small general stores. We, four friends and I, had rented a newly built four-bedroom home on three and a half acres of land, with a swimming pool complete with a waterfall in the deep end and a family of black servants. With its round rooms and ultramodern design we affectionately christened

our home the "Mushroom House." We each contributed $60
toward the rent, a monthly sum that included both utilities
and servants. The servants, Maggie and Arthur, were physically and legally connected to the house. They lived in a shack
in the backyard with their two children. The builders of the
house had thoughtfully placed the shack behind a large boulder to avoid spoiling the view from the swimming pool.

South Africa in 1980 was a country of extraordinary ease
and wealth for the obedient white population, and a country of extreme cruelty and oppression for people of color and
their white collaborators. It was a schizophrenic land where
even mundane daily events could be viewed within a variety
of contexts. Most white South Africans, and most visitors,
were forced to live within a saccharine domain controlled by
the government. It was illegal for a white person to have a
nonwhite guest to his or her home, to visit an official "black"
area, to read certain books, to use a "NonWhite" toilet, to use
the "Black" entrance to a store. It was practically impossible
for a white South African to have a nonwhite friend, as it
was illegal for black Africans to legally be in the country of
South Africa without "papers." The government was based
on the principle that any interaction between the races was
proscribed. To most white people, black South Africans, even
though technically there weren't any black South Africans,
were simply servants.

South Africa was a race-based society where Indians
and Pakistanis were legally categorized as Asian, while
Japanese and Chinese were considered White. Oddly—and
interestingly—black Americans were ordained as White.
I knew a black American Peace Corps volunteer who had
a devil of a time coping. He was once arrested for using a
"White" toilet even though it was illegal for him, as an official
white person, to use a "Black" toilet. When I, American and

non-European, once encountered a "Europeans Only" toilet
I threw up my hands in frustration and pissed in the woods.
The South Africans had a name for this unnatural and
deranged state of affairs: apartheid.

One Sunday afternoon, while sitting around the pool
enjoying a *braai*, a traditional South African barbeque, I
began reading a book written by a friend of one of my roommates. The book was titled *Biko*. Although *Biko* was written as a biography of the South African Black Consciousness
leader Steven Biko, the book is usually thought of as a powerful human rights polemic. It was banned in apartheid South
Africa as was its author, Donald Woods. The banning of the
book meant that mere possession of it was a criminal offense.
The banning of Donald Woods meant that he was stripped
of his editorship of the newspaper, the *East London Daily Dis-
patch*. It was illegal for him to write, travel, or be alone with
more than one person at a time, including family members,
for the duration of his five-year ban. After his six-year-old
daughter was severely burned by an acid drenched t-shirt, an
act he attributed to the South African government, Woods
fled to England to continue his anti-apartheid campaign.

My South African education started at the Mushroom
House pool lazing under a semitropical sun, smelling the grill-
ing *boerewors*, drinking in the good life. As I opened the book,
Biko smiled and said, "Let me show you South Africa."

Maseru was a Wild West kind of town. Providing a bit of civilization, it was the entrepôt and capital of the country of Lesotho. Just outside of town there were cowboys riding horses,
general stores selling tins of tobacco, and occasionally snow-
covered mountains. Lesotho was an enigmatic hundred-mile
diameter circle of black Africa embedded in the middle of
white South Africa. Completely surrounded by its larger,
incalculably wealthier neighbor, it was an independent

country, a member of the British Commonwealth and the United Nations. Lesotho was also a haven for those South Africans needing to flee the omnipresent specter of the South African government. Apartheid did not exist in Lesotho.

Not long after reading *Biko* I hitchhiked from King William's Town, close to the birthplaces of Donald Woods, Nelson Mandela, and Steve Biko, to Maseru, 200 miles distant. My hitchhiking host was an amicable Afrikaner who spent four hours cheerfully discussing his political hero, a "German chap" named Adolf Hitler. Not wanting to embarrass him I neglected to mention my Jewish heritage. Going forty-five minutes out of his way, he good-naturedly took me across the international border and deposited me in downtown Maseru and offered to buy me lunch. I declined.

With backpack and camera bag I began to walk the streets of the capital city. Although Maseru was poor and somewhat decrepit, it was a joy to walk its streets. Its people had a carefree air. Men walked hand-in-hand, as did women, but never a man with a woman. The people wore smiles and constantly stopped to offer greetings or idle chatter to other passersby. Within five minutes of beginning my stroll I was interrupted, or rather surrounded, by a pair of young Africans.

"Hey, you American?"

"Yeah."

"Welcome to Lesotho. Welcome to freedom. Can we buy you a coffee?"

I nodded and we headed off to a nearby café. The two were political refugees from South Africa. Wanted by the South African secret police, the hated Bureau of State Security, also known as BOSS, the two had fled the country to the relative security of Lesotho. After I explained that I had just finished reading *Biko,* they exploded in a touching display of excitement while pulling out their own copies of his biography.

"I can't believe you read *Biko*. An American read *Biko*? Wow. What did you think?"

Before I could answer they continued. "When we were living in South Africa we joined the Black Consciousness movement. Biko was our spiritual leader. When the Boers killed him we protested. When BOSS came to arrest us as terrorists we fled to Lesotho."

"I take it you are not terrorists."

They burst into laughter, slapping their knees, slapping my shoulder. "No man. Hey, you must come stay with us tonight." One of them took my pack and the other my camera bag, and we headed out into the sunshine and up a side street.

They lived outside of town in a house made of cinderblocks topped with a green tin roof. They shared the single room with a sister of one of them. In one corner sat a wood-burning stove, used to both heat the house and cook the meals. Next to the stove were a few shelves sparsely populated with a few tins of sardine-like pilchards, a handful of onions, and bags of mealies, the corn meal staple that is the core of all southern African cuisine. A cot in the other corner of the room was reserved for the sister. My two friends slept on the floor.

While the sister prepared the simple dinner, my two newfound friends and I discussed South African politics. Biko, Mandela, Oliver Tambo; the hated pass laws, banning, and indeterminate detention. They had become members of the banned (in South Africa) African National Congress or ANC, the organization nominally headed by the then imprisoned Nelson Mandela. Then came their necessary exile in Lesotho.

Immediately after dinner, with boyish enthusiasm, they dragged me off to a local ANC meeting. We met in a small, dim room made opaque by cigarette smoke. About a dozen college-age men and women gathered around their American guest. The African women were crowned with Afros or tied-back hair; the men were slim and wore buttoned-down shirts with slacks. They talked politics with the serious and earnest demeanor of a university bull session. I was transported back to my college days reveling in the bond that ties together young intellectuals. When their talk moved on to discussion of friends in South Africa, friends who were currently in detention, friends who may or may not be alive, the superficial similarities between their lives and the one I had lived in college disappeared. None of my college friends were thrown in jail for airing political views; none were thrown out of a window on the tenth floor of John Voster Square for voicing a controversial opinion.

The next day, after sharing the floor of the one-room house with my two friends, I left Maseru and morphed from an honorary member of the ANC back into a naive American tourist. But, thanks to Steve Biko, I was beginning to see. Biko was one of those who died in detention at John Voster Square.

Durban sits on the South African coastline and is the largest Indian city outside the subcontinent. During the nineteenth century the British imported many indentured Indians to help work the large sugar plantations that dotted the subtropical coast of Zululand. Along with the manual laborers came an English-trained barrister named Mohandas Gandhi. It was in Durban that Gandhi set out on the path that would eventually lead him to be recognized as the *Mahatma*, or great soul. While living in South Africa for twenty-one years, Gandhi suffered from the racial inequities that would eventually be encoded into law in 1948 as apartheid. It was in South Africa that Gandhi first began his lifelong fight for equality and civil rights; it was in South Africa where Gandhi developed his nonviolent approach to injustice.

A few weeks after my experiences in Lesotho, my friends from the Mushroom House and I decided to rendezvous in Durban. A half dozen of us headed to the coast and took up residence in a cheap Durban hotel just off the beach and the warm Indian Ocean. It was "spring break in Florida," South African style. We hung out in town and, on those few days we weren't on the beach, explored the interior of Natal Province where the Zulu tribe held sway.

We met some Indian friends who worked in the computer industry. We talked shop, we partied, we talked women, and as always in 1980 South Africa, we talked politics. With two days left on our spring break-type vacation, we met our South African Indian friends at their apartment for one last blowout *jawl* (Afrikaans slang for party), drinking beer and smoking *dagga*. Rock music, the common international language of all young people, blasted nonstop until three A.M. We were having a *lekker* (Afrikaans slang for great, cool, unreal) time.

As things were winding down, in an exhausted, drunken, stoned haze, I leaned over to our host and suggested he and his friends meet us on the beach in front of our hotel the next afternoon. My friend froze. Conversation immediately stopped, and the entire local South African contingent turned to stare at me.

"What the hell is going on?" I whispered, my voice suddenly carrying across the now silent room. "Did I say something wrong?"

"You don't get it, do you?" my Indian friend scowled at me.

"What are you talking about?"

"Don't you realize the beach in front of your hotel is a White beach? Can't you understand that if we came to visit you at the beach, or in your hotel, we would be thrown in jail, you dumb shit?" I was stunned that he was pissed off at me. I thought I had started to take on the persona of a South African, and I had naively committed a terrible faux pas.

My computer friends were Indian, or in South African parlance, Asian. Asians were not allowed on White beaches, or in White hotels. They weren't even allowed on Black beaches (of which there were very few) or Black hotels. They were only allowed to frequent Asian Beaches and Asian Hotels. By simply sitting in their now unbearably tense apartment, we were technically breaking the law.

These folks were not African, people of a different culture, people who spoke a different language, people who lived in a different world. These were my co-workers, folks of my world. Yet, for some crazy reason we were not legally able to spend time together. This was absurd. This made no sense.

After an uncomfortable, sleepless night, I woke to a cloudless semitropical Sunday morning. The streets were mostly empty as most of the population was attending church. I decided to walk to a nearby café for a coffee. As I started down the deserted street the import of the previous night's events hit me hard, and I found myself suddenly running down a main street of the largest Indian town outside the subcontinent screaming at the top of my voice, as though possessed, "This country is fucked! This country is fucked!" I was as shocked as anyone at the spectacle created by the mad American. Fortunately, no one called the cops.

Returning from Durban I landed a three-month software-consulting gig with IBM. The firm was able to arrange a permanent resident visa for me. I settled into my new job, situated on the twenty-fourth floor of the tallest building in sub-Saharan Africa and began to take on the trappings of true expatriate in South Africa. I lived in Westdene, a middle class, officially White suburb of Johannesburg, the financial and business capital of South Africa. It could easily have been mistaken for a suburb of Atlanta. The streets were clean; the people were conservatively attired. American and European cars cruised its streets. There were no people of color.

I shared a modest three-bedroom house with three native South African friends: Roy, a jazz bassist, his girlfriend

Foosie, and an aspiring young actress named Elaine Proctor. My circle of friends had gradually transformed from a close-knit group of fellow backpack travelers into a community of South African artists, activists, and bohemians. My day life was very pedestrian. I got up at the same time every morning, took the local bus to work, wrote some code, took the same bus back home at five o'clock. However, after dinner, life changed dramatically.

Elaine was part of an acting troupe that performed at the Market Theatre in downtown Jo'burg. At that time, the Market Theatre was the only truly multiracial institution in South Africa. Within the confines of the small theater the rules of apartheid were relaxed. The government tolerated a mixing of the races and turned a blind eye to normally prohibited political discussion. The Market Theatre was an island of racial normalcy, liberal political ideology, and enormous artistic creativity. Despite, or perhaps because of, the extreme inequity that saturated South Africa, its arts flourished. Universally acclaimed writers such as Nobel Prize winners J M Coetzee and Nadine Gordimer produced highly politicized English language novels that skewered South African society. Talented novelists such as Andre Brink and Breyten Breytenbach created equally damning works in Afrikaans. Playwright Athol Fugard continued the assault on South African institutions with works that led him to be considered one of the great dramatists of the later twentieth century.

It was through Elaine, the Market Theatre, and my other South African friends that I was introduced to an alternative South Africa. In the evenings or on weekends Elaine and I would head to the Theatre. I would look on as the actors rehearsed their lines; the set builders swung their hammers, and musicians practiced their music. We talked about theater and literature. I was invited to join in wild improvisational jam sessions with respected jazz musicians. Within the cloistered confines, actors and staff, Black, White, Colored, and Asian, collaborated to produce piercing, sometimes brilliant dramas and comedies. The Theatre was quite literally the only place in the country where these activities were tolerated. I was anointed as an honorary American ambassador to the Theatre, and as such was able to participate in theater activities on a semiregular basis. Ironically, the Market Theatre was only a few minutes walk from John Voster Square.

After an evening stint at the theater, perhaps at midnight, a racially mixed group of us would illegally sneak into Soweto where we would head to an illicit black-run speakeasy called a *shebeen*. *Shebeens* formed the social core of life in black townships such as Soweto. (The term Soweto is itself an abbreviation of Southwest Township.) We drank and danced. We laughed and played music. As this was still South Africa we also engaged in countless political discussions. For me this was an opportunity to communicate with the black South African intellectual community. I formed friendships with black actors, writers, journalists, filmmakers, and academics. We talked about what an interracial South Africa would look like, one where ability was the entrée to a bright new world. A different, hopeful South Africa was indeed beginning to emerge from the oppressive political gloom.

One Saturday afternoon I happened to ask to Elaine how she got involved with the Market Theatre.

"Let me tell you a story," she said. "My father is a doctor and university professor. A few years ago, while teaching at a medical school in Durban, he became friendly with one of his students, a young black South African named Steven Biko. Even in his college days Biko was politically active. His charisma and eloquence touched everyone he encountered, including my dad. After he died in police custody, the Biko family asked my father, a neuropathologist, to represent their interests at the inquest. He performed the autopsy on Biko."

She paused, and when she resumed, tears were streaming down her face. "Ken, the cops beat the shit out him. I went to the trial; I saw the pictures. It was disgusting. Even though my dad testified that his death was due to a severe beating, the court found that no one was at fault. A few months after the trial my brother Andre joined the ANC. He was forced to flee to Botswana. I can't even tell you where in Botswana, it's too dangerous for you to know. There are no political innocents in South Africa. Rather than join the ANC, my reaction was to join the Market Theatre and channel my frustration and rage in a creative direction. Let something positive come out of Biko's murder."

In her place stood Steve Biko, smiling and calm.

Steven Biko was born in King William's Town on December 18, 1946. He was accepted as a student at the University of Natal Medical School (Black section). In 1972 Biko founded the Black People's Convention that led to the creation of the pan-African Black Consciousness Movement. Biko was first banned in 1973. He was re-arrested and interrogated four times between August 1974 and September 1977. Biko died under police custody on September 12 of that same year.

At first, South African authorities attributed his death to a self-imposed hunger strike. Under international pressure, led by his friend Donald Woods, the South African authorities allowed an inquest to be held. The Biko family requested that Biko's friend and teacher Neville Proctor serve as their representative at the inquest. The official result of the inquest was that Biko died of self-imposed brain trauma. No one was held responsible.

Biko's death created an international outcry that eventually led to the imposition of United Nations sanctions. A referendum to officially end apartheid was held on March 17, 1992. It passed with 68 percent of the white vote. On May 9, 1994, Nelson Mandela was elected President of South Africa. He

led the first multiracial government as the head of the previously outlawed ANC. This was an outcome that fourteen
years before, all South Africans, regardless of race, thought
was impossible to achieve.

Steve Biko and I have a long history. Although I never met
the man, his influence on me was profound. He guided me
through the confusing labyrinth of apartheid South Africa. He
drew me to my friends in Lesotho and their bitter exile from
their home country. He delivered an unexpected gut check
while partying in Durban. Apartheid was not a black problem; it was blight that demeaned all races. After absorbing
the pain of hate and bigotry that had relentlessly beaten down
my spirit, he relented, connected me to Elaine and opened my
eyes to the enormous creative potential and goodness of the
people that lay hidden behind the door of the Market Theatre.

Through the agony of his life, Biko taught me that good
people might be brought down to dark depths of cruelty and
fear. Yet, through his martyrdom, Biko also showed me that
hope is more powerful than despair and inculcated in me an
undying belief in the potential of humanity.

In November of 1980, I was offered a permanent job with IBM
along with South African citizenship. Psychologically exhausted
but spiritually enriched, I turned down the offer, and after living
for close to two years in South Africa, headed back to the U.S.

୬ଏ ୬ଏ ୬ଏ

*Ken Matusow is a Silicon Valley entrepreneur. Between technology
startups and consulting contracts, he takes off to explore the developing world, sometimes for months or years at a time. He also works
as a volunteer to assist technology companies in remote parts of the
globe. Working with groups such as Geek Corps and the International Executive Service Corp, he has assisted and advised technology companies in Bulgaria, Mongolia, South Africa, and West
Africa. He lives in Northern California with his wife, Barbara.*

ERIN BYRNE

✧ ✧ ✧

# Storykeepers

*Alchemy: A power or process of transforming something
common into something special; an inexplicable or
mysterious transmuting.* —Merriam-Webster Dictionary

*I haven't been a saint my whole life,
but I have done this one thing.*
—René Psarolis

As we crossed the Champs d'Élysées, I looked past
Rogier's blond curls and the rumbling beast of traffic
to the triumphal arch beyond, which held hushed shadows
and autumn sun inside its simple shape.

I saw Hitler cut a swath underneath.

I saw the photo of a boy, his shoulders hunched and hesi-
tant, his dark hair parted neatly but straining to spring out, a
wide nose, a shy smile tugging his lip a little up on one side
with the soft shadow of a dimple. What shouts out of the
image of this boy are his eyes, two pinpoints of light in sepia,
as round as eyes can be, as bold as eyes can be.

Hitler had only been in Paris for a day, but his dark forces occupied this boy's childhood.

"Will we recognize him, do you think?" Rogier asked as he loped along in a confident stride that day in October 2011. "I don't know," I said. But I knew I would. And I knew he would ask me about Ginette.

From the first time I went there in 2005, Paris exerted a pull on me. I didn't know if it was the memory of a crackly slide of the Arc de Triomphe on the wall of my high school French classroom, or the pace of Parisian life that matched my pulse, or the stone philosophers whispering secrets to me, but I felt compelled to return, as if there were something essential I needed to find there.

I had been to Paris twice when I read *Suite Française*, a novel written by Irène Némirovsky, a writer of Jewish descent who fled Paris when the Nazis marched in. This book evoked Paris during the occupation so starkly that I began to travel there two or three times a year to do research on that time period. I spent hours in museums with my nose pressed up against glass cases, examining photos, handwritten letters, and mementos of Résistance members. I trailed after historians scribbling details of Göring at the Ritz, or a school in the Marais where Jewish children had been marched out, or an apartment where an Allied soldier had been hidden. I strolled the stalls along the Seine looking for old magazines and books, and read everything I could get my hands on.

At this time, I wrote freelance travel stories and essays about culture, art and politics. I did not know why I fed this growing obsession with World War II Paris. It seemed to have nothing to do with me.

As Rogier and I crunched through red and yellow leaves toward Hotel Argenton, we reviewed our schedule. We would spend the rest of this day with our man. Tomorrow we would film Edouard on location on Boulevard Malesherbes and interview him in my apartment on Île Saint Louis. I glanced over at a sidewalk vendor's stand of vintage black and white postcards, and imagined the stark brutality of occupied Paris.

Edouard Duval was a business associate of my husband's who owned a factory in Gennevilliers, on the northern outskirts of Paris. He and his wife had become friends, and we would see each other several times a year in Paris or Seattle, where I lived. Edouard was tall, distinguished, balding, and reserved with a gentle wit.

I remembered one evening in 2007 when Edouard said he had a story he'd like me to see, the account of Frank "Kirby" Cowan from Arkansas, who his uncle had met during the war. Kirby was now a dear friend of Edouard's who he would visit each time he went to the U.S. Edouard thought I might want to write this story someday.

Kirby had been in a USAF B-17G flying over Paris in June 1944. The plane had been hit, and Kirby had parachuted down to land in a garden near the Aubert-Duval factory, which was at that time being run by Edouard's uncle, René Duval. Three teenage boys had shielded Kirby from the Germans as they rushed him over to the factory, where they hid him behind some barrels. Edouard's Uncle René drove Kirby to his own elegant apartment near the Arc de Triomphe for a few days, gave him a change of clothes (a pinstriped suit and wing-tipped shoes), then took him by métro to an apartment near Hôtel de Ville, on Boulevard Sebastopol.

In Paris in June 1944 anyone aiding an Allied airman would be tortured, then shot.

Inside this apartment lived Résistance members Georges Prevot (a policeman), his sister Ginette, and her husband Jean Rocher. They hid Kirby for a few weeks, along with downed Scottish airman James Stewart, who had been there for over a month. Kirby and James were both caught at a checkpoint on their way out of Paris, thrown into cells in Fresnes prison, and taken on the last train out of Paris to Buchenwald. Kirby was then moved to Germany where he was shuffled from one POW camp to the next. Finally, Patton himself marched in, just a few feet from Kirby, and liberated the camp.

Kirby arrived in a flotilla in the New York harbor, almost one year to the day after his plane had been hit, and returned to Arkansas to live a full life.

Because of all my research, I fit the story into its context. My first thought was, *This is a film*, as I could so easily see all the action. But I didn't know any filmmakers, so I put the story aside, and continued to write about Winged Victory, baguettes, and Parisian fashion.

As the years went by and I continued to travel to Paris, I'd stretch in my airplane seat during descent, look out the window, and imagine Kirby dangling from his parachute, floating down: *I can see the Seine River winding through Paris. The rooftops getting bigger . . .*

The part that tweaked me most about the story was a scene in the apartment on Boulevard Sebastopol: *We'd sit around the table drinking cognac and talking until late.* Ginette, the woman of the house, would have been the one who prepared the dinner and cultivated the ambiance. Something about this woman piqued my interest and held it.

I envisioned Ginette serving the best dinner she could manage on meager wartime rations—perhaps potatoes, a few carrots, maybe turnips—to the four men seated at a table, with a small amount of wine reflecting ruby circles through glasses onto a white lace cloth. I heard Kirby's halting French and George's booming laugh. I sensed the warmth Ginette may have felt at being able to create this mood even in such strained circumstances.

I felt the fire of cognac sneaking its way into each body.

In 2010, Edouard began to take me to the places in Kirby's story. He talked at length about Kirby, who had died the previous year. Edouard had gone to Arkansas to speak at his memorial service.

Edouard drove me out to the factory and showed me the area near the stairs where Kirby had been hidden by the three boys and rushed over to the factory where they had written "Unexploded Bomb" on some barrels to keep the Germans from checking there.

One cold day in January, he took me to 20 Boulevard Sebastopol. The pale green color of the door gave me the unexpected feeling that I'd found a rare ingredient. Above, the door was a plaque:

> Ici Habitaient
> JEAN ROCHER
> Et le gardien de la paix
> GEORGES PREVOT
> Patriotes arretés par la Gestapo
> Le il aout pour faits de Résistance
> Puis déportes dans les camps
> d'extermination, ou ils sont morts.
> n'oublions pas!

Where, I wondered, was Ginette when this happened? Had she come home one day to find her brother and husband gone, along with whoever they had been hiding at the time? I imagined her turning the key in the lock and climbing five flights of stairs with the unsettling feeling she must have had every time she came home. Had she opened the door to find chairs upside down and curtains rustling in the breeze? Or had they taken her as well—some German soldier snatching her arm at the elbow and twisting it as he pulled her down the stairs?

I touched the pale green door and a chill slid down the back of my neck. Why was Ginette not mentioned on this plaque?

The next fall, at a small seminar in France, I met Rogier van Beeck Calkoen, a Dutch filmmaker who was interested in making short films of several of my stories.

The week after I returned from this seminar, I received an email from Joe Cowan, Kirby's son. Edouard had told him about me years before. I phoned Kirby's wife, Cloteen, who said he had not discussed his war experience much until his later years when he had been contacted by a Frenchman putting together a reunion at the factory in Gennevilliers.

The next time I was in Paris, Edouard told me about René Psarolis.

René had been seven years old in June 1944. One evening, in June of 1944, he was walking down his street, rue de la Chapelle, when he heard a deafening roar. He looked up and saw a ball of silver roar overhead and explode nearby. Flames shot into the air as he ran toward the scene. René saw a German, the first he had seen up close, moving three dead bodies into a truck.

This moment shattered René's boyhood innocence.

All through the Liberation celebrations two months later, this boy ran after the trucks, cheering and waving at American soldiers who tossed out candies and gifts. He thought of the men on that plane. He imagined them alive.

René grew up and moved away, and gradually realized that all the men in that plane, even those who might have parachuted down, had probably been caught by Germans and shot. He returned to Paris for a visit in December 1966, when he was in his twenties. He went out walking one dim and drizzly afternoon, and found himself in his old neighborhood. He continued walking as if pulled, and came to a stop in front of something. Through the gray mist, a plaque slowly came into focus.

> à la memoire des 3 américans
> qui le 22 juin 1944
> ont fait le sacrifice de leur vie

pour que leur avion désemparé
ne tomb pas sur les habitations les cheminots des gares
de pajol et de la vilette
reconnaissants

The bomber had veered to avoid the train station, thus many lives had been saved. Who were the three dead Americans he had seen? How many had been in the crew? Had there been others who had fallen out of the plane, or even parachuted down into Paris?

René heard a voice very distinctly say into his ear, "Don't forget us."

This moment caused a change inside René. He began to travel frequently to Paris from the U.K., where he now lived. His family trailed behind him as he perused bookstalls on the Seine looking for old magazines and newspapers containing any news of the crash. He frequented the national library in the Marais, charming the librarian into retrieving boxes of documents from back rooms.

René's questions had transformed into a quest.

Gradually, René pieced it all together. The crew had consisted of ten men. The three he had seen were Lieutenant Jay H. Horn, pilot, Technical Sergeant Henry G. Morris, and Staff Sergeant Anthony L. Moncaco. Bodies had landed all over Paris and the surrounding area: Bois Colombes, Saint Ouen, Clichy, Gennevilliers.

He contacted historian Claude Foucher, who told him there were two survivors: Steve Manzek and Frank "Kirby" Cowan. René could not believe it: two of his heroes were alive.

René put advertisements in newspapers calling for eyewitnesses and contacted officials in the towns where the bodies had landed. He pinpointed the areas where the two survivors had landed, Steve in Saint Ouen and Kirby in Gennevilliers. He located the three teenage boys who had rescued Kirby. He found the current owner of the factory in

Gennevilliers, the nephew of the man who had taken him to the elegant apartment and given him the pinstriped suit: Edouard Duval.

"He saw the plane crash in his neighborhood and has made it his life's mission to collect all the stories of the crew members," Edouard told me. "He is the one who contacted me and told me about the actions of my uncle. I never would have known about it otherwise."

I emailed René and received this reply: *Bonjour Erin, The crash of the aircraft in my neighborhood has been with me since the age of seven and has stayed with me all this time. It is as clear today as it was then . . .*

I wrote back asking if he would send me the details. I asked if he had found anything about the Résistance members in that apartment, especially Ginette. I told him about the persistent questions I had about her. René hadn't found much about that. He had focused his research on the crew, and offered to send me "a few documents." I received packet after packet of photos, telegrams, eyewitness accounts, letters, and newspaper clippings.

This man's meticulous collection of specifics brought these American soldiers to life. René sent pages out of the co-pilot's journal in which FO John J. Murray wrote a few weeks before the crash as he lay sprawled on the grass near the B-17G:

*. . . in a few hours I would be five miles above—in the cold, steely blue of enemy skies. Up there the temperature is 30, 40, or 50 degrees below zero; our planes struggle to fly in the super thin air that causes the weird vapor trails to swirl from the screaming propellers. Without life-giving oxygen man will die in a matter of minutes at this altitude. This is an ethereal world, high above the dazzling white cloud banks, high above the world of man. Men were not made to live up there. Some would die up there today. I might be one of them.*

Murray had landed, dead, in a wheelbarrow in Saint Ouen. René sent me eyewitness accounts of people telling how they stood in front of the body and refused to let the Germans take it. The people wrapped John Murray's body carefully (they all agreed he had very clean fingernails), brought flowers, and sang *"La Marseillaise."*

René collected the details, yes—this body landed on the roof of a theater in Clichy, that one fell out of the plane and landed in the street in Gennevilliers, another shot in the air as he descended toward Asnières. But what René Psarolis did next changed him even more: he began to give these stories to the people who needed them most.

In 1997, René telephoned Steve Manzek and Kirby Cowan back in the States and invited them to Paris for reunions and ceremonies.

He took Steve to the place where he had landed in Saint Ouen, a back alley where people had given him cognac and signaled the V for victory sign. Steve had sauntered down the street waving and flashing back the sign, two fingers spread under his nose. He had immediately been captured and gone on to endure a nightmare scenario out of which he was lucky to emerge alive.

René took Kirby to the garden where he had landed in Gennevilliers, and introduced him to those three teenage boys who had rescued him, now men in their 60s. He presented Edouard, who held a ceremony and reception at the factory. Kirby went back to the apartment on Boulevard Sebastopol and saw the plaque above the green door.

"All I've said for the past fifty years," said Steve in a televised interview filmed then in which a starstruck René translates, "is that I wanted to go back to the place where I landed."

Kirby nodded and mouthed the word, *closure.* René looked at him, and his smile held something of the boy.

René had plaques put up all over Paris to mark the landing positions of the men. A plaque was placed underneath the one René had come upon that day in 1966, listing the names of the ten crew members, and others were erected in Saint Ouen, Bois-Colombes, Gennevilliers.

René worked with Kirby and Steve to find the families of the crew and invited them to come to Paris.

The widow and grown son of Henry Morris came. Morris was one of those who had gone down with the plane, one of the dead bodies that seven-year-old boy had seen. Morris's son, who had been a baby when his father had gone off to war, had buried his face in the foliage near the plaque and sobbed.

Bob Murray, the co-pilot, John's brother, thanked the people of Saint Ouen for the care they had shown his brother. Two of the women who had been twelve years old at the time opened a bottle of pink champagne. He said that yes, his brother had always kept his fingernails clean.

Not all the families were found. There is a plaque on a street in Bois Colombes, where Anthony Vigliante, an Italian from New York, landed, dead. Perhaps one day a family member of his will stand in front of it.

Everything René sent me I sent to Rogier. Gradually, it dawned on both of us that René was our real story. We agreed to focus on him in the film, and I decided to write a novel based on him.

René phoned me one day. "Something you wrote made me know I could trust you with this story. It's why I sent you all these documents and photos," he said. "You want to know about Ginette. I don't know much about that part of the story, but I know you will find out."

René agreed to meet Rogier and me in Paris.

That sunny day in October we walked into Hotel d'Argenton
and waited a few minutes in the small lobby. All we had to
go on was the old, sepia photo. The minute René walked
through the door we recognized him by his round, dark eyes
under heavy French lids, shining with the same eagerness in
his seventies as they had at the age of seven.

He unfolded his own story for us. When René met Kirby
and Steve for reunions and ceremonies in 1997 and the following years, these events had been a highlight of his life, for these
were his heroes. He said often that he knew he would not
have survived another winter if not for the Allies. I believed
him: by June of 1944, no meat had come into Paris for eight
months, and children were not growing. People had died of
cold the previous winter.

René's most lasting memory is a night at the Ivy Hotel
when he and Kirby stayed up talking. It must have been four
or five in the morning, he said.

We filmed him telling the story of the crash, lapsing
into childhood phrases. We filmed him in the library in the
Marais, and on the streets of Paris. We filmed Edouard outside his Uncle René's apartment, telling the story of how his
uncle took Kirby on the metro to Boulevard Sebastopol, and
how, when Kirby raised his arm to hold onto a strap, his GI-
issued wristwatch nearly gave him away to two Germans sitting nearby. We filmed Edouard and René reminiscing about
their friend Kirby.

"I was just a little guy who didn't want to let go," said our
Storykeeper.

For his collection and sharing of these stories, René was
awarded the medal for Veterans of Foreign Wars from the
United States.

These days, René emails often, and sometimes telephones me.
We discuss the film, which is finished and currently being

shown in film festivals throughout the world, and my progress on the book. But, like a golden apple dangling from the
thread of a branch, the question hangs.

"What have you found, my little one? About Ginette?"

René recognizes the pull of her story on me. He knows
the inner alchemy that creates a quest. He offers advice and
encouragement, and often challenges me: "You can probably find traces of her brother Georges at the gendarmerie."
"This is how you get people to retrieve extra documents; you
must be bold." "I see you have this photo on your website, is
this her?" He has taught me how to pursue a story, collect
scattered fragments, and gather details. But there's one more
thing René Psarolis inspires me to do.

In addition to *Storykeepers*, I am working on a novel, *The
Red Notebook*, about Parisians in the Résistance who hid
Americans—one woman in particular who lives with her
brother and husband on Boulevard Sebastopol. It's possible to
work on both books at once because I spent years doing the
research.

When I am done with both books, what I would most like
to do is to find a distant relative of Ginette's, someone connected with her somehow, who has never heard the details
of her actions. When I meet that person, whom for some
reason I think is a young woman, I envision inviting her to
my apartment in Paris and sharing these stories with her.

I will tell her that I tracked down and contacted James
Stewart, the Scotsman who was with Kirby in the apartment
with the green door. James told me that as he was shuffled
along in Fresnes prison a few days after being caught, he
looked down a long hallway to see Georges, Jean, and Ginette.
On the same day her brother and husband were taken to
Buchenwald, where they would be killed, Ginette was taken
to Ravensbrük, and remained there until the end of the war.
Then James found her a job as an au pair in his village in

Scotland, and settled her in a cottage near his own for a few years before she eventually returned to France and died.

This young woman and I will talk about the meaning of the phrase on the plaque outside 20 Boulevard Sebastopol, *N'oublions pas*: Do not forget. I will ask her if she has stories she can't forget or questions that persist and answers she seeks. Then we will sit around the table drinking cognac and talking until late.

- Lieutenant Jay H. Horn, pilot: Down with plane.

- First Officer John J. Murray, co-pilot: Body landed in wheelbarrow in St. Ouen. People wrapped his body, sang "*Le Marseillaise.*"

- Lieutenant Steve J. Manzck, navigator. Upside down in plane. Landed in St. Ouen. Captured. Died, 2003.

- Lieutenant Harry O. Ubbins: Landed on rooftop in Clichy. Broken ankle. Captured. Died 1987.

- Technical Sergeant Henry G. Morris, aircraft engineer: Down with plane.

- Technical Sergeant Frank K. Cowan, radio operator gunner: Landed Gennevilliers. Passed through Paris. Caught at checkpoint leaving Paris. Fresnes, Buchenwald, POW camp in Germany. Died 2009.

- Staff Sergeant Anthony L. Monaco: Down with plane.

- Staff Sergeant Anthony F. Vigliante: Body landed in Bois Columbes.

- Staff Sergeant Lester N. Weimer: Died in plane. Body fell out and landed in Gennevilliers.

- Sergeant Clifford N. Mc Creary: Shot in the air. Landed badly wounded at Asnières (south of Gennevilliers). Taken by German patrol to Beaujon Hospital in Clichy. Died of his wounds in the early hours, June 23.

- A third survivor, Lieutenant Harry O. Ubbins, died in 1987, before René learned the details of the crash.

❧  ❧  ❧

*Erin Byrne writes travel essays, short stories, poems, and screenplays. Her work has won numerous awards, including 2013 and 2012 Travelers' Tales Grand Prize silver and bronze Solas Awards for Best Travel Story of the Year, and appears in a wide variety of publications, including* World Hum, Vestoj, Burning the Midnight Oil, *and The Best Travel Writing anthologies. Erin is the writer of* The Storykeeper, *an award-winning film about occupied Paris. She is occasional guest instructor at Shakespeare and Company Bookstore in Paris, and is co-editor of* Vignettes & Postcards From Paris, *an anthology of writings from the bookstore, first in a series. Erin is currently working on* Wings From Victory, *a collection of her travel stories about France,* Vignettes & Postcards From Morocco, *and her novel,* The Storykeeper of Paris. *Her screenplay* Siesta *will be filmed in Spain in 2015.* www.e-byrne.com.

MICHAEL SHAPIRO

☙ ☙ ☙

# In Search of
# Dylan Thomas

The elusive poet brought Wales to the modern world.

"This is not a museum," says Annie Haden, the vivacious Dylan Thomas enthusiast who has restored the Welsh poet's childhood home in Swansea, an industrial city on Wales' south coast. "I'm the oldest thing in this house!"

About sixty years old, Annie, who tells me to call her by her first name, is displaying some Welsh hyperbole—she's not the oldest thing in this loving memorial of Wales' best-loved English-language poet. There's a typewriter from the 1920s, colorful drawings based on phrases from Thomas' poetry, antique copper kettles, even oblong filament lightbulbs that looked like something fashioned by Thomas Edison.

But she's right—it's not a museum. Annie, who has spent years refurbishing Thomas's first home, is intent on making this a living, breathing house, a place where the writer's admirers can eat, drink, recite poetry, play music, and stay the night.

"Would you like a drink?" she asks me. "It is a Thomas house after all."

When I visited, the nation of Wales was gearing up to celebrate the centennial of Thomas' 1914 birth, so I thought I'd
explore the coastal homes where he wrote and found solace,
the beaches that made his spirit soar, and perhaps a favorite
pub or bookstore. Like many of his countrymen, I appreciate Thomas' work, though I can't say I fully comprehend it
all. I'm hoping that visiting places that shaped and inspired
him will give me a deeper understanding of the artist and his
words.

Thomas, who died before his fortieth birthday, is often
remembered as much for his excessive drinking and woman-
izing as for his art, but his poems, including "Do not go gentle
into that good night" which he wrote for his dying father,
have stood the test of time.

> And I fly over the trees and chimneys of my town, over the dock-
> yards, skimming the masts and funnels . . . over the trees of the
> everlasting park . . . over the yellow seashore and the stone-chasing
> dogs and the old men and the singing sea. The memories of child-
> hood have no order, and no end.
> —Reminiscences of Childhood

Located in the Uplands suburb of Swansea, Dylan Thomas'
birthplace is a handsome Edwardian two-story house on
the steep part of Cwmdonkin Drive. Out front attached to
the white stucco facade is a simple round plaque reading:
"DYLAN THOMAS, A man of words, 1914-1953, was born
in this house."

I arrive on a rainy afternoon a few hours after touching
down at London's Heathrow; the brick-red tiles in the entry-
way are so worn they're noticeably bowed. "We didn't want
to restore it because it's part of the history of the house,"
Annie says.

She puts a polished copper kettle on the stove. The time
between the great wars, when young Dylan grew up, Annie
says, was an "era when people never got rid of stuff like old
copper kettles. People see relics and say, 'My gran had one of

those.' That's what brings 'em right in." As we talk over tea about the home's restoration, I can tell Annie loves words as much as Thomas did. "I'm a stripper," she says, pausing for effect, "and scrubber of wood."

We climb a wide and time-smoothed wooden stairway to the upper floor and peer out the window of the back bedroom. Annie recalls Thomas' poetic phrase about "ships sailing across rooftops." In the bedroom once shared by Dylan's parents, she points toward a row of houses, the Bay of Bristol in the distance. Because of the sloping hill down to the sea, it appears that boats bob atop Swansea's roofs. "You get it," Annie says, "when you see the view."

In Dylan's little room, illuminated by an antique gas lamp, a collectable copy of *A Child's Christmas in Wales* sits on a small table. Lines from that book are painted on the walls. Annie asks if I notice anything. I read the lines and ask if one might have a mistake. She brightens and says there's not just one mistake but several "because there's nothing more empowering for a child than to say to an adult, 'you've got it wrong.'"

She looks me up and down and asks, "How tall are you?" I tell her five-five. "Well then, you're a half inch taller than Dylan." I concede I'm really five-four-and-a-half. She seems pleased that I'm the same height as her beloved bard.

"I know Dylan," she says. "I'm his mother now." Then Dylan's mother retreats to the kitchen to bring out lamb "that's come nine miles to be with us tonight," fresh pastry-crusted salmon from the nearby River Tawe, potatoes, and a divine bottle of French Cotes du Rhone. Later she'll top off the feast with a fresh-baked rhubarb-fruit tart.

I suggest the house is a labor of love, but Annie is quick to correct me. "It's a labor born of frustration," she says. "This boy of ours hasn't been acknowledged and he should be."

Annie says I can choose where I'll sleep and invites me to stay in Dylan's tiny boyhood room. But the room is barely bigger than the single bed, so I opt for the guest room at the front of the house, which young Dylan called the "best room."

Overlooking Cwmdonkin Park, where Dylan's legs and imagination ran free, the spacious best room has a fireplace and brass candlesticks, a sink with a pitcher for wash water, a photo of Dylan and his wife, and a little crib. A book of Thomas' poems waits on the nightstand.

> Do not go gentle into that good night,
> Old age should burn and rave at close of day;
> Rage, rage against the dying of the light.
>
> And you, my father, there on the sad height,
> Curse, bless, me now with your fierce tears, I pray.
> Do not go gentle into that good night.
> Rage, rage against the dying of the light.

His parents' first language was Welsh, but Dylan was raised speaking English so he would not sound working class, Annie says. Dylan took elocution lessons to get rid of his Welsh accent and read poems in the bathroom to train his voice because he realized it's "not just what you say but how you say it."

Many of Wales' early and modern poets write in a strict-meter form of Welsh, but Thomas became internationally known because he wrote so eloquently in English. Yet it was Thomas' undeniable, intrinsic Welshness that gave his poetry so much strength, Annie says. "The meter and structure is old Welsh in form and the English loved it."

Annie tells me that Thomas wrote hundreds of poems in this house, with his greatest output coming between the ages of sixteen and twenty. He worked in the morning and drank late, Annie says. Unfortunately Thomas couldn't hold his alcohol, perhaps because he's now believed to have been a diabetic, so he became a "performing monkey," she says.

"Obnoxious behavior became his calling card. In London he was a performer. That's not creative, and it's tiring. He had to keep coming back and recharging here—not just this house, this town," she says. "He'd say when he was on the train to London (that) he wasn't going to England, he was leaving Wales. He was leaving his heart, he was leaving his safety."

Like a protective mother, Annie denies that Thomas was an alcoholic. There's "such a lot of work of such high quality that alcoholism is not considered." I refrain from listing all the great writers who overindulged in alcohol. Annie refills my glass with Cotes du Rhone, and I ask about Thomas' most famous poem, "Do not go gentle into that good night" written as Dylan's father, a frustrated poet, lay dying.

"Listen to it from a child's point of view," Annie says. "His father wouldn't give Dylan the words he needed like 'well done' or 'I'm proud of you.' The work between father and son wasn't finished."

Keri Finlayson, a poet and frequent visitor to No. 5 Cwmdonkin Drive, tells me that young Dylan sat upstairs and listened to the sounds of voices floating up through the vents of his two-story home. "I like the thought of words flowing around static objects," she says. "I think of the boy in this tiny room, or in the bath learning to project" his voice.

Annie tidies up the kitchen, shows me how to turn up the heat, then bids me goodnight. I'm alone in the room where Dylan Thomas was born, his words on the nightstand for company.

The next morning I stroll along the lush byways of Cwmdonkin Park, where a dead tree standing more than thirty feet high has been carved into the shape of a pencil to honor the bard who grew up across the street.

At Swansea's Dylan Thomas Centre, a stone's throw from the Bristol Channel, are photos of long lists of words Thomas compiled as he wrote. He placed scrolls of rhyming words before himself like an artist's palette, selecting just the right shade for the meaning he wished to convey.

Audio recordings play in corners of the center. As I listen I understand that, similar to James Joyce, the best way to comprehend Thomas is to hear his work read aloud, ideally in his own voice.

Thomas' work has been called "thrillingly incomprehensible," but I can hear what the Welsh call *hiraeth*, an ineffable longing, and it all starts to make sense. Read aloud, Thomas' poetry becomes music. Which makes me think that Bob Dylan, who took his name from the Welsh bard, is his natural heir: a musician who turns songs into poetry.

Now that most of Swansea's industries have declined, the city no longer harbors the smokestack stench of Dylan's time, but still I'm eager to explore the places to which he escaped as a teen. He called his bohemian group of friends the Kardomah Gang—they took their name from the café where they gathered.

In summer, the ruffians would camp out for a week or two by Rhossili Bay, drinking in the fresh air, clear night sky and copious amounts of ale and whiskey. Today the place attracts ice-cream-cone-toting families who hike among the bleating sheep on the lush green bluffs, gazing out at the broad crescent of sand and a pair of islands called Worm's Head, accessible by a land bridge for less than an hour at low tide.

> When I think of that concentrated muttering and mumbling and intoning, the realms of discarded lists of rhyming words, the innumerable repetitions and revisions and how at the end of an intensive five hour stretch (from 2-7) prompt as clockwork, Dylan would come out very pleased with himself saying he had done a good days work, and present me proudly with one or two or three perhaps fiercely belaboured lines.
> —Caitlin Thomas, Dylan's wife

When Thomas was twenty-three he left the sanctuary of his family's Swansea home and moved to another seaside abode, a place he called the Boathouse in Laugharne (pronounced Lahrn) overlooking Wales' west coast. Walking up a stone path on a drizzly morning, I first arrive at his "word-splashed hut" perched like a bird's nest on a cliff above the sea.

The converted shed where Thomas created some of his best work was exposed to Wales' tempestuous storms and crashing ocean sounds. The room remains a churning sea of manuscripts, discarded drafts of verse, empty cigarette packs and literary journals.

Farther up the stone path is the house where Dylan, his wife Caitlin and their children lived. It feels like a small ship, with low doorways (five and half feet high, just enough for Thomas). The house has been converted into a homey museum, called The Dylan Thomas Boathouse at Laugharne. In the parlor is a grand radio from the 1930s. While Thomas was traveling—to London, New York or Paris—his children would gather round the radio and listen to their father recite his poetry and stories on the BBC.

At the front desk I meet Maggie Richards, who grew up in Laugharne in the 1950s. She tells me Thomas' play for voice, "Under Milk Wood," which has been called "Ulysses in 24 hours," was based mostly on Laugharne. Thomas changed the name to Llareggub, which spelled backwards is Bugger-all. The first performance of the play in Laugharne was in 1958, she says.

"That's how I got interested as a small child—I used to go and see these," Richards says. After a time the community stopped performing the play, but the Laugharne Players regrouped in 2006. "We're doing it again this August," says Richards, who directed the play in 2009, "but if half the players can't be there, it might be a one-woman show."

The scent of baking draws me to the basement kitchen where two young women are making *bara brith*, a lightly sweet Welsh bread. I ask about it, and they cut me a slice to taste, on the house. Walking back down the rain-slickened path, I head to Brown's Hotel which housed one of Thomas' favorite pubs. He spent so much time there he gave the pub's phone as his contact number, but the hotel was closed for renovations.

Nearby is Corran's Books in a weathered stone building with a bright blue door. Owner George Tremlett, author of a biography of Caitlin Thomas, says Laugharne is where Dylan Thomas matured as a writer.

"His early work wasn't very good" Tremlett says. "It was here that he found whatever it was he needed to make the mix." What made this town so right for Thomas? "It's an egalitarian town," Tremlett says. "The rich man counts for very little here. And it's very easy going—I think that fitted him like a glove."

In his last years Thomas and his family moved to New Quay, a seaside resort that has created the Dylan Thomas Trail, a set of sights related to the poet. Number 8 is May's Designs where the owner, a young ebullient woman named May Hopkins, has painted Thomas quotations on the walls. "When one burns one's bridges," reads a Thomas line, "what a nice fire it makes." Another says: "He who seeks rest finds boredom, he who seeks work finds rest." Says Hopkins: "That's up for the girls who work here so they can take the hint."

The shop sells driftwood, paintings, and photos of Dylan and Caitlin. Hopkins is proud that Thomas lived in her town. "I do like his work," she says, "but I don't understand a lot of it."

I walk along a concrete pier and look out to the "fishing-boat bobbing sea" that inspired Thomas in his last years. A lone bottlenose dolphin gracefully arcs above the water, a seal clasps a silver fish that flaps in vain.

> It is the measure of my individual struggle from darkness toward some measure of light.
>
> —"Poetic Manifesto"

Before leaving Wales I attend a lunch with Thomas' grand-daughter, Hannah Ellis, who says that Dylan "clearly had a very happy childhood." However his world was shattered in February 1941 after the German blitz leveled much of Swansea, leaving 230 dead and 7,000 people homeless in mid-winter. "Our Swansea is dead," he writes in "Return Journey," a BBC radio play. The play isn't simply an elegy for his hometown, Ellis said, it's his attempt to rebuild Swansea with his words.

Like Annie Haden, Ellis believes her grandfather hasn't received the recognition he deserves. She hopes the upcoming centennial celebrations will change that and introduce a new generation to his work. "When I tell someone I'm Dylan Thomas' granddaughter," Ellis says, "I don't want them to say 'Who?'"

After almost a week in Dylan Thomas' Wales, I have a much better sense of the poet, but there's one last place I feel compelled to visit: the stately National Library of Wales in Aberystwyth, where some of Thomas' possessions remain. I sit with a curator, with the delightfully Welsh name of Ifor Ap Dafydd, in a high-ceilinged room. Ap Dafydd shows me a map of downtown Swansea that Thomas drew, a betting slip with odds on horses, a Pan American airline ticket, and a letter to his uncle thanking him for a gift and praising the Disney movie *Dumbo*.

The curator then unwraps a leather wallet containing Thomas' passport. "Can I hold it?" I ask. Ap Dafydd hesitates, then consents. I slowly turn the yellowed pages and see stamps for France, Italy, and Iran, where Thomas traveled in 1951 to write a script for the Anglo Iranian Oil Company.

Then there's the final stamp: a New York entry into the U.S. in 1953, where, five days after allegedly boasting he'd knocked back "eighteen whiskeys, a record," Thomas died at St. Vincent's Hospital.

After that last stamp, the better part of the passport is blank, no mark of a return to Britain. I survey the grand room in this house of words that Thomas helped build. "So many empty pages," I say in a low voice as a wave of sadness washes over me. "So many pages left unfilled."

*Michael Shapiro is author of* A Sense of Place: Great Travel Writers Talk About Their Craft, Lives, and Inspiration *and writes about travel and entertainment for* National Geographic Traveler, Islands *and* American Way. *The Dylan Thomas story appeared in the* Washington Post *and his stories about Wales, Peru and Guatemala, and interviews with Jane Goodall and Studs Terkel can be found at www.michaelshapiro.net*

≈ ≈ ≈

# Found

When Slovakian men in sunglasses know your name.

A tiny maroon Vauxhall pulls to the side of the road
ahead of me and taps its horn twice. I hoist my backpack with sunburned hands and jog behind my long shadow
to the back of the sedan. A middle-aged man in military high-
top wingtips steps from the driver's side and speaks to me in
what I presume to be Czech. Not that it makes any difference
if it's Czech, Polish, or Hungarian. I am The Young American
In Europe, he who only ever knows one language. This man
looks like the Slavic version of Humphrey Bogart: short and
serious-looking, he boasts the same formidable forehead lines
and brooding black mob-eyes. I shrug, feeling guilty about
my linguistic shortcomings and try to pronounce my hitching destination, "Zilina?" Bogart furrows his brow into great
trenches, confused. I pronounce "Zilina" three more ways
before he snaps into understanding, "Ahhhhhh Jii-leee-na,"
he gives a curt nod. Opening the trunk, he throws my backpack in.

This is my first ride in two days of hitchhiking in eastern Czech Republic, the borderlands of Slovakia. I should
be ecstatic, kissing Bogart's wingtips in gratitude, but I am
edgy. My fear is not of thumbing in a strange country or of

my rapidly dwindling cash funds. Nor is it from having no second languages except the words I butcher from a pocket Euro phrasebook. I am not even bothered about hopping in the car with Slovakian Humphrey Bogart even if he does turn out to be the gun-running proprietor of a gambling den in Casablanca. These are accepted risks. But I am scared about the tent.

Until a recent drought of rides, I had been traveling with my brother, Joe. We had hitched the length of six countries without too much trouble. (Admittedly Belgium is three hours border-to-border. We'd squandered a week there developing a taste for Belgian blondes.) We had little trouble getting rides in western Europe. As long as we had showered in the past seven days, someone would stop for us within an hour or so, and sometimes we didn't even have to stick out our thumbs. Folks we rode with occasionally offered us a place to stay, an extra bed or a floor. But most nights, we hiked outside town to illegally pitch our bright yellow tent in woods by the highway, on farms, or in public parks. Our sworn mission was to travel without trains, buses, planes, hotels, hostels, or even campgrounds. Since Joe had just graduated college and I still had two years to go, we were content roughing it to save what little money we had. And we wanted the dirtbag cred, to stuff our greedy pockets with stories and taste the road in all its sun and filth, even if that meant eating Nutella sandwiches and canned sardines three times a day.

Our destination was the northern mountains of Slovakia. An international hitchhiker's gathering was being held in a town called Liptovský Mikuláš, and we planned to hitch every mile there from our start in Cork, Ireland. The troubles came east of Prague. We were quickly introduced to the Stoic Slavic Driver, a genotype of the eastern European races that involves but is not limited to a) scowling deeply while b) driving with the fierce concentration of a military general.

The Stoic Slavic Driver wholly lacks the patience and the frivolous inclination to look at the foolish hitchhiker on the side of the road. Because surely that fool is either some half-wit tourist, a bottom-feeding cling-on, or a gypsy. Joe and I just happened to be two of the three. So perhaps we'd over-drawn on our celestial luck, and being stranded was exactly what we deserved. But just desserts don't curb indignation. After the second full day of fruitless thumbing on a busy road populated by hopelessly Stoic Slavic Drivers, our nerves and patience were scarce. We decided it would be expedient to split up and meet in the next town over—Zilina. "Meet at the entrance of the highway E50," we agreed, looking at a desper-ately wrinkled and stained map of Slovakia. This simplistic resolution was rash: neither Joe nor I had a cell phone. We each carried half of the tent so if we didn't rendezvous by sunset we'd have either a bag of poles or the skin of a tent to sleep with. Also, neither of us really knew where Zilina was, let alone the entrance to the E50, or that Zilina is one of the biggest cities in Slovakia. However, if we were in the habit of considering complications, we wouldn't have been stranded in Eastern Europe. So for the first time in months, we split up.

The first ride is with Humphrey Bogart. He ushers me to the rear of his tiny maroon Vauxhall and opens the door with the grim ceremony of an English butler. In the rear are two young girls, probably Bogart's daughters. One is sitting in a car seat, maybe two years old, and the other looks ten or eleven. The younger one looks up at me with off-angle pigtails, gives me the kind of delightful toothy smile possessed only by chil-dren, then goes immediately back to chewing the face off her Kermit the Frog doll. The older girl has fake red fingernails and offers me a coy smile. Bogart tells the older one to make room and I cram in, conscious for the first time in weeks that my b.o. is probably at mummifying-corpse levels. A woman in the front seat, by her looks the mother, turns around and smiles at me. "Ahoy," I say, feeling like an idiot. Strange hello for a landlocked country. The mother says a few more words to me, but Bogart addresses her in Czech, probably something like, "He doesn't know shit," and the mother laughs and stops talking. We grind gears into first, and I wonder how long it will be before I see Joe again.

The Kermit the Frog doll speaks Czech in his obligatory kazoo-like Wisconsin accent, but his batteries are low so his voice begins to deepen into what sounds to me like a Russian KGB officer. Mother lights a cigarette, props one foot onto the dashboard and begins painting her toenails, alternately green and blue. Some eastern European version of Raffi plays through buzzing speakers while Bogart and his wife talk. The language is guttural and staccato, beautiful. Pigtails sinks her teeth into KGB Kermit's eyeball. The older girl with the red fingernails turns to me and asks, "How are you?" in heavily accented English. I smile broadly, grateful to hear English even if this is all she knows. "I'm great," I say. "How are you?" She smiles and gives me a thumbs up. The girl's broken English is amazingly good. She tells me her name is Sabina. She has taken two years of English in school. Her vocabulary is limited and she takes a long time forming sentences, but she knows enough to talk at length. Sabina tells me her mother is from Poland and her father is from Romania, but she and her little sister were born in Slovakia and the Czech Republic.

"So you know at least three languages, not including English?" I ask her. She nods. I had never been more ashamed to be a native-speaking English major. Then she asks the question I hoped she wouldn't.

"And what languages do you know?" I hang my head and hold up one finger. She is as astonished at my handicap as I am by this young polyglot. Bogart turns around and asks Sabina something. She turns to me. "My dad wants to know where you have been in the Czech Republic."

"Well," I say, preparing to butcher all place names, "I was in Plzen, Velké Meziříčí, Brno, Olomouc, Prague—"

"Aaaahhh" Bogart interrupts, shaking his head, "Prague shit." The mother and I laugh. Pigtails laughs wildly, seeing her mother laugh.

"Sorry," Red Fingernails whispers, "the only English word he knows is 'shit.' He's like a child." Bogart consults Red Fingernails again. She sighs and turns to me, "Dad wants to know what kind of Czech beers you have had."

"Well," I say, "I really loved Pilsner Urquell and Primus." Bogart nods approval in the rearview mirror. "Ummm, I had Staropramen—"

"Nooooooo!" Bogart breaks in. He smiles, pausing for dramatic effect, "Star-o-pra-men shit," he exclaims, hitting the steering wheel with every syllable.

I am dropped off in the empty lot of a sprawling industrial park outside Zilina. I thank the family with another of my few words of Czech, and they drive off waving. Miraculously, I find an entrance to the E50 by walking in a random direction through parking lots and abandoned strip malls. But no Joe. I know that I am probably on the outskirts of the city, that the E50 is nothing but a beltway with a dozen entrances. The gray city sprawls into the skyline ahead. I shake my head, beginning to grasp the stupidity of our plan. I sit for a moment and wait for the dread of uncertainty to creep over me like a cold sweat. But I feel nothing. If anything, I feel light, cool, even elated. This is my first time away from Joe in months, and I am giddy with aloneness.

My shadow is long, and I chuckle at my options for the night's accommodation: overgrown cement planters in front of an empty strip mall, under the raised highway belt, or possibly under a footbridge I passed on my way to the highway. To defer my night's grim possibilities, I buy a greasy sandwich at a gas station and eat in the empty parking lot, watching the red sunset. The sandwich tastes like ketchup on stale bread but I eat quickly, my mind wandering to thoughts of my hometown in West Virginia: the odd meow of my cat, Pickney Benedict, the cherry tree's branches reaching toward my bedroom window, the angle of Dad's guitar resting on the wall, the broken whistle of the family teakettle, a blackened copper-bottom Paul Revere. I ball up the oily brown paper and stand to take a walk under the highway.

Ornate and colorful graffiti tags plaster massive cement support beams: here is a sinister purple octopus eating a school girl in a plaid skirt, here a gray alien giving the peace sign, here a thirty-foot goldfish with fat Buddhas sparkling in its eyes. The deep thundering white-noise of the highway above resonates in my chest. Great mountains of trash shuffle and flap in the dusty wind. I spot a few clearings among dense Japanese Knotweed plants and consider sleeping among the forest of weeds. The piles of trash have been sorted into junk-yard hangouts: bike jumps made of plywood and cinderblock, couches with springs sticking through mouldering fabric, wet sleeping bags and rotten pillows on cardboard. I hear voices nearby. Behind the next support pillar I walk through squatter's village, constructed mostly of blue tarpaulins, dull corrugated iron sheets, and cinderblocks. There are maybe a dozen hovels and tents. Two dark-haired young women sit in front of a patchy abode. A *Space Jam* blanket hangs in a window behind them, swaying in the breeze. Both women are beautiful, with dark olive skin and black hair. They look like sisters. One holds a bundled baby on her chest, patting its back. They stop talking as I walk by and look at me with bewilderment on their faces. I know this is no place to sleep. Darkness descends as I backtrack out from under the highway, toward the footbridge.

A quick black stream runs under the bridge, and the air is cool and damp. The red brick platform by the water should be comfortable to sleep on even without a tent. As I step onto the platform an acrid stench pierces my nose. I switch on my headlamp. Neat piles of shit lay everywhere on the brick, evidently a latrine for the homeless. My shoes are caked in it. My optimism hits the fan like a shit cocktail. Weary of my enormous backpack, I begin hiking to the nearest gas station, uncertain why I'm going there or what I will do next.

A weird logic fuels to this severe brand of travel, an attraction to feeling lost, unable to communicate, even unable to find a place to sleep. The unease creates a pendulum of emotion in extremes, like a chosen form of bipolar disorder. The normal cycles of fortune and misery are concentrated. The typical rotation of good and bad days or years shifts into cycles of hunger and plenty, night and day, weariness and rest. The common platforms of normalcy are dissolved: a day is divorced from schedule, home, school, work, family and is replaced by a tangible absence of time, a forced union and trust in strangers, and the complete abnegation of a "normal" sense of control.

Yet this traveling lifestyle has a rare brand of control: the dirtbagger can choose to go someplace, to trust in chaotic forces: in probability, in the belief that random strangers will share that goal and help him find wherever he's going. This willful vulnerability is a trust that shifts the default view of "strangers" from suspicion, anonymity, even paranoia, to a necessary openness. After a time the openness becomes natural; strangers seem more like unmet friends than threats. The kindness I received from so many people in strange lands wore down a cynicism I'd unknowingly internalized from common and simplistic platitudes like, "Don't talk to strangers." I don't advocate unconditional, blind trust, but the world is mostly strangers. Everyone forms their own balance between overly insular caution and foolishly vulnerable trust. It is worth con-sidering where one lies on this spectrum and whether giving more trust might give back a friend or a story.

I walk to the gas station with a bounce. I have direction. At the station I meet a German hitchhiker who knows no English but has Google Translate on his phone. We have a conversa-tion by passing it back and forth, though some translations come through the program a little Yoda-like, "Jim my name is. Meet you it is nice to." Jim allows me to map directions to the Zilina train station on his phone, and I write them on my arm in blue Sharpie. It's a ten-kilometer walk, but with street names like "Ulica Vojtecha Spanyola," and "Nanestie Ľudovíta Stúra" my arm is quickly covered with directions, wrist to elbow. I decide to break the sacred pact against non-hitching transportation, to take a train to Liptovský Mikuláš, where Joe will surely end up for the international hitchhiker's gathering. Something about the shit under the bridge pinched a nerve, and I wanted to get the hell out of Zilina.

The walk is strange and dim, a dreamy daze of narrow winding streets and buzzing yellow lamps. I am comforted to have a direction, to be moving. I smile to the murky road ahead. Bats flit and dip overhead, hunting the swarms of insects gathered around purring street lamps. Once a bat catches a bug, it crookedly careens back to its colony, a circling cloud above the hangar of a car repair yard. It's around mid-night, no signs of people anywhere. I walk down the middle of a well-lit road and not a single car passes. No muffled music plays from apartment windows, no children cry or dogs bark or sirens whine. Even the windows are dark in apartment buildings and houses. Like curfew hour in Pinochet Chile, surreal, portentous. I feel that I am walking in a painting of a strange empty cityscape, the lonely subject of a Hopper piece. It feels more like an elaborate stage set than a city.

The theme and variation of every building is a red-brick shoebox with small uniform windows, right angles, and a bland stoic facade. The neighborhoods are tight and angular; their effect is neat, moralizing, and utterly dismal. No doubt the architecture is a vestige of Eastern Bloc Czechoslovakia. After an hour of walking, I pass an urban graveyard, a city of towering stone monuments. A great stone mausoleum stands in the center of the grounds, decked with ornate buttresses, chiseled portals, and Arabesque stained glass. Burning candles in red glass vases rest at the bases of many of the stones. Some candles are tall and wide, others are small tea lights. Some are only flickering puddles, but the effect is striking: a city of dim blinking ghosts. I stroll through the aisles of Dobrovodskýs, Chrobáks, and Polievkas. Their sleepy red spirits cast my shadow in a hundred shifting angles. I sit on a wooden bench. All is quiet. A weary peace washes over me. The deep gravity of sleep loosens my limbs, and I droop like a slack marionette. The moon is a half crescent, piercingly bright in this flickering graveyard. I squint at its bruised profile, then look down at my long moon shadow. I wonder whether this moon is growing or disappearing. The scrawls on my arm tell me I'm halfway to the train station.

When I finally arrive at the station I feel raw, burned, like a crushed cigarette. The lobby of the sad white building is bright with buzzing orange fluorescent lights. I blink and squint. It's around two A.M., but one ticket counter remains open. Miraculously, the slow-blinking woman behind the glass knows some English. "Four euros to Liptovský Mikuláš," she says, yawning deeply. Overjoyed at meeting a fellow English-speaker, I begin to tell her why I am buying a ticket, "And-so-I'm-traveling-without-my-brother-and-we-are-hitchhiking—and . . ." The woman looks at me with furrowed eyebrows, a mix of genuine concern and fright. I shut up and hand her the money. She probably has no idea what I'm saying. The train is scheduled to leave an hour and a half later, so I walk around, looking for a place to sleep.

In one corner sits an old woman, perched on a heap of possessions, her face a field of wrinkles. Shouts and drunken protests echo through the cathedral ceiling as two fat policemen escort a scruffy old man from the station. An arm under each of his, the police drag the drunken man two steps for every lazy stride he takes. His matted head hangs forward, bobbing and spitting curses. As they pass, I catch a whiff of the fresh stain down the crotch of his pants. I sit on the floor, back to the wall, and hug my backpack. An old Asian man stands by a row of coin lockers with what looks like his life's belongings. His eyes are deep-set, as if trying to hide in his head. His face is leather-dark and wrinkled. When the police walk through the station, the Asian man pretends to put his things into the storage locker. He stops immediately when they leave. All night, I think, all night this man must perform this desperate act to keep from being thrown out into the street.

The lights in the station are too bright to sleep, so I move to a bench outside by the tracks. Nearby the fat policemen take a smoke break. The blue smoke lifts into a fluorescent lamp, turning orange and twisting like flames before wandering off. Far away a train whistles. The half-moon passes behind a cool wall of cloud. I drift to thin sleep, lying on a small bench.

I feel a light tap on my shoulder from some far-off place. I hurtle back to my body like a baseball to a glove and snap upright. A man is standing above me in a cheap black business suit. He is tall and thin, gaunt, with a dark complexion and a long nose. Thin lips smile straight white teeth at me. The man offers his hand formally to shake, as if I am a politician or a businessman. I scowl, dubious, still curled on the bench. He speaks Slovakian as he crouches and opens a black attaché case. Inside are rows of sparkling chrome wristwatches, knives, lighters, and Woolworth-type jewelry spangled in plastic rhinestones. The man talks rapidly, pointing out the features on a wristwatch with a massive bejeweled face. I shake my head, unable to fathom why a suited man is selling his gaudy wares to a filthy traveler sleeping on a bench. "No," I croak, "no." I laugh a little at the absurdity before laying back down. The suited man closes the case and walks on. What the hell? I drift back to a strange, dreamless sleep.

I wake to a hand resting on my arm. I jolt up. Two women are standing in front of me. The one with her hand on my arm takes two steps back as I sit up. The women are pleasant-looking, dark-skinned, maybe Indian. One is thin with black hair tucked behind large ears. The other is very fat and stands farther back. Neither of them look older than twenty. The smaller woman begins to speak to me. I shake my head, "I am sorry. I cannot understand." The thin woman thinks for a moment then repeats herself slowly, carefully enunciating each word. "No, no," I chuckle, rubbing my eyes, "I don't understand slow or fast Slovakian." She purses her lips, then rubs her thumb and forefinger together in the sign for money.

"*Euro se prosím, Euro se prosím,*" she says, rubbing her belly, miming eating something with a spoon.

"Oh, hungry," I say, and rummaging through my pack I pull out a loaf of bread and a jar of jam, and offer it to her. She looks surprised, then laughs, a good-natured laugh. She shakes her head and asks for money again. I say no and offer the bread once more but she is not interested. She sits close to me on the bench, our shoulders touching. Her eyes are narrow with concentration, as if she is trying to remember a word. After a moment she puts a small hand on my leg and says, "Sex?"

"Jesus Christ. No," I say. She mimes fellatio. "No, no, no. Nothing." I take out my wallet and hand her a few euros. "Please go now," I point to the station. The women leave together and are immediately followed by a morbidly obese blonde girl who shuffles up to my bench in broken flip flops. "Pleease," she moans, "Pleeeeeease," in a deep voice. I shake my head, but she repeats her moan at least ten times, dragging it out longer each time, "Pleeeeeeeeease." I say nothing, and we spend a moment in silence, looking at each other. She is young, probably a teenager. She's so fat her facial features are swallowed into inflated folds. The girl wears a yellow flower print dress, ballooned like a living Botero statue. She opens her mouth as if to plead again, but instead turns around and shuffles off on swollen feet. My three night visitors remind me of demented versions of the ghosts in *A Christmas Carol*, and I laugh out loud, just to hear the sound.

The train finally comes to platform six. It rumbles in a sea of percussion, a free-jazz drum solo. Restless and squeaking, it speeds in, brakes screaming. The colorful graffiti on the cars blur together, a sickly rainbow. Aboard, the hall is tight and hot, the passenger booths full. Almost everyone looks asleep. My unwieldy backpack bumps peoples' shoulders. "*Prominte, prominte*," sorry, sorry, I whisper. I sit in a car with two snoring men and an old man in an enormous tweed suit. The suit is clean and pressed, but four or five sizes too big. He pushes the sleeves back to keep them from swallowing his hands. The old man's lips purse inward, implying a lack of teeth. His hands are massive arthritic paws, each finger a swollen bratwurst. They look like false hands, part of a horribly realistic Halloween costume. The man studies me for a long time before reaching under his seat and retrieving a two-liter bottle of pineapple soda. He unscrews the cap with deliberation and takes a great bubbling guzzle. The soda is exactly the color of piss: an opaque mustardy yellow. He wipes his mouth and examines me again. He clears his throat and says something, then laughs heartily at himself, an airy wheeze of a laugh. His smile is great, all lines and folds. I smile and nod lightly. This is all the acknowledgement the man needs. He breaks into full-scale monologue, a dam unleashed, talking a garrulous river of words. The old man motions charismatically with his grotesque hands, only breaking his narrative to take excited chugging gulps of pineapple soda. One sleeping man beside me wakes from the noise, scowls, and puts earphones in before settling down again and resting a newspaper over his face. For the train's hour ride, the old man never stops spouting stories. Of course I don't let on that I can't understand a word he says. What does it matter? He needs someone to listen, so I let him speak. Liptovský Mikuláš is called over the intercom, and I stand to go. The man takes one of my hands in his and says something very solemn. I look into his watery dark eyes. My hand is a child's again, a tiny slipper of a hand. His reminds me of my grandfather's, dark and peppered with sunspots. For all I know he could be a philosopher, a Slavic Socrates concluding his theory of good and justice. He could be a Buddhist sensei or a madman expounding some theory on corporate mind-control through dermal microchips. I smile a "nice to meet you smile" and grip his monstrous hand in return.

Exhaustion warps time, a heady drunken squint. The brain feels squeezed, leaky, bleeding. I walk through the train station of Liptovský Mikuláš, trying to blink myself to consciousness. My head throb counts off four A.M. over and over. I slam through the doors of the station as the train's whistle reaches my spine. I hum "King of the Road" but don't mean it. I'm angry, interrogating myself: *Why the hell didn't you get a boring internship this summer like a normal undergrad? At least you'd be paid instead of wandering aimlessly in eastern Europe, looking for a place to sleep, asking to be mugged. What the fuck are you doing this for?* I want a logical end to the surreal madness of this day, a neat outro with fade-out music, roll credits. But there is no conclusion here, and certainly no logic. There is only engagement—one foot after the next. I walk in what looks to be the direction of town. A few condemned houses with black eyes and graffiti tattoos lean on either side of the road, peeling and softly breathing in the wind. An ancient truck sleeps in the driveway. Vines and tall grass grow over it, the soft hand of abandonment, gently pulling it back to the earth. I crouch next to the truck and look under. Nothing but high grass. I wonder if anyone might bother me if I crawled under there to sleep. I look around.

In the road behind me stands a man, fifty yards away, looking my direction. He is a muscular young man with a shaved head, no shirt or shoes. The street is empty. I stand up and walk on. The man walks behind me. I turn down a side street, he follows. I turn again and hear him behind, closer. I reach back to my pack and unbuckle the sheathe on my buck knife. An idea sparks into my head, a strange thought like the cliché last question of the jumper, did I leave the oven on? I can scare this guy. He's expecting a frightened tourist, a timid kid easy to corner. I look back. The shirtless man is still following me, closing in. Before I can think again, I whip around and shout "HRRAAA!" with thunderous aggression. The man stops, face contorted in bewilderment. We look at each other for a moment. I take a step toward him and unsheathe the buck knife. Six inches of steel flash in the streetlamp's yellow light. "HRRAAA!" I shout again, and walk toward him faster, gripping the knife with white knuckles. His eyes widen. He pivots, running, sprinting. His footsteps fade and silence envelops the street. I bend over with laughter, tearing up and shaking with adrenaline. I don't want to laugh but I have to.

I walk to the town center, edgy, delirious with fatigue. The buildings are made mostly of a heavy dark stone, blocky and menacing. A Gothic cathedral stretches skyward, its blackened spires peopled with grotesque gargoyles sticking out their long fat tongues. Further on, colorful blocks of apartments shoulder each other, pastel blue, yellow, and green, neat and vivid as the Copenhagen waterfront. I pass the massive town hall in a grassy quadrangle. The clock over its entrance reads five-thirty. The town is larger than I expected, much more beautiful, and utterly hushed. I wander, dizzy, seeing little, hearing only the creak of my boots. I find a walking path somewhere in the suburbs near a black river and lie nearby under a tree. I shimmy into my sleeping bag and sink to black sleep as the horizon blushes peach.

I wake to the shadows of cyclists passing a whirring strobe. The sun is bright, the sky cloudless. I remain sprawled out, back turned to the eyes of passersby. I feel no shame lying in the open; embarrassment takes energy. But I am low, hungry, and wearied at the thought of not seeing Joe for days or more. Soon I pack and head toward town, stopping in another park to sleep in cool grass under the shade of a statue—a bronze man in an academic gown looking down disapprovingly. Awake again, the sun is high. I walk to the town square, now thick with people. My plan is to sit someplace obvious until Joe happens upon me. Stupid, stupid plan, I think, sitting down at an outdoor coffee shop. I order an espresso and watch pedestrians pass on the busy sidewalk. I order another. The table is decked in a white cloth and elaborately folded napkins. This is probably the nicest café in town, and I look like Tom Hanks from *Castaway*. When I lift the demitasse, I see a light gray stain where my arm had rested on the white tablecloth. I pretend to be cultured anyway, sipping gingerly with the obligatory pinky extension. Content as the foil to The White Tablecloth, I continue ordering espressos to the apparent displeasure of the maître d'.

I feel the shallow shaky energy of caffeine. A beautiful little boy toddles by speaking kid-Slovakian to his mother who wears sunglasses so massive she looks like a fly. Young men kick around a soccer ball in a city park nearby, their shouts echo. A little girl and her mother splash in the basin of a public fountain, laughing. Two men in sunglasses walk down the sidewalk, their steps in sync. They look like punk versions of FBI thugs, like *Matrix* henchmen. They stop and glance around for a moment. One points in my direction, toward the café. They walk closer, in unison. I look around at the surrounding customers, sure I am about to see some mob action or a white-collar arrest. I brace myself for a Dashiell Hammett fight sequence complete with revolvers, karate, and screaming women, but the men stop in front of my table.

"Are you Ben?" one asks in a heavy accent. He removes his sunglasses.

The road is a twilight zone unto itself, a chaotic, serendipitous, lucky, accidental land. Being on the road often has no immediate point, except as a conscious rejection of control. The only immediate sense that can be made of the random joys and sufferings of dirtbag travel is through a remodeling of memory, cutting loose threads, and framing the scattered, loud collage into digestible anecdotes. The "purpose" is made much later, after memories are consolidated, forgotten, measured, weighed, packed, and served over and over at bars and dinner parties. Their meaning is created as memories are added, neglected, and remolded. Often, the road stories that seem to make the most sense are the most manicured, the closest to fiction. There is a surreal insanity to fresh uncondensed accounts of the road, a randomness that defies the logic of imagination. It has been nearly a year since I was in Slovakia, and I have told parts of this story many ways, ending at different places, omitting details, injecting meaning at odd angles. But each time, I say that I was glad to hear my name at that coffee shop in Liptovský Mikuláš. It was as if the impulse to make sense of being lost was speaking directly to me. "Are you Ben?" A call to be found.

Years before hitchhiking in Europe, I wrote a short story about a lonely old man, a farmer without a wife, children, or friends. He sells his farm in Maine to buy a motorcycle and rides across the U.S. On the way, he meets many people and has long conversations with all kinds of folks: kids, construction workers, drug dealers, priests, fishermen, travelers, and prostitutes. At the end of every conversation before saying goodbye, the old man asks each person to guess his name. He gets many responses: "Rigoberto" from a tomato-picker in Florida, "Jochen" from a German professor in New Orleans, "Ken" from a Texan rancher. The old man asks because he has lived alone so long he has forgotten his own name. He wants to pick a new one that suits him. In New Mexico he stays with a family of migrant farmers who know no English. They call him, *"el perdido."* Though he does not know what it means, he thinks El Perdido is fine, and goes with Perry for short. Later he finds that his new name means, "the lost one." Perry is content being lost. He feels more at home on the road than he ever did as a lonely farmer, and he never goes back to his land in Maine. Perry stays on the road for nearly a year, motoring all over the U.S. and Canada. He loves riding through the night and looking at the stars, because even when he goes twice the speed limit, it looks as if he's standing still. Eventually Perry dies happily in Alaska when he crashes into a moose crossing the road. But his mission is complete, he dies as Perry, The Lost One.

"Are you Ben?" the man asks in a heavy accent. He removes his sunglasses. This will be a good one, I say to myself. This is the ending I wanted.

"Yes," I say, grinning.

"O.K., we are local police. There's no trouble. We just met your brother. He's looking for you."

～～ ～～ ～～

*Ben Aultman-Moore is a West Virginia native earning a degree in creative writing at West Virginia University. His work has appeared in the literary journals* Calliope, Haggard *and* Halloo, *and in the upcoming issue of* The Poetry Bus. *He spends summers farming and hitchhiking, singing to cows, and reading under his favorite sombrero.*

JESSICA NORMANDEAU

~≈ ~≈ ~≈

# Southern Sandstone

A young woman justifies a passion for rock climbing and
struggles to find its place in her life.

## I. VERTICAL WORLD

I am 115 feet above ground and 5 feet from salvation, but
my body shakes so violently that the rock face just inches
from my nose is blurred into an earthy shade of peach, and
I am rendered momentarily immobile. Nothing is there to
catch my fall but a 10-millimeter rope and some precariously
placed pieces of gear. My right foot, stemmed out against the
adjacent corner, begins to slip from the thumbtack-sized hold
it rests upon. I shift my weight left and stabilize, relying on
the friction created between the sole of my rubber climbing
shoe and the cliff.

Beads of perspiration form in the creases on my forehead
and along the vertebrae of my spine, though the air temperature tops off around fifty degrees. My palms also start
to sweat, so I remove one from the ledge I hold on to and
reach behind my back to dip it in the bag of chalk tied with a
black nylon string around my waist. I repeat the same gesture
with my other hand, tighten my hold on the rock and reassess
the situation, looking to my next move. The anchor is close,
and if I am able to follow this crack system just a bit longer, I

can reach out to a large flake of rock with my right hand. I'll need to hold on long enough to extend my left arm and clip my rope into two metal rings permanently bolted in the rock above. If I don't stick the move, if my arms give out or my feet slip out from beneath me, I am looking at a twenty-foot fall sideways into a rock face.

I am climbing a very famous route named Rock Wars, which runs up the side of a sandstone cliff at The Long Wall in Kentucky's Red River Gorge. The general predicament of my situation is attributable to my being on lead in a traditional form of climbing, called "trad" for short. What this means is that clipped to my harness is an assortment of multicolored and variously sized pieces of metal gear called nuts and friends. Friends the latter truly are, for when I pull a trigger, the four lobes of each metal piece marvelously swivel in toward one another, decreasing the friend's size. When the trigger is held and the friend is placed in a rock crack of an appropriate width then released, the lobes of the friend push outward against the rock with a tremendous amount of force, acting as a miniature and temporary point of anchor. A nut is similar, though without moving parts, and can be slotted into a like-sized constriction in a crack. Once a lead climber places a nut or a friend, she clips the rope tied to her harness through a carabineer threaded through its end. Her rope runs through the carabineer as she continues to climb upward, and if she were to fall, she would fall only twice the distance between herself and her last piece of gear.

Trad climbing can be as safe as a laundromat or as dangerous as washing shirts in a shark tank, the trouble being that more than a few poorly placed pieces have popped out of cracks in the years since this form of climbing came to be, and sandstone itself can crumble and break, for yes, it is composed primarily of sand. This is not my only point of concern, for in my immaturity as a climber I did not plan well enough ahead and am out of friends, having climbed up and to the left of my last placement. To fall from here would be bad enough if my last friend holds; if it fails, then my downward plight would be long enough to make a final prayer or shriek a handful of profanities before my rope catches me. The alternative would be a ground fall.

"Dude, you've got this." I look down to the bottom of the cliff where Sel, my climbing partner, is belaying me. His head is resting on the hunch of his shoulders and his blonde dreadlocks are spilling out of a slouchy gray hand-knitted hat.

"Come on, Jess, send it!" he offers encouragingly. I try to respond but only whimper. How I'd really like to reply is by yelling, *I don't want to fall. I don't want to fall! I don't want to be here, I want this to be over, I want to get down!*

I start to move, my arms tired and pumped so full of blood they are visibly swollen in size. The veins in my forearms are frighteningly raised, and the scabs covering my once nicely manicured fingers are reopened and joined by new fissures in my skin. I leave drops of blood in the crack, viciously red against the white trail of chalk accumulated through decades by many hundreds of climbers' hands. I cross one arm over the other, move my feet higher, sink my right hand into the promising jug of a hold and reach with my left to clip into the anchor.

"TAKE!" I scream to Sel, signaling for him to pull in the extra slack of rope.

## II. CLIFF BAND DREAMSCAPE

Thirteen hours ago I left school in upstate New York, fourteen of us total, filing down South in four cars packed full of ropes, cook stoves, and duct tape-patched puffy coats. My route is marked by the flux of city light—driving by night through Rochester, Buffalo, Cleveland, Columbus, Cincinnati, and finally Lexington. The skyline of each metropolis emerges beyond the highway guideposts, unnamed stories shooting out of this flat western land. Lexington is the last stretch of urbanity before we reach Slade, Kentucky, and it is here that I rise from my back seat slumber that carried me unconsciously through most of Ohio and all of Illinois.

The landscape now rolls itself into hills and valleys, the road winding along the courses of rivers and over bridges where water withers slender. Everything is shrouded in pastel blue fog, as if someone took the artist's dust and threw it in the air to filter out sunlight before coming to rest upon the spring earth. On the eastern horizon the sun is rising like an overcooked heirloom tomato, pregnant with ideals of its own enormity and the pigment of dominion over southern lands. Soon the fog will burn off and the blue dust will dissipate, revealing grasses greener each day along the miles of fenced-in horse pastures stretching on.

Nearing Slade, the hills and valleys gnarl with vegetation. Rhododendrons and enormous beech trees occupy the lowlands, their trunks spiraling clockwise from years spent following the sun's path low in the southern sky. I am entering the Red River Gorge, an intricate canyon system spread over forty-four square miles and much of the Daniel Boone National Forest of eastern Kentucky. The Red is marked by natural sandstone arches, waterfalls, and rivers still carving out canyons. This is why I am here, for the sandstone walls of the gorge that cater to venturous desire as much as geological wonder.

Many of the walls are overhanging, forming stretches of caves along their bases, and riddled with holes of incomprehensible dimension. Some pockets are the size of human bodies, and some as small as index fingers. It is amazing how people hang faithfully from that one extremity until finding something more positive to grasp. The most remarkable routes up these walls look like stretches of golden honeycomb;

others are laced like flower buds where iron deposits have bedded in the rock. The cliffs of the Red emanate the wooden warmth of a kitchen counter and all the terror that a chopping board is to turnips and chives. As a climber I am drawn to them like strange insects are to the nectars that sustain their lives. I may distract myself from this passion for a while, go out seeking love or pollen, but after a time I return to see what I can make of the rock, or rather, what it can make of me.

It's not explicable, this attraction, why it affects some of us and not others. I'd say that climbing feeds an instinctual desire, and that I am better for it, but I'd also say that the manifestation of fear is a great deal of what makes climbing so stunningly beautiful. This is an uncomfortable realization to come by. Why must I endanger my life to feel that I am fully living? Is this recklessness a byproduct of youth, or unsound humanity? No, maybe neither, for being on the wall, hanging on for life (or greater self-preservation) is more akin to a dance than a battle, and the polka and tango are no plagues of the mind. When I move vertically, other troubles are left on flat earth. I don't remember the names of many climbs I've done, but I remember the lines and the moves I had to pull in order to finish them. I remember how I've shifted my weight on arêtes to reach the next hold, and how it felt to reach an arm in darkness toward the heart of a cliff, each crack characterized individually.

Driving into Slade I am but one in a car of four, a group of fourteen, and a community of hundreds that flocked to a backwoods small town in Kentucky this week for the promise of fear and adventure. So the sun lifts higher, burning away the smoky fade of the hills, and we begin to dance.

## III.  MOONSHINE AND MIGUEL'S

Of all the climbers who spend their days scaling the walls of the Red, a good number spend their nights at Miguel's Pizza.

In this little oasis for dirtbag athletes, one can find a restaurant, gear shop, basketball court, camping, showers, and laundry service (though use of the latter two is largely frowned upon—I myself was pressured into relinquishing clean hair for the nine-day duration of my stay). The restaurant front is painted sunbeam yellow with the iconic blonde and mustached image of a face blazing over a hand-carved door. Picnic tables are scattered out front, and down a small hill stretches a field crosshatched with puddles and bamboo. Everything about the place beckons, *yes, you are tired and hungry, your hands are dirty and your biceps are sore. Come, pitch a tent, order your pizza with avocado, olives and mango salsa, yes, we have vegan options too. Come, come let us take care of you so you may do again tomorrow exactly what you've done today.*

Our ragtag group sets up camp on an oblong knoll next to a marshy pond. A cardinal watches us from a thicket of bramble bushes; it is the first colored bird I have seen in many months. There is Jimmy, with his long curly hair that earned him the nickname Chewbacca for the trip. Cassandra: our token Californian with long legs, a blonde braid and easy attitude. Then Timmy and Sel, both wearing muddy hiking boots and pleasantly smelling like they have been playing outside since the snow first started melting up North. The others are off cooking, shooting hoops, and flipping through the guidebook, already searching out tomorrow's place to climb.

When night falls, we build a fire on a high patch of ground between two marshes, burning dead branches and pizza boxes. A bottle of moonshine is passed around in a glass jar; pale cherries bob around like eyeballs in formaldehyde, tasting of welding torch and orchard. I hand off the jar and someone chirps in, "Dontchya worry about the germs, that moonshine'll kill any kinda bacteria." I believe him, and I don't doubt that it would kill me too if I fell into the jar, or, its contents in entirety fell into me.

A group of Tennessee climbers begins to sing and strum a guitar.

"Oh yeah, Chattanooga is the best," one tells me. "You can climb all year long, and in the summer when it's hot, you can climb the cliffs out over the river and jump off 'em!"

"So what are you doing here?" I ask. No one has a good answer, but we all know that no matter how good the climbing is at home, climbing in the Red is probably a little better. Every time a pizza box is tossed on the fire it throws heat into the circle, burning my face and melting all memory of snow-drifts left behind up North.

"Aslan! Aslan!" another kid from Chattanooga yells at a giant Pyrenees mountain dog.

"It's Ivory," the owner corrects, not amused. A couple talks about the latest hard climbs to be done in Yosemite and several groups compare this morning's road conditions on the approach to different crags. Another pizza box pitches embers against the backdrop of night. The crowd moves a few steps away, the cold of early spring at their backs, then gravitates forward as the fire cools. Moonshine stirs remembrance of the day's climbs. I think back to the thick forest that surrounds us, and the giant cavern within the PMRP climbing area; standing way back inside and looking out, the gorge framed by an enormity of rock. My eyes start to close with fatigue, and so I move through the darkness toward the little patch of ground I've claimed with a sleeping bag and a pile of fleece for a pillow.

In the morning we wake to a carnival of tents in every shape and size that sprang up overnight in Miguel's fields like the first colored daffodils of the year. It takes me some time to wrestle off my sleeping bag and reach out into the cold for my boots.

## IV.  A CONSTELLATION OF SCARS

"You know, studies have been done that show that cities grow in exactly the same way as disease," Jimmy chirps in on our way back through Cincinnati. He says it with conviction, and we don't disagree. We're all a little bitter to leave our sandstone jungle gym in the woods and return to the cold. In Ohio I awake to snow whirling across the highway lanes. I curl up against the car door and look out the window at opposing lanes on the flat highway and the country unfolding without ripples behind. My body hurts all over from nine days of abuse on rock walls. My shins are bruised, my knees are scabbed, my hair is woven with enough chalk dust, twigs, and grease to make a suitable home for baby raptors. I look down at my hands, and they are in the worst condition. The polish is entirely gone from my nails, and my knuckles are scattered with scabs like cosmos. Every climbing trip renews the rawness of my skin; I don't mind it really, even if I am beginning to look more like a dappled fawn than a girl. These scars are the mark of the breed, and tied to each is the weight of the history of a climb.

I start to think again of the why. Why do I do this to myself? It is scary, yes, and fun. But it is also a way to move in this world. The climbing community is a mobile one, and for many the only restrictions they place upon their freedom are the ones that keep them safe. I think that by climbing routes, and sending them, that is, climbing them clean without falling, I feel as if I have conquered something. Though I'll never really possess the places I visit and am too transient a rambler to settle into one as a home, the send gives me a sense of ownership. But the reality of this feeling exists only in the way that I own my dreams, because I can't really, they are not mine. What happens in the night and on the rock is not tangible enough to be stamped, only treasured. I think that is why I keep beating on, because there is something shadowy and recalcitrant in climbing, and no matter how hard I push myself, there are ways unknown to push harder.

## V.  RETURN TO HORIZON

"Gotchya," Sel yells back.

My rope is tight to the anchor, and just in time, for my muscles and tendons have nothing left to give, and when they release, I sit back into my harness and rest. The sense of relief ushered in with the completion of every climb spreads through consciousness of my physical self. I push my feet against the rock, colored with unmixed tones of flesh: raw umber, alizarin crimson, burnt sienna, cad red. Below, the forest undulates over the uneven terrain of the gorge; green evidence of life returning to the flora. I am aware of the pallid white sky and the landscape of what I just climbed, but the pain that will come to my hands has not yet returned, and though I am conscious of cold air, adrenaline forms a second skin. I look down the expanse of rock to Sel, his head still resting on his shoulders. I lean back and push out from the rock.

"O.K., ready to lower," I call down. The rope runs through the carabineers of the anchor, and when I put my cheek against it, I hear the vibrating whir of fibers rolling over the metal. I come to the ground and steady myself on two feet; now my fingers are stiffening, and goose bumps are elevating my skin.

"Nice job, dude."

"Thanks," I say. "So what's next?"

❧  ❧  ❧

*Jessica Normandeau was raised in Vermont where she pilfered cherry tomatoes from her mother's garden, chased cows from the back yard, and waited for the snow to fall each winter. She spent last summer driving a Volkswagen Beetle converted to run on recycled vegetable oil (from dive bar frialators) on a rock-climbing trip across the country. She currently resides in Canton, New York, where she is studying English Creative Writing as an undergraduate at St. Lawrence University.*

⚞ ⚞ ⚞

# The Bloom of Cancer

Matters of life and death send her packing.

Fifteen years ago, I wrote a wish list at a time when I thought my life would either be taken by cancer or by my own hand. I'd been ill for several years due to tumors growing like trees in my body, their branches twisting my organs until they stopped working. Many surgeries later, the tumors had all been removed except for small pieces, which I had hoped would die on their own. But instead they returned, stronger and hungrier, consuming everything, consuming me.

My body was not owned by me during that time. I was only an anxious observer, who worried about bills that lay unopened on the kitchen table next to printouts of platelet counts. Exhausted by medications, angered by doctors, I spent my days terrified, my nights in a dull dreamless sleep.

Cancer is a lonely business. People don't really understand what cancer means: sometimes it means you will die. It's not popular to say so, but it's true. Everyone tells you "you will beat it," but no one wants to talk about the fact you might not. But you, *you* have this truth with you every day: you wake up in morning, and it is there. It follows you wherever you are, this unnerving feeling that you are rotting inside. It stares back at you in your vanity mirror as you brush your teeth, making you cover all the mirrors in your house. It sits next to you as you drink your liquid meal replacement because you can't eat solid food anymore. It crawls into the phone line as you try to talk to friends, contaminating the conversation until you give up and stop calling anyone at all.

One morning, I realized I had to make a choice: end life or find life. I remember that day so well that I can recall details from it still. I was lying on the floor of my living room, and I'd been lying there for a long time. Overnight. I was cold, because the fire in the wood stove had gone out, but I didn't care. I was so ill I'd soiled my clothes with urine, because by then, I'd become incontinent. My hair was tangled and dirty, since I hadn't showered in over a week. I had on a maternity dress that someone had given me, an ugly flesh-colored peach dress, the color of a Band-Aid, and I hated it. My tumors had come back and my abdomen was so swollen I couldn't wear any of my own clothes.

My dog was hungry and pawing at the back door, and I made myself get up to feed him. Then I saw how he looked at me: his eyes were wide and alert to a stranger. *Me.* I went and looked at myself in the bathroom mirror and saw someone in hell. Right then I knew I had to pull myself together. There was no one else to do it but me.

I cancelled my chemo. I threw away the medications. Driving out to the countryside with my journal and a blanket, I stretched myself out in a field surrounded by sheep and sunshine. It was in that same field that my bucket list was born, a list that kept me alive and saved my soul from sorrow.

From the start, I knew my list had to be that of a visionary: impossible tasks, a maze of places and things that required my full participation, a belief in the magical qualities of the Universe. Choosing tasks that were far away or took a long time to accomplish meant promising myself to be healthy and whole again. I knew I needed a list that would propel me out into the world, shot like a cannon into a neighboring country, led only by the desire to have more time.

I wrote until the light dimmed, the grass buzzed with night insects, the way back to my car hard to find. But while creating that bucket list, my pain, aloneness, and my fears were replaced with the gift of forgetting. I forgot who I was and decided who I would become.

Once home, I taped copies of my new bucket list everywhere: the refrigerator, the bathroom mirror, the dash of my car. I tore the list into narrow strips, one task on each bookmark, placing them in every book I owned, my wallet, the silverware drawer.

Slips of paper, everywhere, reminding me that I needed to live, scribbled with jumbled words, *wishes*:

- Skydive solo in the Nevada desert just after the sunrise.
- Spend an entire day at the top of the Empire State building and have a five-star meal delivered.
- Jump off a pirate boat into the sea.
- Build a cross on the top of a mountain along the Camino de Santiago in Spain.
- Nap in Vita Sackville-West's white garden while reading Virginia Woolf.
- Become a Buddhist monk.
- Feel quicksand.
- Join a Catholic order of nuns.
- Be entirely alone in a desolate landscape of another country.
- Snowshoe in Canada.
- Be the star of a parade.
- Eat dinner with a famous artist.
- Work on a banana plantation.

- Plaster a city with poems in the middle of the night.
- Ride a train car to an unknown destination.
- Spend the night at the bottom of the Grand Canyon with an astronomer who can explain the stars.
- Travel around the world alone, taking my time.
- Be an artist.
- Experience nature.
- *See everything.*

These and hundreds more prompts to do the things of my wildest imaginings, crazy dreams that required endless resources of time and money I didn't have.

I was still sick, but my days were full of plans and preparations, and I began whittling down the list with surprising success, in no particular order. Some things were hard to manage, but explanations usually opened doors. Money was useful, but not entirely important: the sheer *will* needed to actually do something seemed to make it possible to do it, whether it was expensive or not. Other tasks proved impossible or ridiculous in retrospect: pirate ships were terribly hard to find, and the top of Empire State building didn't allow food of any kind, so I'd had to make do with a hastily gobbled hot dog that I smuggled in under my jacket. Sometimes I changed my mind: being a nun sounded lovely until I had realized I couldn't even wear lip gloss, and snowshoeing turned out to be more torturous than fun.

The list kept me alive. I didn't think about being sick any more. I treated my body like it was well, forcing it to do things it had never done: skydiving, white water rafting, ballroom dancing. And six months later, somewhere between talking stars with an astronomer in the Grand Canyon and almost getting arrested for plastering poems on streetlight posts in my city at two A.M., I felt better. The doctors told me I was better, too: *the cancer was gone.*

The bucket list had become a tool that changed me from someone who had obsessed about mere surviving . . . into a strong woman who didn't care so much about living as she did about thriving.

*I'd bloomed.*

Five years later, I found myself traveling around the world alone, with a single task left to complete at the bottom of my bucket list. It sat, dangling like a loose thread, demanding to be pulled. Part of me wanted to pull that thread, close the chapter, and start a new story that had nothing to do with cancer. The other part of me was scared to complete it, thinking that once the list was finished, my life might be finished too.

The final thing on my list was to spend a month at the Louvre in Paris. I'd never even been to Paris, I didn't speak French, and all I knew about the Louvre was that it was filled with beautiful art that most people only had a few days to see. A month at the Louvre. Impractical, luxurious, out of reach.

Yet despite an utter of lack of funds on my round-the-world adventure, I suddenly had an unexpected delay in Paris, forced to stay there for three months as I awaited a visa to arrive for India. I knew no one, except for a glum Parisian art student, who had scribbled her telephone number on a napkin one night as we both tried to sleep in the Mexico City airport on our way to other places.

Led by a desire to actually sleep indoors rather than a park bench, I called her. By some twist of luck, she had a brother who was out of town, who happened to have an empty apartment near the Bastille. I had the apartment for three months if I wanted it. I viewed this at once as both a miracle and a warning: the end of the list which had, in my mind, kept me alive. Perhaps the end of me.

*    *    *

I set off at sunrise the next morning, fed by a warm baguette and the subtle light of the city. Gray to lemon yellow to gold. With light rain as my only company, I walked through Paris until I reached the famous pyramid, splashed with water nymphs in the form of diamond-colored drops, surrounded by Japanese tourists holding candy-colored umbrellas. Rain mixed with tears on my face as I sobbed, my face tracked with tears I'd never allowed myself to cry since forcing myself to get up off my living room floor all those years ago.

There was no need for a tour, plan or guide: the month stretched before me, and unlike the rushed tourists who had to chase down the usual suspects in between flights, I had the extravagance of time. That first day I spent with the first sculpture I saw, the *Winged Victory of Samothrace*. A human figure with wings, perched on the edge of a boat, I imagined her taking flight each night after the Louvre closed. And as I sat on the stairwell looking up at her, I realized that this was not the *end* of me, but rather the *beginning* of me.

The month went by slowly, like a painting as it takes shape under the hand of a painter with only one canvas and a thousand ideas, each day layered with new colors and textures.

For thirty days, each morning I would walk through the city, stopping to buy my baguette and coffee, pretending to be offended when the waiter laughed as my grim attempt at French was replaced by sign language. Farther on I'd dodge the trash trucks and the early morning graffiti artists to get a place in line at a bakery hidden in an alley, where I'd buy a warm croissant from a baker who smelled like cherry pie. When I'd finally arrive at the square of the Louvre, the pickpockets would smile at me in greeting, while the flower seller pushed a nosegay of bruised violets or tiny pink roses into my hands. At the entrance of the Louvre, the staff would wave me in, as they squabbled in furious French with the illegal ticket sellers just outside the doors.

After a few weeks, I could walk into the museum with my eyes closed. I knew the feel of the handrails, slightly worn yet smooth and cool. I heard the sound of the security guards shifting their feet, the hum of vented air, the sigh of shoes walking on marble. Each painting and sculpture seem to have waited for my arrival, dressed in their finest draperies and gilded frames, like flags in an endless procession of gladness.

The women of the Louvre invited me to walk past the crowds into their private chambers. Teasing. Whispering. Welcoming. The Mona Lisa, small and stained green, her plucked eyebrows raised quizzically at the crowds who came to admire her. Gabrielle D'Estrees caught forever fondling one of her sisters, no doubt wishing she hadn't. Marquise de Pompadour, impossibly coiffed and powdered, permanently poised in pastels. La Grande Odalisque, her body stretched before the world, waited for gossip and visitors. Here were women unapologetic about being women: whole, incomplete, messy, divided, fertile, plump, merchant, slave, prostitute, servant, old, nubile, lost, found, owned, free. I sat before them, held their gaze evenly, without blinking. Our stories were not the same, yet I found myself in each one of them.

On my last day at the museum, I said goodbye to these painted women I'd met, who at first had seemed two-dimensional and flat, but really had come to life and become friends. Then I took a different route back to the apartment and found myself on the banks of the Seine. I walked along the river, my thoughts on that woman who, many years ago, sat in a field and wrote out a list to save her life. I'd carried her list with me around the world, and as I took it out of my bag, my hands shook so badly it seemed as though the paper would take flight.

One last gesture, one last goodbye, one last promise made to that woman who was me so long ago. Her list was finished, and somehow I felt her end had come as well. I held the journal tightly and tore that final page of my past out. I folded it into a small paper boat, and set it in the Seine. It floated, small and white, like a dove, a peace offering to my old self. My eyes followed the little white boat as it moved down the river, past the barges, until it was gone. She was gone, too.

She finally got what she had wanted the whole time: to be free and not defined by cancer.

*And I, too, was free. I still am.*

~~ ~~ ~~

*World traveler Amy Gigi Alexander writes tales of place interwoven with memoir and social commentary.* Her work has been published in numerous literary magazines as well as National Geographic India, BBC Travel, World Hum, Lonely Planet, and others. Her award-winning travel essays have been translated and published internationally. Her work focuses on being an empowered woman, a solo traveler, and finding the good in the world. Her website is www.amygigialexander.com

PETER VALING

~≥ ~≥ ~≥

# The Lapham Longshot

Nothing ventured, nothing gained.

I wasn't making any headway freelancing in Canada. A decade of effort and risk had come to little more than a contact list of editors who weren't interested or couldn't pay. Before trading in pen for hammer, or any tool with which I could earn a living, I decided to give America a try and thus go out with a bang. I decided that I would attempt to impress myself on at least one editor at a publication with money and clout in New York. I sent, in manilla envelopes, a selection of clippings and awards to Graydon Carter at *Vanity Fair*, to David Granger at *Esquire,* and to David Remnick at *The New Yorker*. I described myself as a writer in the art-of-fact tradition of Gay Talese and George Plimpton and sealed the portfolio with a photograph of myself that would do either writer proud. The effort cost $105 in copies and postage. It amounted to nothing.

Then an acquaintance in the know suggested that I drop in on Lewis Lapham in person. I sent Lapham one of my manilla envelopes and waited. Meanwhile, I researched the legendary man of letters at the library. Lapham had headed *Harper's* for years, and upon retirement founded *Lapham's Quarterly*, a publication into which every four months he distilled millennia of literary insight into topics ranging from Magic Shows to Arts & Letters. During his career, he had published writers as divergent as Tom Wolfe and Christopher Hitchens, but what excited me most about the elderly scribe was that he proclaimed himself open to young talent (though he didn't think much of what was currently on offer). Oh, yes, and he smoked. Lewis Lapham was my kind of editor, and it didn't take much beyond a gut feeling for me to convince myself that great things would come of us meeting face to face.

I sold the idea to my wife as a package. The trip would be an addendum to our weekend-long honeymoon, a break from our kids and an opportunity for me to relaunch my writing career. Besides, we had never been to New York. We booked flights and a week in a one-room, walk-up tenement house in Manhattan's Lower East Side. Then one morning in July, we departed for New York without hearing a word in response from Lapham.

The first two days in New York I didn't think of Lapham much. I'd check my email at a café each morning and then put work out of my head for the rest of the day. It was easy to do. Lee and I are walkers, and in the mornings we'd dress up, have something to eat on our bed and step out of the door of the tenement to see of the Big Apple what there was to see. We began with concentric circles of our neighborhood. In recent decades, the Lower East Side has undergone gentrification, with million-dollar condos replacing much of the once-working-class-turned-bohemian/skid-row Bowery. But the Jewish stamp on the borough has remained. Locales like the Eldridge Street Synagogue have been restored, and a host of trendy businesses run by young Jews have returned to the place of their forefathers. Indeed, some of these businesses had never left. The knishes we ate at Yonah Schimmel's Knish Bakery were delivered up warm by the very same pulley-operated dumb waiter that had delivered them up from the basement a century ago. Sitting there eating the simple, doughy snack, surrounded by yellowed clippings of Jewish celebrity patrons from Woody Allan to Barbara Streisand, I entertained all sorts of thoughts. I thought about Lee crying at the foot of the bed at three A.M. the previous night because I, drunk, wanted to sleep without AC, while she, sober, couldn't handle the heat wave and the noise from the street. I thought about the Jews who had once lived in that tenement house, packed to the rafters and poor as mice. They must have had some wicked rows. Jews described by Blaise Cendrars in *Easter in New York*, his poetic tribute to the turn-of-the-century New York street, came to mind as well:

> They sit in shops, under copper lamps,
> Sell old clothes, books, arms and stamps.

Yes, the bakery got my strong sense of nostalgia rolling, and it rolled along with me as hand-in-hand Lee and I strolled down boulevards and through alleys and parks. We poked into a tailor shop here and a bookshop there, and passed plaques commemorating Mark Twain and Brendan Behan on the pillars that marked the entrance to the Chelsea Hotel. The nostalgia lingered still. We tried to retire to the storied lounge for a nightcap, but it was under renovation, so we walked on until we arrived at Times Square. Even it, lit up as it was with ads for a dizzying swirl of products, held appeal for me. I asked a husky beat cop for directions to Jimmy's Corner. He had never heard of it. We eventually found it in the "Dive Bars" section of our NYC city guide and spent the remainder of the night drinking draft in New York's famed boxing bar. The handsome, well-spoken bartender appeared out of place. He was holding the bar down for the founder, his father, Jimmy, who was out of town cornering a fighter. Would he run this institution once his father retired? I asked. No, he was finishing a law degree in corporate law at Harvard and the bar would eventually be sold.

Two days passed like this and then another two. Still no word had come from Lapham. This was no surprise, as according to the *Quarterly* website, the editor was currently out of town for a few days at a librarian's conference in D.C. We were, however, in New York and would make the most of it. We devoted a day to fine art. Instead of going to a large gallery like the MOMA, we spent the morning at the Frick, an old mansion that had once belonged to a steel baron but which had been converted into a museum that held a small but varied collection of Vermeers, Titians, El Grecos, and Goyas. We were among few visitors in the stately rooms, and the docents didn't reprimand us for edging close to the paintings we liked. My afternoon plan was to walk farther up Central Park to Rockefeller's mansion, now converted into the Neue Gallery. I wanted to view some Klimpts and Egon Shieles. I also wished to surprise Lee with lunch at the Cafe Sabarsky, which served Viennese pastries in an atmosphere that combined live classical music with a view of Central Park. Both gallery and café were closed, however, and we made do with concession food at the Park.

We spent the afternoon on a hilltop overlooking the Hudson River. That we had reached the Cloisters was a miracle, as we had trudged the barren, winding road for over an hour in 40-degree (104°F) heat. When finally we crested the hill and the fragments of the Spanish monastery became visible, we collapsed under a small group of wilting trees and expelled what felt like our last breath. But to inhale again was divine. The river breeze blew up from the other side of the hill scents from hundreds of rare herbs and flowers. We recovered quickly and crossed the heavy stone threshold of the Cloisters. Several hours passed. By the time we exited, the temperature had become bearable. The walk down the hillside and then back down through Central Park was lively with conversation. The Cloisters was a treasure house of art from old Christendom, something we had not encountered since we were kids backpacking together through the towns and cities of Europe. The fifth day in New York thus came to an end, the two of us merrily making our way through a darkening Central Park, talking about God and art and God in art. Except that I ruined it with an attempt to contact Lapham. My acquaintance had told me that the editor would often spend late hours in his office, and that bit of information, emboldened by a few drinks at Jimmy's, led me to the one payphone in the city that still worked. I dialed. The phone rang, and I pictured old Lapham hunched over his desk, reading my clippings by the light of a solitary Tiffany-shaded bulb. The phone continued to ring. Later, on the rooftop of our tenement, Lee and I had our second holiday fight. I had apparently smooth-talked her into another poorly planned, hare-brained adventure.

What could I do at this point but to raise morale, and what better place to do it at than at the racetrack? I had staked around two grand on this Lapham longshot—what difference would a few more dollars make? So in the morning, after checking my email, we set out for the Belmont. In this postmodern New York City of spotless, air-conditioned subways and anti-busking bylaws, this was no easy undertaking. The direct train to Belmont had been cancelled due to a declining interest in thoroughbred racing, so along with a few elderly men, we boarded the first in a series of buses bound for the track.

Even a bright summer's day couldn't deliver Belmont from its gloom. The dead mounted on the walls well outnumbered the few living in the stands, and my heart sank deeper when I compared the slovenly present to the elegant past. For over a hundred years, the Belmont has hosted the third leg of the Triple Crown. It was supposed to be regal. High and low society were supposed to mix in its stands in the same way they mixed in a Toulouse-Lautrec painting. I sank down in my seat, corn dog in one hand, plastic cup of beer in the other, and played a race. I cashed a 9/1 win. The spent horses cantered by, sweat-soaked in the sun. Someone screamed an obscenity at one of the jockeys. I thumbed the fresh roll of bills in my pocket.

We now had some money to burn, and much of the day remained. We bussed it from Elmont through Queens and then hopped onto a subway to Harlem. There was no plan, so we walked up one street and down another, took breaks in the shade of doorways and drank tall beers out of paper bags. While loitering around one intersection, a neighborhood-wide water fight erupted in the heat. Kids pried loose a fire hydrant and were using trashcan lids to direct the stream of water against each other and at passing traffic. This was a happy corner of town, and we would liked to have stayed there longer, but Lee and I were hungry from all of the walking we'd done. At Amy Ruth's Restaurant, we stuffed ourselves with Southern fare and then dragged ourselves to the nearest bus stop. As the bus turned a corner, a spray of water doused our laps through an open window. The kids were still at it.

Lee had been generous not to mention the main purpose of this trip since our rooftop argument, and I was doing my best to keep failure from my mind. We arrived at Coney Island just as the sun had begun to set. I wanted to feel happy, to feel like I had felt watching those kids, but the old seaside amusement park slated for demolition only pushed me into a deeper funk. On the boardwalk, I listened to Chopin nocturnes banged out by a tourist on a piano that looked like it had been delivered up by the sea until Lee grabbed me by the arm. "Honey, let's go for a roller coaster ride!" Up we creaked along an ancient latticework of wood and bolts. Each

scream-filled apex opened up to a different blurry vista—to
the now-dark and empty beach and its shimmering shoreline;
to a cluster of forlorn highrises jutting out from behind the
Ferris wheel; to an ocean that was flat black and hemmed in
by the lights of New Jersey.

I had run out of days. We were flying home in the afternoon, and I still hadn't seen Lapham. But I had dressed for
the occasion. At the entrance of 33 Irving Place, Lee kissed
me and wished me luck. I stepped into a small, turn-of-the-
century elevator and pressed 8. I didn't know if Lapham
would be in his office, or what I would say to him if he were.
I wanted to forge a connection between us based on the man's
intimate involvement with the disappearing world of letters
that I have loved for so long. It was no longer about anything
else. What, after all, was I here to ask of him—a job? In hind-
sight, that's exactly what I should have asked of him—a job
that would support my family while allowing me to read old
books. But in all the time that I had spent planning this trip,
the obvious had eluded me, and it eluded me still. The elevator door opened.

I wasn't thinking clearly at all. I was going through the
motions—knocking on doors, talking to faces.

"Hello, I'm here to see Lewis Lapham."

"Is Mr. Lapham expecting you?"

"No, but I'm a writer. I was told that he'll see young
writers."

"Mr. Lapham was sick this week and is catching up. Is
there something you'd like to leave with me?"

There was nothing but sweat in my hands. "My plane
leaves this afternoon, back to Vancouver. Please tell him that
Peter Valing is here to see him."

The secretary was merciful. She sat me in a cubicle and
told me that she would ask her boss if he had a few minutes to spare. My eyes darted around the high-ceilinged and

book-cluttered office. There were liquor bottles arranged on a nearby table. I peeked over the dividing wall. There behind a glass wall was Lewis Lapham. He was seated behind a large, cluttered desk and he looked as elegant—albeit a bit older and now bespectacled—as he looked in the photo on the *Quarterly* website.

A minute later I was shaking hands with him.

"Mr. Lapham, thank you for your time. I know I've come unannounced, but—"

He didn't cut me off. I just ran out of words.

"Have a seat, Mr. Valing. I understand that you've come all the way from Vancouver."

"Yes," I managed. "And it's the hottest day in New York City history!"

"So you arrived today?" He appeared confused.

"No—I mean it's the hottest day today. I arrived last week."

The phone rang. "Excuse me, but I have to take this," said Lapham. I calmed myself. My eyes searched the stacks of papers on his desk. Quickly I noted the ashtray and the absence of a computer before my eyes returned to the stacks. I counted over a dozen manila envelopes.

"I apologize. I'm a little behind today."

"Oh, that's fine. I'm just happy to be here."

"That's good," said Lapham leaning back in his chair.

I mustered up the nerve. "Last month I sent you some of my writing. It was in a blue duotang—stories about monks and boxers and pigeon catchers. Odd sorts."

"Oh yes, I remember those. You're a talented writer, Peter."

A warmth spread through me like a drug.

"And you have many years ahead of you."

The phone rang again, but Lapham let it ring.

"So what would you like me to do for you?"

I told him that I was making no progress in Canada and that I had sent portfolios to some big magazines in New York but had not yet pursued face-to-face contact with any editors other than him because I had received no response.

"No, don't go knocking on those doors. You won't get anywhere that way anymore."

He paused.

"You say Granger is still at *Esquire*?"

"Yes."

"Do you have a pitch for him? I could give him a call."

"Not at present," I said, cursing myself for not having prepared for such an opportunity.

The phone rang again, and Lapham ignored it.

"I'll tell you what. Just leave this in my hands, and we'll be in touch."

What did this mean? Whatever it meant was much more than I had expected. My gratitude translated into an intense urge to leave this man alone to catch up. We shook hands, and I passed through the glass partition.

I was halfway out of the office when I realized that I had nothing to commemorate this special moment but my word. Then I noticed a box of *Lapham Quarterleys* in the corridor by the elevator.

"May I take one of these?" I asked the secretary.

"Certainly."

It was the Sports & Games issue, and among the contributors I immediately counted Ernest Hemingway and A.J. Liebling.

I did an about face and walked back into Lapham's office. He put down the phone.

"Thanks for this publication, Mr. Lapham," I said. "Would you sign it for me?"

He uncapped his fountain pen and wrote:

*NYC 7/6/10*
*Lewis Lapham*

꙳ ꙳ ꙳

*Peter Valing is the author of the unpublished memoir of living in Belize with his family,* Caye Caulker. *His story about boxing in Africa, "Where the Fighters Are Hungry," appeared in* The Best Travel Writing 2005.

❧  ❧  ❧

# Into the Cold

*Sometimes the chill warms you up to possibilities.*

"This is one of the deepest lakes in Sweden," says Joachim, indicating to the right—towards me—in the passenger seat. It hardly seems like a body of water, but rather like a boundless prairie blanketed with snow. "Many people have drowned here on snowmobiles and they completely disappear under the ice." We are driving along the shore of Lake Malgomai on a February day and the scrape of tire studs beneath our Subaru wagon clashes with the Jennifer Lopez and Pitbull duet thumping on the radio. The horizon is a rainbow of grays—dove to steel to charcoal—like a Benjamin Moore paint strip.

"Do you mind if I turn down the radio?" I ask. The noise level makes it difficult to give the icy gravesite its due. Joachim taps off the power button and silence inflates inside the car. "How deep is it?"

"One hundred seventeen meters," he says. Several fishermen are planted in cleared-out spaces on the surface. They are bundled under earflaps and bulk and their poles stick out from holes drilled into the ice. "And forty-five kilometers long."

Thirty minutes ago, Joachim collected me at Vilhelmina Airport, a one-room outpost in Southern Lapland. He was the only person in the "arrivals" corner of the enclosure and since he was picking up a stranger, his gaze was cautious. The whole scenario should make me wary: I—a lone woman— pile myself and my bags into a man's car, whereupon he tells me of frozen bodies that float somewhere under the lake just a guardrail away, and proceed to drive with him 200 miles on a snow- packed road deeper into forest to the hotel he manages. But I know my instincts well enough to trust them and with few exceptions, those I encounter when I travel alone. Besides, I'm elated to be in the opening moments of a brief disappearing act, the kind I've come to crave and even require. Joachim has no idea that he's in collusion with me as I fade into the folds of Lapland's forlorn geography for a few days, with no plans for anything except to be out of reach.

I've come to Sweden to do a roundup on spas for a glossy monthly, and have spent the last four days in Stockholm getting scraped and pummeled, kneaded and oiled with extracts of birch and lingonberry. I can't lie, it's a peach of an assignment but while there I still inhabit my own familiar skin—of the artist's wife, preoccupied mother, the well- shod magazine scribe under constant harassment from a smart phone.

Until I moved to a wooded corner of New England, I spent my adult life in New York and Paris, or on the road roaming Istanbul's bazaars or Singapore's teeming streets. But as I get older, it's the remote I seek, the far-flung counterpoint to my rural existence, total sequester to erase the static. The more I wander the world's most crowded places, the harder it is to shake the burdens that have become a part of me: of middle age, of ailing parents and growing children, of perpetual financial doom, professional incertitude and—what is perhaps most unbearable—technological overload. It's a time of life that requires contemplation, which I can achieve neither in the context of my home, where I stew and ponder and spin domestic wheels, nor in a nervous urban swarm of bodies all racing to get somewhere. It is a conundrum: I'm seeking to remedy isolation with greater isolation. Some people call it a getaway. I call it salvation.

It bears mentioning, however, that a few hours striking distance from the Arctic Circle would not be my normal, chosen paradise. I loathe the winter, which, in northwest Connecticut, lasts from November to April. At the moment, though, a beach is a hemisphere away, so I plan to stay indoors and wrap myself in reindeer skins for a few blissfully lonesome days. My lackluster enthusiasm for outdoor adventure—or for being outdoors at all—clearly bewilders Joachim and I find myself a touch embarrassed by it.

"You don't want to ski?" Joachim asks, incredulous.

"I never learned how," I say.

"What about the snowmobile?" he asks.

"I don't think so," I say, meaning, "Are you fucking kidding me?"

Joachim tries not to look confused. "We can take you in the Caterpillar up to Mount Klo verfja llet, or you can go in the helicopter. That would be very nice, to ride in a helicopter. It's very beautiful to see the mountain from the top."

How many more ways can I—politely—say, "No, thanks?" He's the owner of a winter resort and his new charge is disinterested, a complete dud. I want him to believe that I'm happy, and that my sense of adventure, however paltry to the naked eye, is already satisfied by this excursion north. I don't need to chase powder on a Catski, courting avalanches and frostbite. No one except a friend in Stockholm knows my whereabouts. I don't require much more.

"I'll think about it," I say. "Does the hotel offer massage?" I'm not sure my muscles can withstand another beating but at least it's an activity.

Joachim lights up. "Yes, in fact we have a new person starting today," he says.

"That's great," I say.

"You can also go for walks," he says.

"Really, I'll be fine."

It's mid-week, so, Joachim tells me, the hotel is all but empty. There is a fireplace that I can curl up next to and stoke for the next three days. "You will be very happy in the restaurant," he says. "We have a nice wine list and we carry a small-batch local gin which is wonderful."

"Now, you're talking," I say.

Joachim fills me in on the region. The indigenous Lapp people, known as Sami, have changed along with the rest of the world. Many still herd reindeer, the cornerstone of their livelihood, but instead of doing so on foot across the wide Arctic expanses, they use trucks and helicopters. You may still find dogs and sleds, but the culture is less nomadic and population much dwindled, and the virgin expanses of Lapland are largely for tourists.

Eventually, Joachim takes the exit ramp towards the town of Borgafjall, a sprawling flash of electric white even more intense than the landscape we've just traversed for the past three hours. He points to two distant peaks that are the town landmarks. "That's Klo verfja llet," he says. "Locals call them 'The Tits,' or more often, 'Anita Ekberg.'" Clouds obscure one of them, the right breast perhaps, but they are wispy ones, like linen curtains on a spring day, and the sky otherwise is sapphire blue. It is not yet eleven A.M. and the sun is low on the horizon.

"This is good for tonight," he says. "You can see the Northern Lights only when the sky is clear."

"What are the chances of seeing them?" I ask. It's the middle of February and because the air tends to be less moist than earlier in the winter, it is, in fact, the optimal viewing time. Borgafjall is in Vasterbotten County in Southern Lapland, about sixty miles from the Arctic Circle. When electrically-charged solar particles collide with atmospheric gases as they are drawn to the North Pole, this creates the Aurora Borealis. In fact, I learn, the eleven-year cycle of solar activity is predicted to peak in what is dubbed the "Solar Maximum" right now in the winter of 2013—so the auroral activity, according to Joachim, has been in full disco throttle. But he knows better than to promise a guest a show. I look warily at the sky.

Hotel Borgafjall is a low-slung yellow structure built by an English architect, Ralph Erskine. Inside, there is a pleasing midcentury vibe—a bright seating area around a mod white wood stove. Joachim's wife Gertrud leads me to my room and I pass a vitrine where stuffed wildlife from the area is on display: an Arctic fox, a lynx and a snowy owl with its disturbing gaze both cross-eyed and direct.

I had heard there are some clean, modern rooms but I don't get one—perhaps I overstressed my limited budget in my correspondence with Joachim. It will be fine for sleeping but it is awkward in a kind of vertical way—very tall, very narrow and very small. I make my way across the dorm-like upper floor back to the aesthetically fascinating main part of the building. There is a funky, suspended staircase and painted white I-beams bisect the rooms and ceilings, which jut and angle in no particular direction. I have found my home: the dining room, as welcoming as my little quarters are not.

Gertrud, who also works in the kitchen, obviously got the dope from Joachim on their boring new guest.

"You would not like to go to the slopes today?"

She places warm bread and butter made, she says, locally, on the table. The fire sparks invitingly.

"Actually, I have a lot of work to do," I lie. Another woman approaches the table and introduces herself.

"I'm Johanna," she says. "We have horses. Would you like to go riding in the forest?"

"That's so generous of you," I say with a smile shellacked on my face. By now my apathy has insulted them, their hotel, and in fact the entirety of Lapland if not Sweden. "Actually, I don't know how to ride horses."

I've been on a horse exactly once—the same number of times I've been on skis. I begin to wonder if there is anything I actually do know how to do.

"The horses are very nice and gentle," Johanna says.

"Old and close to death would be better," I say.

They laugh. "Tomorrow then."

There is no point in any further refusals, so I accede to their persistence. "Maybe a short ride."

The afternoon passes slowly so I venture outside for a quick walk. Johanna tells me it is very cold, so I depart in mittens, a hat and the boots I carried overseas for Stockholm's snowy sidewalks. Still, the air deals me a body slam when I open the entrance door, as if it's something tactile and in need of wrangling. I speed up to generate warmth. There is daylight, dim and crystalline. I pass by a small church designed by the same architect as the hotel and peer inside. The drifts are higher than I am and under my footsteps, the road makes a sound like creaking floorboards. At first, the air is so pure I burst into loud hacks when I inhale, the city expunging itself from my lungs. My face grows numb while the brief stroll turns into two hours, then three. My body is moving, heated, propelling me forward, further from the hotel. My head is uncluttered and I don't pass a soul on the road.

There is little to see but a bleached landscape embellished in parts by a green-black treeline. Though the vista is uniform, every new angle from every corner turned startles me just the same. Sweat prickles my stomach and back and pools in the waistband of my jeans when I veer towards foreign territory: the ski area.

It was strange to grow up in New England and never learn to schuss down a mountain. My father is an Italian from Tucson who worked every weekend of my childhood. While my friends hauled off for Vermont on Friday afternoons, I stayed home and baked Toll House cookies, waiting for our annual getaway to St. Croix or Barbados come February. Skiing wasn't in his, or subsequently our, vernacular. So when we moved to the countryside, I was determined that my kids should tackle what I had not. For a few years, I dragged them on Wednesdays and Sundays to the mountain near our house and had them kitted out for lessons. At one time, I thought I'd join them, but instead, opted to toast my bones in the lodge by an ancient fireplace at tables encrusted with ketchup and grease. I always worried until I saw their little bodies at the bottom of the run.

Inside the ski shop, the surroundings are familiar from when my children were small. Skis line up wall to wall, kids with pink faces trudge in boots. I even recognize the wet, worn carpet underfoot. Behind this equipment rental room is a snack bar, with antler chandeliers poised above the tables full of skiers exuding the hale flush of exhaustion. I wished for a fraction of their spent physicality. My lips unfreeze to sip hot tea and nibble on a slice of chocolate cake, and passing back through the store, I turn back and head for the counter where a man is bent over a metal contraption waxing skis.

"Do you offer lessons for cross country?" I ask.

"Yes, but our teacher is away for the week," he says.

"Is it hard?" I ask, "I mean, to do?"

"Once you get used to it, it's like walking but you'll need to practice," he says. "You've never done it?"

"No," I say. "Can I reserve a pair of skis for tomorrow?"

I fill out a form, leaving my name and a deposit of SEK 100, and depart the lodge with a written commitment to teach myself to cross-country ski the next day. I'm no longer brooding when I get back to the hotel, where I plunk down in the lounge and never crack open my book. There are only a few of us at dinner, including the new massage guy whom I had booked for the following day. The meal is magnificent— even the sliced reindeer. I'm ashamed to tell these nice people that I don't eat meat, either, or fish, but I swallow all of it, as well as Arctic char from Malgomai and my wine, happily. It's been an entire day since I've checked my emails or my dwindling bank balance. No texts from the kids far away at school. Exhausted, I drift off to my room to get ready for bed.

Just before switching off the light above my bed, I remember the Northern Lights and Joachim's prediction that the conditions were ideal. I'm warm, buzzed, deliciously at peace but I force myself into boots anyway, as well as my coat, mittens and hat. The hotel bar is hopping, and I pray no one glances outside to see the woman with a down coat thrown over her nightclothes looking up at the sky.

I walk around, filling myself with freezing air, seduced by the thought of the warm bed I just abandoned, tempted by sleep. I jog to the road to fight off my apathy, to promise myself a deep slumber if I can be patient for once, to persist in this bitter cold a few more minutes. Instead I go inside and slide into bed. It's ten o'clock. I can't fall asleep.

To see the Northern Lights requires commitment I don't feel obligated to muster up during this, my time to clear the head and shun responsibility. But I lurch out of bed again anyway, begrudgingly, and pile on the layers, slip on my boots and leave without a hat. The wine has leeched from my system and now I'm colder and emptier. I stroll briskly to the road. I spin around and observe the waif of a new moon and the stars, chrome studs shimmering against a deep violet sky. The chill lodges in my joints and my ears tingle from the sharp, windless air. I wave my arms to keep the blood flowing.

I know, the Aurora Borealis is a crapshoot, like spotting a pod of whales in a boat off Cabo. I cannot fight my fatigue anymore so I wander back to the front door, buying a little time with my slow, deliberate steps. My neck aches from craning it skyward. The air crackles so softly it almost hisses, and I turn to the source of the noise. To the north, above the hotel apartments, I see a corner of the heavens illuminated with a swoosh of green light, ghostly and ethereal. The colors seem to brush against my frozen face and undulate against the pitch-black stretch of horizon. I hear a bustle of people and voices, including Johanna, the staff closing out the kitchen, who emerge to watch the spectacle. We all stand silently as it flares to reveal a rolling arc, watery flashes of neon green and pale blue still isolated to one fragment of the sky. The lights contract from a brush stroke to a thin yellow-green ribbon and when it disappears, I dare to breathe again.

The next morning, Johanna insists on taking me for a horseback ride. I try to refuse her but there is a softness about her insistence and frankly, I'm somewhat worn down. The lethargy I desire looks like a problem to them, a petulance that needs rectifying with bucking up, Swedish optimism and more suggestions. As she drives me to the stables, Johanna confirms it's been a banner season for Northern Lights. "It was a small one last night," she says, "but I never get tired of seeing it," she says.

The wind blows in icy puffs, yesterday's sun has vanished, and I'm about to mount a horse for the second time ever (the first being behind a resort in Tucson, rattlesnakes and all). It smells of hay and the cold, and the animals, of the Northern Swedish breed, are enormous. She introduces me to my ride and I love him immediately, despite the fact that he's a giant and seems hearty and not at all dead. I don't reveal to Johanna my next piece of bad news: that I'm allergic to cats, dogs, hamsters and yes, horses, the latter of which have always rather scared me. I did have an urge to ride, once, when my daughter started taking lessons, but I suppose I chickened out and bagged that, too.

"See how kind he is?" she says. "His name is Besten, which means Beast."

"Not encouraging," I say. Did I mention? He's massive. "It's also means 'the best,'" she says.

Johanna strokes him and whispers both to me and to him. "You'll be fine, I promise." She hands me a brush and shows me how to groom his fur, where to scratch him. I catch him squarely in the eyes. "Friends, O.K.?"

Johanna mounts her horse with ease and rides bareback. She drapes a saddle over Besten, I don a helmet that is too small over my wool cap, and we ride into the woods. I am terrified and exhilarated. The horse trots too quickly over deep snow but soon I settle into his pace and even urge him on faster, over rocks and brooks, past thickets of birch and rows of giant spruce that seem to close in on us. We go up and down a few steep hills, and when my body lurches perpendicular to the ground I love Besten even more for not letting me tumble off. We have ridden a few miles when Johanna leads us into a pine glade for lunch, where we tie up the horses. She reveals cheese sandwiches and a thermos of coffee and we settle into a snowbank. The jagged treeline is rimmed by a blackish sky. I think of nothing but as I am: far, far away.

I envy Johanna's ease with the horses and the forbidding terrain. I envy her competence and knowledge and clarity of purpose. She has bought a house in Borgafjall with her husband who runs the ski area and simply loves this magnificent place. "So why did you decide to come here?" she asks.

"You mean, and not ski?" I ask. We laugh. "Just for a break," I say.

"Life is very complex," she says as we fix our eyes on the frozen horizon and prepare for the hour's ride back to the stables.

Back at the hotel, I'm restless. I reluctantly eat elk sausage for lunch and feel my stomach churning in the aftermath. I wander outside in my usual cold weather get-up in the direction of the ski trails. My acquaintance in the shop welcomes me with my equipment, unfortunately freshly waxed, that I cart over my shoulder back to the hotel. I dial my husband.

"Hi, I'm in Lapland," I say.

"You're what?"

"In Lapland and I just rented cross country skis." He skis almost every morning on the trails near our house. "Can you give me some pointers?"

"Wow," he says. He's never once convinced me to join him, despite asking me daily. He only reluctantly accepts the fact that, even if I live in New England, I hate being outside in winter. "I'm amazed."

"Yeah, me too. It's cold but for some reason, it's not bothering me," I say. "So I figured, why not?"

"Way to go," he says. "Lift the heel of the back foot as you push forward on the front leg. The poles are key."

"Here goes nothing," I say.

Gertrud directs me to the trails right behind the hotel. Shortly, I'm winded, dripping perspiration, crawling then sliding, struggling to keep my legs parallel and loose and gradually I pick up speed. Strapping Swedes with gaunt cheeks and high-tech outdoor gear whiz past me. The route slopes downward and I accelerate for about two hundred yards before I lose control and fall face-first into the snow. I get up and click my skis back into place, but before long, I'm spent. It is strange to see my feet in ski boots as they trod through the snow. In them, I'm a different person, all legs and strength and heartbeat, without a thought except to walk steady and not to slip on the ice. I see my breath but I don't feel the cold.

The sky is dark enough to hide Anita Ekberg and at the hotel, I meet up with Johanna, who reminds me of my massage. "You are O.K.?" she asks.

At dinner, four snowmobilers on a guy's getaway invite me to their table and offer to share their fine Bordeaux. "You have never been on a snowmobile?" One of them, an executive for a mountaineering equipment firm, asks me.

"You have to come with us tomorrow, we are going twenty-five miles to Saxnos," another says. We debate it after dinner by the fireplace, over cognac and the local gin. Too dangerous, I maintain. Nonsense, say they. It's the Nordic way of life!

"Even the Sami people use snowmobiles now," one of them exclaims.

At breakfast, they're all there, my drinking buddies, in swell outdoor attire—orange, green, Gore-Tex, microfiber efficiency. "You can still change your mind," one of them says. I laugh. "Thanks anyway."

They leave and I finish my coffee alone. Just how I wanted it, right? But the northern air is clearing my head, making me dare to face something I've never braved before: the outdoors. The cold. Air so clean it makes my head weightless.

"Joachim and are going out on the snowmobile to put some restaurant flyers on the trail," says Gertrud, who sits at the next table. My stomach grips tightly because I know what's coming next. "Why don't you come?"

I'm not getting any thinking done, nor have I been able to submerge myself in a pool of isolation. But I'm healthier than I was when I arrived two days ago and it's easy to see why.

"As long as it's safe," I say, thinking of Lake Malgomaj and the reckless adventurers. "Please, go slow."

I hold onto Gertrud while Joachim speeds up ahead. The acrid odor of exhaust wafts around us, and I worry about befouling the virginal air, but not as much as I fear calamity. "Slow" for her is too fast for me, and I squeeze her. When she takes a sharp corner we dip towards the ground like a listing ship, and I imagine the motor slicing into my frozen neck. But always, she rights the machine, laughing, sailing into the white. "We're fine, don't worry," she reassures me.

We park the snowmobiles and climb to a cluster of round wooden Sami huts which are buried under a cap of snow. The blackened remains of fires darken the interiors. They are long abandoned. We climb from one to the other and peer behind the disintegrating doors and soon resume our trek.

Gertrud zooms, allowing me to firm my grasp as we rise higher on the mountain. Joachim hammers flyers advertising specials for the upcoming weekend into stakes. They are expecting a full house and, he tells me, these same trails will be packed. Today, they are empty.

When we stop, the cold, which has already lodged into the creases of my cheeks, nose and lips, wends its way under my coat, even under the ski pants Johanna lent me, even beneath the layer of thermal fabric closest to my skin. The couple has stopped for *fika*—the Swedish ritual of drinking coffee. We are in a clearing, in full view of the blinding white tits of Anita Ekberg, under a sky so blue and so packed with atmospheric gases that this night, we may see the whole horizon transform again into a halo of liquid light.

Gertrud splashes a drop of milk into my cup. The hot drink relieves the prickly Arctic air that surrounds us in every direction. The cookies, too, warm me, the sensation of sugar against tongue, the comfort of sustenance. None of us rushes to finish our coffee but soon I clamber back onto the snowmobile and clutch onto Gertrud. The elements are relentless, just as they are under a Caribbean sun from which eventually you need to seek shade.

As we ride back, the sky clouds over quickly. There will be no Northern Lights tonight, but I am certain there will be something else to stumble upon and surprise me. I don't quite recognize the person these people have turned me into over the last days but I'm getting fond of her. In fact, I might like to spend a little time with her—walking, riding, gazing— engaged in anything, actually, but contemplation.

❧ ❧ ❧

*Marcia DeSanctis is the author of the* New York Times *Travel Best Seller* 100 Places in France Every Woman Should Go. *She is a former television news producer who has worked for* Barbara Walters, ABC, CBS, and NBC News. *She is also an award-winning essayist whose work has appeared in numerous publications including* Vogue, Marie Claire, Town & Country, O the Oprah Magazine, More, Tin House, and The New York Times. *Her travel essays have been widely anthologized, including four consecutive years in* The Best Women's Travel Writing, *and she is the recipient of three Lowell Thomas Awards for excellence in travel journalism, as well as a Solas Award for best travel writing. She holds a degree from Princeton University in Slavic Languages and Literature and a Masters in International Relations from the Fletcher School of Law and Diplomacy. She worked for several years in Paris, and today lives in northwest Connecticut with her husband and two children.*

# Acknowledgments

"Friends Who Don't Bite" by Jill K. Robinson published with permission from the author. Copyright © 2015 by Jill K. Robinson.

"The Vanishing Art of Losing Your Way" by Sarah Colleen Coury published with permission from the author. Copyright © 2015 by Sarah Colleen Coury.

"The Marco Chronicles: To Rome, Without Love" by Elizabeth Geoghegan originally published in Shebooks. Reprinted by permission of the author. Copyright © 2014 by Elizabeth Geoghegan.

"What Is that Thing?" by Michael Coolen published with permission from the author. Copyright © 2015 by Michael Coolen.

"Inside the Tower" by Keith Skinner published with permission from the author. Copyright © 2015 by Keith Skinner.

"Notes into Lines" by Hannah Sheldon-Dean published with permission from the author. Copyright © 2015 by Hannah Sheldon-Dean.

"Into the Hills" by Matthew Crompton published with permission from the author. Copyright © 2015 by Matthew Crompton.

"Show Me, *Shouyu*" by Kelly Luce published with permission from the author. Copyright © 2015 by Kelly Luce.

"Fish Trader Ray" by Lisa Alpine published with permission from the author. Copyright © 2015 by Lisa Alpine.

"My First Trip to the Homeland" by Tania Amochaev published with permission from the author. Copyright © 2015 by Tania Amochaev.

"The Tea in Me" by Bill Giebler published with permission from the author. Copyright © 2015 by Bill Giebler.

"Code 500" by Stephanie Elizondo Griest originally appeared in the Fall 2013 issue of the *Oxford American*. Reprinted by permission of the author. Copyright © 2013 by Stephanie Elizondo Griest.

"Diego Forever" by Kelly Chastain published with permission from the author. Copyright © 2015 by Kelly Chastain.

"Woman Rain" by Katherine Jamieson originally appeared in 2011 in *Meridian: The Semi-annual from the University of Virginia.*

# About the Editors

**James O'Reilly**, publisher of Travelers' Tales, was born in Oxford, England, and raised in San Francisco. He's visited fifty countries and lived in four, along the way meditating with monks in Tibet, participating in West African voodoo rituals, rafting the Zambezi, and hanging out with nuns in Florence and penguins in Antarctica. He travels whenever he can with his wife and their three daughters. They live in Palo Alto, California, where they also publish art games and books for children at Birdcage Press (birdcagepress. com).

**Larry Habegger**, executive editor of Travelers' Tales, has visited almost fifty countries and six of the seven conti nents, traveling from the Arctic to equatorial rainforests, the Himalayas to the Dead Sea. In the 1980s he co-authored mystery serials for the *San Francisco Examiner* with James O'Reilly, and since 1985 has written a syndicated column, "World Travel Watch" (WorldTravelWatch.com). Habegger regularly teaches travel writing at workshops and writers' conferences, is a principal of the Prose Doctors (prosedoctors.com), and editor-in-chief of Triporati.com, a destination discovery site. He lives with his family on Telegraph Hill in San Francisco.

**Sean O'Reilly** is editor-at-large for Travelers' Tales. He is a former seminarian, stockbroker, and prison instructor who lives in Virginia with his wife and their six children. He's had a lifelong interest in philosophy and theology, and is the author of *How to Manage Your DICK: Redirect Sexual Energy and Discover Your More Spiritually Enlightened, Evolved Self* (dickmanagement.com). His travels of late have taken him through China, Southeast Asia, the South Pacific, England, and Ireland. He is also an inventor with one patent to his name and another on the way.